RELATIONS
OF
RESCUE

The Search for Female Moral
Authority
in the American West, 1874–1939

PEGGY PASCOE

New York   Oxford
OXFORD UNIVERSITY PRESS
1990

Oxford University Press

Oxford   New York   Toronto
Delhi   Bombay   Calcutta   Madras   Karachi
Petaling Jaya   Sigapore   Hong Kong   Tokyo
Nairobi   Dar es Salaam   Cape Town
Melbourne   Auckland

and associated companies in
Berlin   Ibadan

Copyright © 1990 by Peggy Pascoe

Published by Oxford University Press, Inc.,
200 Madison Avenue, New York, New York 10016

Library of Congress Cataloging-in-Publication Data
Pascoe, Peggy. Relations of Rescue
the search for female moral authority
in the American west, 1874-1939
Peggy Pascoe. p.   cm.   Includes bibliographical references.   ISBN 0-19-506008-3
1. Abused women—West (U.S.)—History—19th century.
2. Women's shelters—West (U.S.)—History—19th century.
3. Church work with abused women—West (U.S.)—History—19th century.
I. Title.   HV1446.A17P37   1990   362.8′292′0973—dc20
89-36475   CIP

2 4 6 8 9 7 5 3 1

Printed in the United States of America

For My Mother and Father
and in Memory of My Brother Bob

Acknowledgments

For their help in completing this book, I am indebted to a whole host of archivists, librarians, and historians. The research could not have been carried out without the people who guided me to diverse local and national organizational sources. I am grateful to Valerie Matsumoto, who first told me about Donaldina Cameron; to Reverend Harry Chuck, who gave me permission to examine confidential case files at Cameron House; to Judy Yung and Mildred Martin, who shared with me their personal research notes and photographs; and to Valerie Sherer Mathes, who directed my attention to Susan LaFlesche Picotte. Archivists and librarians at the repositories listed in the bibliography provided me with scholarly assistance and friendly hospitality while I did my research; much later they patiently responded to long-distance requests for fact-checking and photographs. From beginning to end, I relied heavily on the outstanding Stanford University Libraries, where I received exceptionally fine assistance from American History bibliographer, Jim Knox, and from Hallie Perry and Sonia Moss of the Inter-Library Loan department.

Several institutions provided the prerequisites for writing. Generous financial support came from the Stanford Graduate Fellows program, the David Potter Fund, the Giles M. Whiting Foundation, and the Woodrow Wilson Foundation's Charlotte W. Newcombe Dissertation program. The University of Utah History

Department obligingly allowed me to design a teaching schedule that facilitated rather than delayed completion of the manuscript; a Career Development Leave from its College of Humanities allowed me uninterrupted time for final revisions.

The editorial staff at Oxford University Press provided a delightful introduction to the world of book publishing. I am especially grateful for Rachel Toor's thoughtful suggestions and enthusiastic encouragement and for Gail Cooper's meticulous copyediting. I also want to acknowledge the *Journal of Social History* for permission to use material from my previously published article, "Gender Systems in Conflict: The Marriages of Mission-Educated Chinese American Women, 1874–1939," *Journal of Social History* 22 (Summer 1989): 631–652.

This book developed in an atmosphere of abundant support and thoughtful criticism from colleagues. The Women's History Dissertation Reading Group at Stanford acted as a sounding board for my first tentative ideas and carefully critiqued several chapters as I wrote them; I want to thank its members—Sue Cobble, Liz Cohen, Gary Goodman, Yukiko Hanawa, Susan Johnson, Becky Lowen, Sue Lynn, Valerie Matsumoto, Julie Reuben, Penny Russell, Linda Schott, Frances Taylor, and Katherine Weinert. Several people gave helpful advice about particular parts of the manuscript, among them Al Camarillo, Pam Elam, Gail Hershatter, Susan Johnson, Waverly Lowell, Mary Odem, Stacey Oliker, Beverly Purrington, Mary Rothschild, Jack Tchen, Anne Walthall, Ann Waltner, Anand Yang, and Judy Yung. Dave Gutiérrez and Valerie Matsumoto offered their ideas along with the kind of understanding support that comes only from long friendship; they got me through the rough times. At various stages, several people— Mari Jo Buhle, Carl Degler, Estelle Freedman, Joan Jensen, Gerda Lerner, Patty Limerick, Anne Firor Scott, Regina Morantz-Sanchez, Richard White, and one anonymous reader—took time away from their own work to read the entire manuscript; I have learned a great deal from their perceptive suggestions for improvement.

In the widest possible sense, my understanding of history has been nurtured by two women who embody the highest ideals of the community of feminist scholars. Gerda Lerner introduced me to these ideals and impressed upon me the transforming possibilities of women's history. Estelle Freedman, my graduate adviser, offered criticism, advice, and encouragement at every stage of my work. I am constantly grateful for her wise academic counsel, her extraordinary personal integrity, and her devotion to feminist scholarship that is at once critical and humane.

Contents

Introduction

The Search for
Female Moral Authority

Because we live in a time when few things seem as questionable as moral certainty, the emergence of a self-consciously "moral" version of feminism must be counted as one of the most striking developments in contemporary American society. Even before the defeat of the Equal Rights Amendment, some feminists had begun to question the validity of egalitarianism as a model for male–female relations. Over the past decade, many more shifted their tactics from tearing down the barriers between the sexes to advocating "cultural feminism"—the attempt to identify and define the distinctive values of a "women's culture" and to show how the adoption of these values might lead to a better world.[1] As Hester Eisenstein concluded in a recent survey of the field, "feminist theory has moved from an emphasis on the elimination of gender difference to a celebration of that difference as a source of moral values."[2]

Examples of this phenomenon range all the way from the carefully stated arguments of psychologist Carol Gilligan, who maintains that women speak about morality "in a different voice" than men, to the blatantly oversimplified pronouncement that "women relate, women create, women heal"—to borrow the chapter titles from one cultural feminist account.[3] In recent years, cultural feminists have proposed a list of "women's values" that includes intimacy, creativity, cooperation, and nonviolence. A daring few have begun to use the term *feminine* with approval.[4] Popularizing their program with the slogan "the future is female," cultural feminists placed the regeneration of "women's values" at the center of their agenda.

Such an agenda does not, of course, appeal to every feminist. Socialist feminists object to cultural feminists' placing primacy on gender rather than class oppression.[5] Most feminists who study sexuality hesitate to advocate "morality." Like many Americans, they associate the term *morality* with a repressive Victorian sexuality they would prefer to bury in the nineteenth century.[6] Postmodern theorists influenced by "French feminism" also disdain cultural feminism; they call for a "post-gendered" society and question whether the category "women" can be defined at all.[7]

Nonetheless, the excitement generated by Carol Gilligan's *In a Different Voice*, to take only the most obvious example, indicates that the issue of morality holds new significance for American feminism—indeed, for American society.[8] Even the critics agree that cultural feminism has provided an enormous impetus to feminist political activity in the United States. Cultural feminist assumptions lend support to the movements to legislate against pornography, to reduce nuclear arms, and to save the environment. As of this writing, cultural feminists speak for a large group of women who believe that women's values differ greatly from men's, and that a livable future depends on elevating "women's values" to a position of long-denied cultural authority. "It is clear," noted Adrienne Rich in 1986, "that among women we need a new ethics; as women, a new morality."[9]

The cultural feminist program is something of a reversal for mid–twentieth-century feminism, a movement that started out to eliminate rather than to celebrate gender difference. It is also a sharp challenge to modern culture, the set of assumptions that has been largely dominant in American society since the 1920s.* Modernists

---

*When I refer to modern culture, I refer to a set of values, attitudes, and beliefs that characterizes much of America from the 1920s to the present. As recently defined by historian Daniel Joseph Singal, "modern" (or, as he dubs it, "Modernist") culture has been dedicated to re-joining the dichotomies Victorian culture established between such supposed opposites as human and animal, civilization and savagery, man and woman. Suspicious of any single system of morality, mod-

define their culture as the near-opposite of the Victorian one that preceded it: they tend to confuse morality with sexual repression and to belittle moralists as prudish neo-Victorians. In such a context, cultural feminism seems to go against the grain, to be nearly inexplicable.

Yet, for the historian, what is most significant about contemporary cultural feminism is not its departure from the recent past, but its consistency with a familiar theme of American women's history. The particular list of women's values in vogue today is unique to modern America, but the program of using gender difference to strengthen women's voices in society has nineteenth-century roots. This book explores one of those roots—the activities of Protestant missionary women in the American West.

To modern minds, of course, contemporary cultural feminists and Victorian missionary women could hardly seem farther apart. For one thing, the two groups propose distinctly different lists of women's values. Victorian missionary women celebrated female purity and piety. Modern cultural feminists, however, go out of their way to avoid being associated with sexual "purity" or with self-righteous Protestantism.[10] Most would deny that they echo the ethnocentrism of Victorian women in the American West.

Yet the obvious differences should not blind us to the similarities. Both groups advanced the same plan of action: they tried to valorize "women's values," to give women's moral judgments authority in societies that largely ignored or dismissed their concerns. Both also faced daunting challenges: To what extent is it possible to promote "women's values" without ultimately reinforcing limited definitions of womanhood? To what extent is it possible to establish reciprocal relationships between women who face each

ernists value experience and authenticity; they disdain the appearance of innocence Victorians valued so highly. Like the Victorian culture that preceded it, "modern" culture is only one of many cultures in twentieth-century American society, but it has achieved substantial dominance in our own time. It is important to add that I do not use the term *modern* to refer to the end products of "modernization," a social science concept predicated on a linear progression from "traditional" to "modern" societies that I would deny. (See Daniel Joseph Singal, "Towards a Definition of American Modernism," *American Quarterly* 39 (Spring 1987): 7–26; and Singal, *The War Within: From Victorian to Modernist Thought in the South, 1919–1945* (Chapel Hill, N.C., 1982), 3–10.)

other across sharply drawn, socially enforced racial and cultural boundaries? At a time when the contemporary search for female moral authority attracts such a large following, we need to explore the roots of these dilemmas in an earlier period in American history when women fought to give "women's values" social authority.

This book begins in the 1870s, when middle-class Protestant women joined together to try to establish female moral authority in the cities of the American West. Appalled by the overwhelmingly masculine milieu of western cities and influenced by the Victorian belief that women should be pious and pure moral guardians, they set out to "rescue" female victims of male abuse. While their projects took many forms, the most common was the establishment of rescue homes, institutions designed to provide a loving, homelike atmosphere in which unfortunate women rescued from predatory men might live under the watchful eyes of white, middle-class Protestant women. Creating a network of rescue homes in western cities, Protestant women carried on what they called "woman's work for woman" for more than fifty years.[11] Not until the missionaries' Victorian assumptions could no longer stand (in some cases as late as the 1930s) did the institutions falter.

The search for female moral authority was not unique to missionary women in the American West. Several historians have identified elements of what I call female moral authority in the temperance, prison reform, and antiprostitution campaigns of the late nineteenth century.[12] For the most part, however, they have relied on the timeworn assumption that these movements exemplified Victorian "female moral superiority." The term *moral superiority* needs serious reconsideration. The phrase itself distorts understanding by playing into contemporary stereotypes; for few people seem less appealing to modern sensibilities than the self-righteous women too frequently equated with Victorian moral reformers. Much more important, the use of the term *superiority* encourages contemporary readers to exaggerate Victorian women's social power. Even when Victorian women argued that they were morally "superior" to men, it is by no means clear that Victorian society as a whole accepted their claims. Victorian women reformers knew what they wanted, but they did not necessarily find what they were searching for. What they had was moral influence, not social power; what they sought was to turn their influence into authority.

If the concept of "female moral superiority" will no longer suffice, its well-known western variant, the notion that women were "civilizers" of the West, is even less adequate. Despite the best efforts of recent historians of western women, the image of (white) women as civilizers remains a staple of western lore.[13] As historian Susan Armitage explains, their "very presence on the frontier [is thought to be] enough to make rough and rowdy men think about polite behavior and the establishment of civilized institutions like schools, churches, and libraries."[14] The enduring belief that Victorian women "cleaned up" the wild West rests on the racist assumption that the West only became "civilized" when white women entered it. Furthermore, it encourages disproportionate attention to their activities after they arrived on the scene. Indeed, in holding on to the "white women as civilizers" theme, too many historians have overlooked one of the best reasons to study the American West—that it is an arena of signal importance for the study of intercultural relations.[15]

It is true, of course, that Victorian missionary women had every intention of "cleaning up" western society. To them, the West, with its reputation for male-dominated cities, gold rushes, gambling, prostitution, and polygamy presented a conspicuous challenge to the moral values of nineteenth-century women. For this very reason, the search for female moral authority, a nationwide phenomenon, emerges in sharp relief in the American West. But the historian has an obligation to present a picture of the society as well as the individuals in it. As Protestant women in the West knew all too well, their attempts to effect change were always contested. Indeed, it is in their relationships with the men who held the power and could ignore their influence and with the women who held different interpretations of the term *morality* that the meaning of the search for female moral authority emerges. Accordingly, this book focuses on three aspects of the Victorian search for female moral authority in the American West: its benefits and liabilities for women's empowerment; its relationship to systems of social control; and its implications for intercultural relations among women.

To what extent can a campaign for female moral authority empower women? In identifying and playing on the Victorian "women's values" of piety and purity, nineteenth-century Protestant mission women tapped a vein rich with strategic advantages. Their search for female moral authority allowed women to turn familiar—even culturally approved—ideas about female nature into tools to challenge male power. So appealing was this approach that missionary groups were the largest women's organizations in the country from the 1870s to 1900; larger than their close cousin, the Woman's Christian Temperance Union, and far larger than the more thoroughly studied suffrage organizations.[16]

Because Protestant women in the West argued for women's "advancement" but rarely mentioned equality, their attempts to raise the status of women can easily be overlooked. Gerda Lerner offers a relevant insight when she distinguishes between the struggle for women's rights, meaning the fight for legal and property rights equal to those of men; and efforts for the emancipation of women, meaning "any struggle designed to elevate [women's] status socially, politically, economically, and in respect to their self-concepts."[17] Josephine Donovan interprets the work of turn-of-the-century women's organizations as a form of cultural feminism that offered a vision of female emancipation based on the assumptions of Victorian women's culture.[18] Following Lerner and Donovan on these points, I would offer "the search for female moral authority" as a better description of the goals of Protestant women in the West than "social feminism," a term that, like "female moral superiority," still appears in the literature but has long since outlived its usefulness.*

---

*The term *social feminism* was first proposed by historian William O'Neill, who distinguished between what he called "extreme" feminists, who advocated suffrage, and "social" feminists, who advocated other reforms and for whom "women's rights was not an end in itself." Many scholars subsequently adopted the term *social feminist* to describe women's club members, settlement house workers, temperance workers, and moral reformers. As critics have commented, however, this categorization makes an artificial distinction: many women activists advocated a variety of reforms. The adjective "social" trivializes women who worked for reforms other than women's suffrage but fought for women's emancipation in their own way. The inadequacies of the term are particularly apparent when dealing with women's moral reform or temperance groups; consequently, historians of these groups have repeatedly struggled to find alternatives. Thus Barbara Epstein calls

Strengthening "women's values" empowered some Victorian women, but it had disadvantages as well. In the end, reliance on a particular formulation of women's roles—no matter how appealing in the late nineteenth century—entrenched rather than challenged gender definitions. Moreover, because Victorian missionary women believed that "true" women were pure and pious, they had a great deal of difficulty understanding women who did not share these values.

To fully comprehend their predicament, we have to develop a more sophisticated conception of the connections between the search for female moral authority and systems of social control. Over the past three decades, the term *social control* has acquired a very specific—and very problematic—meaning for historians. During this period, historians reexamined a variety of reform movements. Not as willing as their predecessors had been to take reformers at their word, they brought to their work a healthy skepticism fed by modern doubts about the moral and religious frameworks of Victorian reformers. In the process, some historians reinterpreted everything from prisons to public schools as attempts by middle-class reformers to impose social control on potentially disruptive underclasses.[19] This revisionist perspective, which stresses reformers' power over others, has become the conventional wisdom on nineteenth-century reform efforts. It is now virtually impossible to think or write about Victorian reform without confronting this "social control" interpretation at every significant juncture.[20]

This social control framework has the advantage of paying close attention to reformers' access to economic power, an important

temperance workers "protofeminist"; Ruth Bordin believes they engaged in a "quest for power and liberty"; and Jack Blocker argues that temperance and suffrage were "separate paths toward protecting the interests of women." (See William O'Neill, *Everyone Was Brave: The Rise and Fall of Feminism in America* (Chicago, 1969), x; idem, *The Woman Movement: Feminism in the United States and England* (London, 1969), 32–70; Barbara Epstein, *The Politics of Domesticity: Women, Evangelism, and Temperance in Nineteenth-Century America* (Middletown, Conn., 1981), 128–37; Ruth Bordin, *Woman and Temperance: The Quest for Power and Liberty, 1873–1900* (Philadelphia, Pa., 1981); Jack Blocker, "Separate Paths: Suffragists and the Women's Temperance Crusade," *Signs* 10 (Spring 1985): 460–76; and Katherine Harris, "Feminism and Temperance Reform in the Boulder WCTU," *Frontiers* 4 (Summer 1979): 19–24) concern for all who study relatively powerless groups. It has, however, some significant disadvantages, too. First, revisionists' critiques of social control have been based almost exclusively on rather vaguely defined class differences, with the middle-class assumed to be in opposition to all others. Since differences of race and gender cannot be entirely encompassed by a class-based model, the revisionist framework fits some groups better than others. Thus, while a conception of social control based primarily on class dominates the study of social welfare movements in general, it has been adopted with far less enthusiasm by historians of racial minority groups and has become increasingly problematic for historians of women.[21]

Along with many other historians of women, I have come to believe that the revisionist social control framework limits understanding by distorting women's experiences.[22] Certainly, the urge to impose middle-class moral authority on the underclasses was one theme of the ideology of Protestant missionary women. At the same time, the rhetoric of home mission women featured another, sometimes contradictory, theme—the need to establish the moral authority of women *vis-à-vis* men. Missionary women sought to establish, not just moral authority in general, but female moral authority in particular. To understand this search for female moral authority, we have to probe the interaction between class-based systems of social control and gender systems, the ways societies create, maintain, and reproduce ideas about gender.[23] But even this is not enough; we then have to explain how both systems bear on overlapping racial and cultural hierarchies. Only when all these factors have been taken into account can we go beyond the limitations of revisionist thinking to understand social control in the largest sense of the term.

We must then recognize that systems of social control are better understood in the plural than in the singular. Most American historians apply the term *social control* primarily to nineteenth- and early–twentieth-century reformers, inadvertently leaving the impression that social control itself was a unique invention of middle-class white Victorians. In fact, it is possible to speak of multiple systems of social control in any given society or time. We need to understand Victorian culture, not in isolation, but in the context of what preceded it, overlapped with it, and replaced it.

In exploring the late nineteenth century, we have to pay attention, not only to (the dominant) Victorian culture, but to its relations with other cultures within American society, too.

Only when we begin to do this are we in a position to challenge the last major disadvantage of the revisionist social control framework—its tendency to portray those being controlled as putty in the hands of reformers. In the social control drama, the subjects of reform are cast in a particular role: they function as victims whose powerlessness is the surest indictment of reformers' control. As a result, they appear as shadowy figures who have little individual agency and few choices about their lives. Such a picture is far too simple; for, while the power dynamics between reformers and reformed were never equally balanced, it is in the relationships between the two that we see the making of history.

And this brings me to the third—and most important—concern of this book: the implications of the search for female moral authority for intercultural relations among women. Historians have usually examined the set of "women's values" favored by Protestant women as part of the history of white, middle-class women.[24] Victorian women themselves, however, would have dismissed such a categorization. Like contemporary cultural feminists, they assumed that the particular set of "women's values" they advocated was, or should have been, characteristic of all women. Accordingly, they established rescue homes for women of many other races, classes, and cultures, working on the assumption that all women wanted to share Victorian gender values and would do so if placed in favorable circumstances.

To the extent that these Victorian "women's values" were seen as salient by women of other cultures—or could, however shakily, be construed as congruent with the gender prescriptions of those cultures—matrons and rescue home residents forged cross-cultural bonds. That this happened much more often, and with more genuine affection, than we might suspect suggests the limits class-based social control thinking has placed on our understanding.

But there was another dynamic at work as well, one in which the Victorian formulation of "women's values" constrained interaction between missionaries and their charges.[25] In intercultural relationships, the search for female moral authority took on additional meaning. Conceived as a way to strengthen women's authority in relation to men, it came to express mission women's authority over the very women they hoped to serve by establishing rescue homes.

To explore these three concerns about Protestant women's search for female moral authority in the American West as broadly as possible, I have used four case studies. Three of these are rescue homes: the Presbyterian Chinese Mission Home in San Francisco, California, founded for Chinese prostitutes in 1874; the Colorado Cottage Home in Denver, Colorado, founded for unmarried mothers in 1886; and the Industrial Christian Home in Salt Lake City, Utah, founded for polygamous Mormon wives in 1886. The fourth is a mission project undertaken for the Omaha Indians of Nebraska by the Connecticut branch of the Women's National Indian Association. Taken together, these four mission projects reveal the range of Protestant women's concerns and allow an analysis of the wide variety of factors that influenced relations among women.

The Protestant women's groups that sponsored these and other rescue projects left abundant records. Because I wanted to go beyond the missionary record itself, I sought out projects for which local sources, ranging from biographical data to newspaper coverage of rescue home scandals, would be available. At a critical point in the research, I stumbled on the case files of the Chinese Mission Home in San Francisco, lying forgotten at the bottom of a storage closet. These records proved to be a hitherto unexplored treasure trove.

In part because of the richness of these sources, I was able to devote much of this book to the relationships between Victorian missionary women and their clients—Chinese, Indians, Mormon women, or unmarried mothers. In the case of the Chinese Mission Home, I was faced with the problem of protecting the confidentiality of the women whose letters were included in rescue home files. Frequently my information about rescue home residents comes from public sources (such as newspapers or mission periodicals) that identified rescue home residents by name: in these cases, I have used the names already made public in the sources. When, however, my source of information about a rescue home resident is an in-house case file, I have assigned the file a number and used pseudonyms in the text (marked by asterisks in the notes).

This book is divided into three main parts. The first two chapters survey the origins and ideas of the Victorian search for female moral authority. Chapter 1 explores its roots in Victorian middle-class gender ideology and the unique conditions of western cities in the 1870s and 1880s by chronicling the establishment of the four mission projects. Chapter 2 outlines the ideology of female moral authority elaborated by Protestant women between 1874 and 1900. The middle three chapters focus on the ways relations between home mission matrons and rescue home residents were structured by—and in turn affected—nineteenth-century systems of social control. Chapter 3 examines the maternalistic attitude of rescue home matrons, the motivations of rescue home residents, and the patterns of institutional interaction between the two groups. Chapter 4 analyzes the position of mission home matrons and trusted ethnic minority assistants in relation to Victorian ideas of race and culture. Chapter 5 explores the constraints rescue home residents faced in trying to establish homes outside the rescue homes. The last chapter, Chapter 6, outlines the institutional and cultural forces that led to the demise of rescue work for women in the early twentieth century. Finally, an epilogue explores the legacy of the Victorian search for female moral authority for contemporary cultural feminism.

I am only too well aware that, in exploring the past to unearth the roots of present dilemmas, I challenge traditional scholars who advocate a kind of pure history purged of its contemporary associations and understood solely on its own terms. I have come to believe, however, that such a purist stance merely disguises and mystifies our inevitable involvement with the present. For the moment, let me simply say that I understand history as a kind of conversation between the past and the present in which we travel through time to examine the cultural assumptions—and the possibilities—of our own society as well as societies that came before us.

ORIGINS
AND
IDEAS

1

Institutional Origins

The search for female moral authority flowered in the 1870s and 1880s, but its roots are back in the early–nineteenth-century benevolent activities of Protestant churches. As the farming towns of the Northeast recast themselves into commercial cities, the forces of economic transition and religious revivalism combined to create a crucible for middle-class Victorian culture.[1] Seeking economic advancement, men turned their energies away from self-sufficient farming and toward the accumulation of capital to establish commercial enterprises. While businessmen were preoccupied with creating a commercial economy, clergymen joined forces with moralists to produce a proliferation of Sunday school, tract, and Bible societies. Men formed the backbone of most early evangelical societies, but the revivals that rushed over the so-called Burned-Over District in the first three decades of the nineteenth century attracted women in such numbers that many congregations were "feminized," becoming organizational bases for charitable activity by women.[2] Middle-class and élite women, inspired by evangelical faith in human perfectibility or by a sense of *noblesse oblige,* provided charity for people left adrift in the burgeoning, and often bewildering, commercial urban environment.

Female benevolent activity emerged at the juncture of gender ideology and class formation in early–nineteenth-century America.

Benevolent activity provided women with an opportunity for moral stewardship roughly parallel to the commercial leadership exercised by local merchants. At the same time, benevolent women expressed their adherence to the values that separated middle-class women from men during and after the economic transformation to commercialism.

A "cult of true womanhood" forged during these years held that "true" women could be recognized by their virtues of purity, piety, domesticity, and submissiveness. Middle-class rhetoric described Victorian women as the embodiment of innocence, purer and more pious than their male counterparts; Victorian men were thought to be tainted by the competitive economic struggle for survival. One consequence was that white middle-class women of the period had so much in common with each other (and, some would say, so little in common with their male counterparts) that historians have identified a veritable "women's culture" among them.[3]

The Victorian association of women with piety and purity was a significant innovation. Although nineteenth-century Protestant churches could not claim the same degree of social authority their Puritan predecessors had enjoyed, they remained central institutions, fountainheads of Victorianism. As recent historians have made clear, sexual restraint—conceptualized as purity in women and self-control in men—was highly prized by Victorians.[4] Nineteenth-century Protestant women held neither final religious authority nor the political power of the vote, but by virtue of their identification with piety and purity, they enjoyed unprecedented influence.

The values of piety and purity provided the terms through which middle-class women worked out their relationship to community life over the course of the nineteenth century. In city after city, and towns and villages as well, women formed groups dedicated to charitable purposes. In benevolent work, women used their identification with piety to establish an arena of semipublic activity for themselves. Much of this activity was quite conventional, remarkable only because it involved the organization of women rather than men. Hundreds of churchwomen formed sewing circles and "cent" societies in order to contribute to missionary and relief programs directed by churchmen.[5]

As early as 1797, some women established their own benevolent projects, usually designed to aid widows and orphans. In New York City, for example, women established the Orphan Asylum and the Asylum for Lying-In Women, and contributed as well to a Society for Relief of Poor Widows and an Association for the Relief of Respectable Aged Indigent Females.[6]

By the 1830s and 1840s, other, more daring, women channeled their benevolent impulses into ambitious campaigns for social reform. Some formed female antislavery societies that worked in tandem with male antislavery groups. Still others organized female moral reform societies dedicated to eliminating prostitution. Members of one such group, the New York Female Moral Reform Society, made themselves notorious by bursting into brothels to hold prayer meetings and by publishing the names of men known to have seduced young women.[7] Relying on women's emergent claims to moral guardianship, female moral reformers in New York and Massachusetts used their political influence to demand that state legislatures make the seduction of unmarried women a crime.[8] Although women reformers were held at arms length by more traditional evangelical women, both agreed on the need for female benevolent institutions: significantly, the Female Moral Reform Society established a House of Reception to shelter and reform repentant prostitutes.[9]

The burst of energy that infused this first wave of female organization passed quickly through the commercial cities where it had begun.[10] In the meantime, however, female benevolent societies popped up all over the Midwest, and female benevolent institutions became commonplace. By mid-century, institutions for widows and orphans were being joined by homes for working girls; refuges for "fallen" women would soon follow.[11]

This city-by-city extension of benevolent work created a firm foundation for the national expansion that took place after the Civil War. During the war, middle-class women organized a large-scale program of war relief work: its success inspired benevolent women across the country. After the war, a new burst of Protestant evangelicalism, this one strongly flavored by American nationalism, rejuvenated charitable organizations. Postwar organizations of women were national in scope and much more independent than their prewar predecessors: they seemed to spring up everywhere.

Protestant women formed so many organizations in these years that one twentieth-century commentator labeled the 1870s "the church women's decade."[12] Breaking away from denominational missionary organizations administered by men, evangelical women formed their own missionary societies, this time devoted to projects chosen by churchwomen rather than churchmen. The women of "foreign" missionary societies focused on countries in which they discerned the "wail" of female voices crying for help in eliminating practices such as polygamy, wife-bartering, and female infanticide.[13] The members of "home" missionary societies adapted the foreign missionary slogan of "woman's work for woman" to minister to groups within American borders.[14] Not surprisingly for women raised in a culture that prized sexual restraint, they zeroed in on groups whose behavior seemed to them to raise the spectre of unrestrained sexuality; among them unmarried mothers, Mormons, American Indians, and Chinese immigrants.

Enthusiasm spread quickly from denominational to interdenominational women's groups. Soon Protestant women applied the term *home mission*, which originally designated one of two fields of missionary work, to a wide variety of evangelical women's organizations. Before long, they invested the phrase *home mission* with ideological significance. Home mission women interpreted the "home" as the ideal Christian home of Victorian rhetoric. They believed that, since unrestrained sexuality threatened women's moral purity, women had a special "mission" to sustain Protestant moral values by "rescuing" female victims and teaching them to emulate the family and gender roles of white, middle-class Victorian culture.

By the late nineteenth century, Protestant evangelical women engaged in "woman's work for woman" all over the country. Outgrowths of Victorian women's culture, home mission organizations tied local women into national women's networks with a good deal of organizational independence. Like the female moral reform societies that had been their clearest predecessors, they preached Victorian female values of piety and purity in an attempt to set moral standards for their communities, their regions, and their nation. It was this burst of female reform activity, the search for female moral authority, that led mission-minded Protestant women to direct their energies westward in the late nineteenth century.

Eastern Women and Western Projects: The Connecticut Indian Association

A distinctive and often volatile mix of cultures, the West seemed to home mission women "a specially interesting field for missionary effort."[15] In part because middle-class Victorianism was not yet dominant there, missionary women envisioned the region as a prime arena for the establishment of female moral authority. Both eastern and western Protestant women leapt into the field in the 1870s and 1880s. Four home mission projects—one each in Nebraska, California, Colorado, and Utah—suggest the range of the search for female moral authority in the late–nineteenth-century West.

The Connecticut Indian Association illuminates the process by which eastern women came to focus on the problems of western areas. The Connecticut Indian Association was a branch of the larger Women's National Indian Association, formed in 1879 in Philadelphia.[16] Mary Bonney and Amelia Stone Quinton, the founders of the national group, had been moved to action by two particularly heinous white offenses against American Indians. The first was the 1879 invasion of Oklahoma Indian Territory by white land-seekers called "Sooners."

The second incident concerned the Poncas, a small tribe in northern Nebraska. Government officials had carelessly transferred Ponca lands to their enemies the Sioux, then tried to solve the resultant problems by forcibly removing the Poncas to the unfamiliar Indian Territory. After a third of the tribe died, Ponca chief Standing Bear led a desperate group of his followers back to their homeland, only to be arrested and ordered to return to Indian Territory. While the Nebraska courts pondered the legal issues raised by his arrest, Standing Bear and Susette LaFlesche, a relative from the nearby Omaha tribe, went on an eastern speaking tour to raise interest in the Ponca cause. Their dignity and determination—as well as the novelty of their appearance in native costume—catapulted them into the limelight, making Indian reform a *cause célèbre* among eastern reformers. Susette LaFlesche, known to fascinated audiences as "Bright Eyes," helped fan the flames of outrage that enabled the infant Women's National Indian Association to expand its membership and add auxiliary branches.[17]

One of the strongest of these auxiliaries was the Connecticut Indian Association. Amelia Quinton had organized a Connecticut branch in Hartford in 1881, but the group accomplished little until 1883, when Sara Thompson Kinney revitalized it.[18] Kinney, the daughter of a doctor, had been born in 1842. Like many of the middle- and upper-class women of her generation, she was educated at a female seminary. Fascinated by the relatively new phenomenon of women doctors, she kept scrapbooks on their professional achievements, but she did not go to medical school herself. Instead, she married a newspaper editor and devoted herself to benevolent work. Like many late–nineteenth-century women, she participated proudly in a number of patriotic women's organizations, including the Daughters of the American Revolution. Her major commitment, however, was to the Connecticut Indian Association, over which she presided from 1883 until her death in 1922.[19]

Kinney was enthusiastic about the prospects for developing missionary work among American Indians. Under her leadership, the Connecticut branch, which retained a great deal of autonomy from its parent organization, pioneered in innovative approaches to promoting "civilized home-life" on reservations. Taking a personalized approach to mission work, Kinney and her Connecticut branch devoted much of their energy to Susette LaFlesche's Omaha tribe. They began by helping the national Association sponsor a medical mission on the Omaha reservation in Nebraska. The mission was staffed by a physician and his wife, who led church services, taught schoolchildren, dispensed medicines, and encouraged the Omaha to visit with them in their home.[20]

Soon the Connecticut association announced its own project, a "home-building" loan program. This revolving loan fund enabled Indian couples who graduated from eastern boarding schools to borrow the money to build houses on reservation land. The unexpected largesse from the home mission women proved attractive to young Indians. The first "home-building" loan financed what proud missionary women referred to as the "Connecticut Cottage"; but before long, so many couples applied for funds that the program was adopted by the national association, where it remained under Kinney's direction.[21]

In the meantime, Connecticut women hatched an ambitious plan to recruit native missionaries. Influenced, perhaps, by Kinney's personal interest in medicine, the society decided to put Indian women through medical school. For their first beneficiary, the Connecticut women chose Susette LaFlesche's sister Susan, an Omaha woman then finishing her studies at Hampton Institute. Susan, who had dreamed of becoming a doctor since childhood, needed financial support to start medical school. Hoping to secure a native medical missionary, the Association paid for Susan's education at the Woman's Medical College in Philadelphia and later underwrote her medical practice on the Omaha reservation.

By the mid-1880s, the members of the Connecticut Indian Association had developed a program for the Omaha that demonstrates the central themes of post–Civil War women's home mission work. The Connecticut branch was a local group with national ties; it was entirely under the control of women. To Victorians, who thought that women were more attuned to the needy than men were, women's organizations seemed especially appropriate for home mission purposes. Because they believed that women were the proper moral guardians of society, home mission women assumed it was their duty to extend middle-class moral standards everywhere. Accordingly, the Connecticut branch tried to bring Omaha Indians into contact with such exemplars of Victorian morality as Protestant missionaries, newly married homeowners, and professionally educated Omaha women.

Like home mission groups across the country, the Connecticut group used the values of "true womanhood" to identify women with morality. As Amelia Quinton remarked, the Women's National Indian Association believed in "the centuries-old and divine call to women, often to lead and always to share in moral movements."[22] As one member of the Association commented when she addressed the 1888 convention, in the late nineteenth century, female "sweetness and light" was needed even more than "great armies or great industries," the comparable social responsibilities of men.[23]

Although the Women's National Indian Association differentiated between female and male responsibilities, its members stopped short of displaying the public anger at men that surfaced among home mission women in western cities. In eastern cities like Hartford, the home of the Connecticut branch, home mission women had long ago fought the battles needed to establish women's charitable activity. They built on strong networks of female benevolence that encountered little overt opposition from their male counterparts. Furthermore, both the subjects of mission concern (Omaha Indians) and the communities to be reformed (reservations) were far removed from the eastern cities in which reformers made their own homes. Despite their benevolent impulses, Connecticut women lacked the personal stake in the future of the American West that, as we will see, motivated home mission women who lived in western cities.

Under these circumstances, Association members saw their work as different from, but largely complementary to, the work of male Indian reformers. Thus the women of the Women's National Indian Association welcomed the advent of another national group, the all-male Indian Rights Association formed in the early 1880s. They hoped that the men would take over the task of agitating for political reform so that women could focus their resources on the establishment of missions. They resolved that they would act as "one society" with the Indian Rights Association, though they prudently retained their financial independence.[24] Their actions demonstrate their basic confidence in the good will of male reformers and community leaders, a confidence that home mission women in California, Colorado, and Utah found they could not share.

Home Mission Women in Western Cities

Like the pioneer women of the Oregon Trail historians have described so eloquently, the women who migrated to western cities in the 1870s and 1880s rushed to re-create the Victorian women's culture of the East by establishing a middle-class Protestant woman's vision of moral order in their new communities.[25] In the emerging cities of the American West, as in the burgeoning commercial cities of the Northeast almost a century earlier, women's drive for moral reform seemed to thrive on the fluidity of emerging class formations. For the short period of time in which class structures were relatively flexible, western cities provided unusual opportunities for new residents to make their mark as community leaders.[26] In the 1870s, they offered a minimum of established charities and a maximum of opportunities for middle-class women to gain community standing through benevolent work. In San Francisco, so many women took advantage of their chances that the city experienced what one historian called a "charities explosion."[27]

Many women migrants to western cities participated in benevolent work as one way to capture social status and ensure their— and their husbands'—standing in the community. Candid personal sources reveal that some women who joined home mission groups sought a better start in western cities after failures elsewhere. Mrs. E. V. Robbins, for example, moved to San Francisco from Chicago, where her husband had, she said, "met with a financial disaster" in the 1870s.[28] One of her first actions was to join the Occidental Branch of the Woman's Foreign Missionary Society, a group of Presbyterian women who sponsored a rescue home for Chinese prostitutes. Robbins maintained her connection with the Board for nearly fifty years. Mrs. P. D. Browne, president of the Occidental Branch from 1877 to 1900 and a woman who established an impressive record of community leadership in California, serves as another example. Like Robbins, Browne came to San Francisco after her banker husband suffered "heavy losses in business" in Montreal.[29]

Like Robbins and Browne, most home mission women for whom biographical information can be found were married; the majority to middle-class men, a few to men who became truly prosperous in western locations. They depended on their husbands, local churchmen, and other middle-class men to support their institutions and used their names to garner support for their mission projects. The women expected the men to make suitable donations to building campaigns and to give advice on business and real estate transactions. They counted on doctors, lawyers, and grocers to donate services and supplies for their charitable work.

Many home mission women engaged in several projects at once; in this, they resembled the "interlocking directorate" of Protestant community leaders historians have identified in cities as distant from each other as Jacksonville, Illinois; and Los Angeles, California.[30] Women who presided over benevolent organizations expected to be regarded as prominent citizens of western cities and to be praised in terms that echoed those applied to merchants and professional men. With so much status at stake, many women set their hearts on acquiring leadership positions in women's organizations. Their successes—and failures—sometimes led to jealousies that lingered for years. In San Francisco, Robbins remembered a struggle over the presidency of the California Occidental Branch in 1874 vividly enough to detail it in a personal journal nearly forty years later.[31]

Yet the multiplication of home mission organizations in western cities represented more than a middle-class quest for status. Schooled as they were in Victorian gender roles as well as class roles, Protestant women approached western cities with a dual vision. On the one hand, they appreciated the opportunities for status these emerging cities offered them and their husbands. On the other, as women who considered themselves moral guardians of society, they feared the Far West's reputation for aggressive masculinity and wide-open immorality.

Denver and San Francisco illustrate the conditions that fostered their campaign to inject female moral authority into western cities. Both cities had retained their frontier reputations as centers of moral libertinism; they were known for saloons, prostitution, and urban vice. Furthermore, in both cities, men far outnumbered Protestant women. Highly visible male social institutions like saloons contrasted sharply with the comparative absence of female charitable networks. For all these reasons, Denver and San Francisco seemed to Victorian women to exemplify the dangers of men's living without the moral guidance of women: in such a situation, even a normally self-controlled man might lose his hold on self-restraint and abandon his commitment to Victorian morality.[32]

The resistance missionary women faced was formidable. Direct opposition came from those who profited from liquor and prostitution, the favorite vices of the mostly male transient population and the *demimonde* missionaries were fond of contrasting with middle-class family life.[33] Even more important, home mission women found that some of the very middle-class men they expected to be their allies failed to share the sense of urgency that propelled Protestant women to establish benevolent institutions for the protection of women and children. As one historian has described them, the men who inhabited San Francisco and Denver tended to be "reluctant citizens" devoted to the search for opportunity and wealth in fast-growing cities, content with imposing only a "minimum of order" on local governments.[34] In western cities, the number of established charities remained minimal, and local governments were in the hands of politicians who tolerated saloons and prostitution. Under these circumstances, home mission projects that might otherwise have expressed only the conventional behavior of benevolent women took on greater significance. They began to symbolize, not just female benevolence, but also female opposition to the male-dominated social order that characterized emerging western cities.

The San Francisco Chinese Mission Home

Presbyterian women established the Chinese Mission Home in San Francisco in 1874 to provide refuge for Chinese prostitutes.[35] The idea for the Mission Home developed from an entirely different proposal put forth by Mrs. John Gulick, a Presbyterian missionary to China. In 1873, Gulick spoke to a small group of San Francisco women on behalf of her pet project, an orphanage in Shanghai. Telling sad stories of the lives of girls and women in China, she elicited enough interest to inspire eight local women to form a women's mission society they called the California Branch of the (Philadelphia) Woman's Foreign Missionary Society.[36]

Despite initial enthusiasm, however, support for the Shanghai project waned and the California Branch languished. Its worried officers decided that, while "woman's work in Foreign lands was a worthy object," they needed "something tangible, something right here at home, to create a greater interest."[37] Still concerned by what Gulick had told them about the treatment of women in China, Presbyterian women found local examples in the case of Chinese immigrant women, many of whom worked as prostitutes. Here was a cause to hold their attention. Protestant women quickly came to see Chinese immigrant prostitution as symbolic of the

San Francisco's Chinatown as it appeared in the 1870s.
(*Courtesy of the Bancroft Library*)

abuse of women that flourished in western cities. Accordingly, they decided to build a rescue home to provide "shelter and protection" for those Chinese women in San Francisco who were, as prostitutes, "refugees from a slavery worse than death."[38]

In the San Francisco of the 1870s, they could not have chosen a more controversial undertaking. The plight of Chinese immigrant women compelled to serve as prostitutes was indeed comparable to slavery. A complex system of procurement had developed in China, sustained by poverty so severe that in some regions parents paid debts by selling their daughters. Young women—some enticed, others purchased, and many kidnapped—were transported to the United States and placed under the control of agents. Agents then sold them either to private "owners" or to tongs that specialized in providing sexual services to the predominantly male Chinese immigrants who sought their fortune on the "Golden Mountain." Some women worked as prostitutes to pay off indenture contracts or to support their families in China; most were completely at the mercy of their "owners." Compared to white prostitutes in San Francisco, they had only minimal control over their working conditions, earnings, and customers.[39]

Along with other Chinese immigrants, Chinese prostitutes were the targets of bitter racial hostility. Many of San Francisco's white working men, victims themselves of depressed economic conditions, were receptive to the polemics of local "sand-lot orators" who used Chinese immigrants as scapegoats for economic problems. In the 1870s, the Workingmen's Party gained control of the San Francisco city government. The class-based rhetoric of the Workingmen's Party frightened some local businessmen, but the new government passed several anti-Chinese ordinances and made anti-Chinese rhetoric a staple of San Francisco community life. Soon agitators began to marshall support for a federal measure for the exclusion of Chinese immigrants. The first exclusion act, which prohibited the immigration of Chinese laborers, became law in 1882, setting the pattern for more than half a century of racist immigration restriction directed at the Chinese.[40]

In this charged atmosphere of class and race hostility, the plan to establish a rescue home for the protection of Chinese prostitutes required a degree of determination that constantly tested the mettle of Presbyterian women. The Chinese Mission Home, presided over by a Presbyterian matron selected by the California Branch, opened in tiny rented quarters in 1874. Before long, the leaders of the Branch, eager to obtain a larger building, heard of a twenty-five-room tenement on Sacramento Street that might serve their purpose. When a missionary group led by Mrs. E. V. Robbins went to look over the property, they discovered, according to one reminiscence, that the landlady, who "had heard that the Chinese were to live there," was so "indignant" that she expressed her disgust "by spitting in the face of Mrs. Robbins."[41] Mission women obtained the building only after the tenants, who were Catholics, were evicted; an action that left "the neighborhood in an uproar" and "a mob threaten[ing] to tear down the building."[42] Trying to avoid more trouble, the women refused to tell the workingmen hired to remodel the building what it would be used for. Their worries had substance. On the day they moved in, a black man who had been helping carry the furniture "saw the Chinese girls

[and] quit work, exclaiming, 'I can't stand that.' "[43] The next-door neighbor, a Catholic, covered five of the mission windows with boards, and children made a game of harassing mission workers.[44]

Despite this opposition—and despite their own considerable fear—the women of the California Branch continued their work. Like other white San Franciscans, they worried that an influx of Chinese immigrants might overrun American institutions, but, unlike them, they opposed Chinese exclusion laws.[45] The use of Chinese women as prostitutes, a visible threat to female purity, seemed to them a greater peril than unlimited immigration. The inculcation of Protestant morality, a visible expression of female piety, seemed to them a more effective solution than legal exclusion.

The women reformers' viewpoint ran counter to that of community leaders, who quickly objected to the enterprise as a challenge to local hierarchies of race and gender. Mrs. Mansie Condit, a missionary, recalled that not only did "political aspirants [refuse] to have their wives and daughters identified with work for Chinese" but Presbyterian pastors also treated the work with "distant reserve" or "openly opposed it."[46] After some pastors refused to allow women of the California Branch to use their pulpits to recruit among churchwomen, the women demanded a formal meeting with churchmen of the Synod. Although one minister boycotted the session because he believed his absence would demonstrate that he would not "countenance women in doing such things," the two groups hammered out an agreement that reduced open animosity.[47]

A few years later, however, the women learned that churchmen's formal acquiescence did not imply acceptance of the women's belief in the importance of maintaining a refuge for Chinese women. The California Branch had proven so attractive to San Francisco Presbyterian women that by the end of its second year of operation, Branch leaders claimed to have enlisted 1,200 women in local auxiliaries.[48] The auxiliaries busied themselves with raising funds, mostly through individual contributions from home mission women. In 1878 the women celebrated a milestone in their struggle for the permanency of the Chinese Mission Home, having purchased, remodeled, and painstakingly paid off the debt on their new property. At their next regular meeting, a delegation of churchmen proposed that the women sell their cherished building in order to help the church purchase a new headquarters. Perhaps, the men suggested, one floor of the new headquarters might be given to the women for their work.[49] This proposal, which died in shocked silence, is an indication of how strongly the priorities of churchmen and home mission women differed. For most churchmen, the women's work was a controversial program that conflicted with the needs of a larger, male-directed mission operation. For the women of the California Branch, however, the rescue of Chinese prostitutes was self-evidently urgent; a route to establishing a female vision of community moral order that held great appeal for white middle-class Protestant women in San Francisco.

The Denver, Colorado, Cottage Home

While Protestant women in San Francisco developed a rescue home for Chinese prostitutes, their counterparts in Denver focused on the needs of unmarried mothers. In 1886, Denver women established the Colorado Cottage Home, a rescue home for pregnant girls and women sponsored by the Colorado branch of the Woman's Christian Temperance Union. Although the Temperance Union is best known for its opposition to liquor, historians of women recognize it as a central organ of Victorian women's culture.[50] Its nineteenth-century members did not limit themselves to the temperance cause but pursued a variety of charitable projects, in line with the "do-everything" policy of its national president Frances Willard, a strong advocate of "homes of reformation, protection, and employment."[51] In Colorado, charitable projects provided the glue that kept the state Union together when temperance victories were few and far between. Colorado Union members sponsored a kitchen garden (to train domestics), a woman's exchange (to allow homemakers to sell handicrafts on consignment), a day and night nursery, and a home for "friendless" women. For several years, the group also sponsored the fledgling Denver Florence Crittenton Home for the rehabilitation of prostitutes. The largest of the Union ventures, and the most popular among members, was the Colorado Cottage Home for unmarried mothers.[52]

Like home mission women in other western cities, women in

Denver drew two pictures of local conditions: one a glowing land-
scape of growth and opportunity, the other a frightening collage
of women seduced and abandoned and children deserted or orphaned. There is little reason to believe they exaggerated the dangers. The best information now available indicates that premarital
pregnancies increased all across the nation between 1870 and
1920.[53] In Denver, where the population nearly tripled between
1880 and 1890, and the ratio of saloons to citizens increased as
well, the situation was ripe with opportunities for seduction and
abandonment.[54]

One young pregnant woman provided the personal connection
that sparked the formation of the Colorado Cottage Home. The
woman, a dance hall employee in Leadville, Colorado, came to
Temperance Union member and missionary Catherine Beach for
assistance. When Beach's efforts to reunite her with her family
failed (her unsympathetic parents suggested she be sent to a refor-
matory), the troubled woman committed suicide in Beach's
home.[55]

In the wake of this tragedy, Beach urged Colorado Union officers
to establish a refuge for "betrayed girls." A handful of the officers
objected, fearful that their advocacy of temperance had already
made them so notorious that they could not afford to take on the
equally unpopular project of rehabilitating "fallen" dance hall
girls. Union leaders held a meeting to pray over the matter. Beach's
arguments apparently proved persuasive: at the end of the day-
long session, the group emerged tearfully dedicated to the concept
of a rescue home that would, as they described it, help them save
defenseless young women from callous seduction and abandonment.[56] Believing that unmarried mothers were, in the main,
blameless women degraded by unscrupulous men, they built the
Colorado Cottage Home to "rescue" and care for pregnant girls
and women.

The Colorado Cottage Home opened in Colorado Springs in
1886 and relocated to Denver in 1888. In this home, as in other
rescue homes, Protestant women hoped residents would learn to
follow the example of the middle-class matron hired to supervise
the institution. The first matron of the Colorado Cottage Home,
local notable Sadie Likens, a former Civil War nurse who was also
Denver's first police matron, attracted such enthusiastic support

Larimer and Sixteenth streets, downtown Denver, at about the time of the establishment of the Colorado Cottage Home.
(*Courtesy of the Colorado Historical Society*)

from the 719 members of the Temperance Union that the institution seemed off to a good start.[57]

Yet, the women of the Colorado Union, like home mission
women in San Francisco, found it difficult to justify their program
to the surrounding community. Denver residents were at best in-
different to their appeals for financial assistance, and the state
legislature rebuffed their attempts to secure public funding.[58] In
1889, Union members, angered by the unwillingness of the Colorado legislature to turn its attention to charities for women and
children, passed a resolution expressing their annoyance. They
declared that they deplored the "lack of principle" and the "ex-
travagances and unwarrantable expenses of the late state legislature," and they pledged themselves to "work and pray for the
hastening of the time when men shall stand shoulder to shoulder
with us in the work of uplifting humanity and honoring God."[59]
In many late–nineteenth-century western states and territories,
Colorado among them, legislators were known for their willingness
to line their own pockets at the expense of taxpayers. Temperance
Union women, however, expressed their anger, not at lawmakers
in particular, but at "men" in general. To them, the legislature's
graft was symptomatic of a larger problem: the indifference of men
to moral reforms advocated by women.[60] The connection was an
easy one to make, for the Colorado legislature flaunted its masculinity by holding its deliberations in saloons.[61]

Only after Colorado women gained the vote in 1893 were Union
members in a position to mount a concerted drive for the moral
and charitable reforms they had in mind. They advocated raising
the legal age of consent, making wives equal guardians (with husbands) of their children, establishing a State Industrial School for
Girls, and securing state appropriations for the Denver Florence
Crittenton Home and the Colorado Cottage Home.[62] Their list of
priorities, so different from those of male lawmakers, illustrates
the vision of social order held by Protestant women trying to establish female moral authority in western cities.

The Salt Lake City Industrial Christian Home

The search for female moral authority emerged even more dramatically in the establishment of the Industrial Christian Home in

Salt Lake City.[63] In Salt Lake City, Protestant women singled out the institution of Mormon polygamy as the most significant symbol of male control over community social order. As they saw it, Denver and San Francisco may have been places where male abuse of women was publicly tolerated, but Salt Lake City was a place where male domination was actually celebrated. National temperance leader Frances Willard expressed the urgency Protestant women felt. In the Mormon capital, she remarked, "the instinct of self-protection, not less than philanthropy, should warn the wives and mothers of this land that each woman degraded means the potential degradation of all women."[64]

In Salt Lake City, local officials who resisted home mission women's efforts to establish benevolent institutions did so for rather different reasons than in San Francisco or Denver. For all intents and purposes, Salt Lake City welfare programs were in the hands of the Mormon church, which, until the first non-Mormon political victory in 1889, firmly controlled local politics.[65] It was the determination of Mormons to retain this control that moved Baptist Cornelia Paddock to lament that "Utah has no system of public charities, and no organized private charities."[66]

One of the central religious tenets of nineteenth-century Mormonism was polygamy, a marriage system in which men could take more than one wife.[67] Estimates of the percentage of Mormons who practiced polygamy vary dramatically. Scholars have found rates of male participation as low as five per cent and as high as sixty-six per cent in different localities; current opinion is that more than a third of all Mormon men (and, of course, at least twice as many women) made polygamous marriages.[68] More important than the actual percentages is the fact that the men who did practice polygamy were, for the most part, respected church leaders whose status in the community helped attract women to the system.

The very existence of polygamy seemed to home mission women to undermine claims to female moral authority. As home mission women saw it, Mormon women were trapped in a marriage system that made a mockery of female purity and virtually enslaved wives. Polygamy, they believed, was a diabolical attempt to reduce the status of women by making women into sacrifices.

Mormons defended themselves from these charges by advancing their own version of female piety and purity; one that did not, however, include a claim to female moral authority. In Mormon theology, moral authority clearly rested with men. In theological terms, Mormon men, all of whom shared in the power of the priesthood, gained salvation according to their achievements and the size of their families, but Mormon women gained salvation only through their earthly protectors, their husbands.

Although many Mormon women found living in polygamy difficult, they endured its trials for religious reasons; they accepted the Mormon belief that polygamy was God's will.[69] Mormon women leaders, however, went further, publicly defending plural marriage. Echoing some of the favorite terms of Protestant missionary women, they contrasted the "purity" of polygamy to the general licentiousness of non-Mormon society. They insisted that polygamous Mormon homes were morally superior, not inferior, to those of middle-class Protestant women.[70]

Home mission women, stung by this attempt to attach the values of Victorianism to polygamy, dismissed all their arguments, and began to promote the establishment of an evangelical "industrial home"—a popular type of Victorian welfare institution specializing in job training—for dissatisfied polygamous wives. Confidently discounting the influence of Mormon women leaders, they predicted that "if a good home were provided and absolute protection guaranteed, the number of women who would renounce polygamy and church rule, and seek shelter under its protecting roof, would astonish you."[71]

By the 1880s, polygamy had become the symbolic issue in a struggle between Mormons and non-Mormons for political and economic control of Salt Lake City. Ever since the 1840s, Salt Lake City government had been exercised by Mormon men who blurred the line between civic and church authority. Non-Mormon (or "Gentile") officials sent by Congress to administer Utah territorial affairs were appalled by this *de facto* theocracy and determined to foster opposition to Mormon rule. In the 1860s and 1870s, the small contingent of federal officials was reinforced by an influx of non-Mormon merchants and miners. In 1869, local Gentiles joined with a group of disaffected Mormons to establish the Liberal Party, the first serious challenge to Mormon civic leadership. Determined but still hopelessly outnumbered, the Liberals relied on sensational antipolygamy rhetoric to bolster their attempts to curb Mormon political and economic power.

Through the 1870s, the antipolygamy campaign was frustrated by the Mormon argument that the First Amendment guarantee of religious freedom protected polygamy. In the 1880s, however, Gentiles gained momentum. In 1882, Congress passed the Edmunds Act, which outlawed polygamy, disfranchised polygamists, and sent a five-member Utah Commission to oversee all local elections. Mormons held on to local power in the 1883 elections, but in 1884, federal officials initiated court proceedings against the first of 1,200 polygamists. In 1887, Congress passed another, still stricter, antipolygamy statute that dissolved the church corporation and increased the extent of disfranchisement.[72]

But for Salt Lake City home mission women, polygamy was not merely the conveniently sensational adjunct to political and economic concerns it seemed to many men; it was the primary issue. Throughout the 1870s, local women's concerns, echoed by evangelical women all across the country, had surfaced in a spate of anti-Mormon novels written by women. Women's novels transformed the anti-Mormon genre, which had earlier functioned as a sort of proto-pornographic exposé of the sexual practices of Mormon families, into a call for middle-class women to eradicate polygamy.[73] The autobiographies of female Mormon apostates lent credence to antipolygamy fictions and inspired the formation of the Salt Lake–based Ladies' Anti-Polygamy Society.[74] Between 1880 and 1883, the Society published a journal, the *Anti-Polygamy Standard*. In a bid to attract the attention of a national audience of evangelical women, the *Standard* featured in every issue a call for "happy wives and mothers" to use their "sentiments and sympathy" on behalf of Mormon women by channeling their political influence into a crusade to outlaw polygamy.[75]

Despite the depth of their feeling, Protestant women in Salt Lake City were a tiny minority who had few financial resources with which to establish a refuge for Mormon women. They made little progress, until Angie Newman applied herself to finding support for the project. Newman, who was born in 1837, was a native of Vermont with a long (if not especially illustrious) New England genealogy. She grew up in Wisconsin, where, after holding a job as a public school teacher and briefly attending classes at Lawrence University, she married dry goods merchant David Newman, with whom she had two children. For the next decade she was a virtual invalid, afflicted with a severe pulmonary condition that improved only after she left Wisconsin for Lincoln, Nebraska, in 1871. While David Newman took advantage of the move to establish himself in the real estate and insurance businesses, Angie Newman applied herself to women's organizations. A devoted member of the Woman's Christian Temperance Union with an active interest in both prison reform and Methodist missionary work, she joined the Woman's Foreign Missionary Society, contributing articles to its publication, the *Heathen Woman's Friend,* and speaking on its behalf.[76]

But it was in the home mission field that Angie Newman would make her mark. In 1876, she took a health-seeking trip to visit some relatives in Utah. Alerted by them to what she called "the substitution of the Harem for the Home in all our western borders," she pushed aside her other causes to devote herself to the establishment of a refuge for polygamous women, taking full advantage of the evangelical and political contacts she had developed over the years.[77] In 1883, she persuaded the Cincinnati-based (Methodist Episcopal) Woman's Home Missionary Society to back the project, securing from it $660 in initial pledges and an appointment as its bureau secretary for Mormon affairs.[78] Over the next few years, however, her personal influence within the Society ebbed. While she recovered from an accident that left her temporarily bedridden, the Society's enthusiasm for the project suffered from the loss of her personal advocacy.[79] In March of 1886, Newman, whose plans were by now even more ambitious, left the Society behind. She called a meeting with a group of Utah residents, including Park City Presbyterian Jeannette Ferry and a core of old members of the Ladies' Anti-Polygamy Society, to form the interdenominational Industrial Christian Home Association.[80]

The new Association was richer in enthusiasm than in money; furthermore, its members knew they would find no kind ears among local officials. They had only one card to play: the fact that Congress, which was known to be sympathetic to anti-Mormon rhetoric, was in charge of territorial governments. Stretching women's political influence as far as it would go, they took the highly unusual step of sending Newman to Washington, D.C., to seek funding from the federal government. In May of 1886, Newman was granted a hearing before the Senate Committee on Education

Angie Newman, home mission lobbyist, temperance advocate, and moving force in the establishment of the Industrial Christian Home in Salt Lake City.

and Labor. Her impassioned descriptions of Mormon women victimized by polygamy struck a responsive chord in the Committee.[81] Shortly afterward, Congress, which was under pressure from Protestant constituencies all over the country to take action against polygamy, agreed to underwrite the project.[82] The delighted Home

Association announced that the Home would extend a warm welcome to Mormon women they hoped to rescue from "enslavement" at the hands of Mormon men.

Having surmounted the problem of Mormon control over local charity, however, home mission women in Salt Lake City ran up against another problem—resistance from non-Mormon men in Utah. The Industrial Christian Home Association had asked a number of prominent Gentile men, including territorial officials, local merchants, and evangelical ministers, to sponsor their organization. When Angie Newman traveled to Washington, D.C., to appeal for Congressional funding for the Home project, she took with her letters of recommendation from several of these men, counting on their public reputations and political contacts to enhance the credibility of her request.[83]

This initial spirit of cooperation between Salt Lake City's Gentile women and men quickly evaporated. Congress agreed to fund the Home but was unwilling to give its financial control to a group of women. Neatly revealing the distinction between the political influence women wielded and the political power they did not, Congress added to the appropriation a provision for the appointment of an all-male Board of Control to oversee the Home Association. The Board of Control consisted of Utah's territorial governor, its supreme court justices, and the district attorney. Most of these men had expressed their opposition to polygamy; some were sponsors of the industrial home project. Yet a dispute between the men of the Board and the women of the Home Association broke out almost immediately.

According to one Mormon reporter who covered the story, the women were "mad as hornets because [the money] was placed in the hands of the board of control."[84] In an attempt to determine exactly what kind of oversight the Board would provide, the women of the Association asked the men of the Board for their assurances that they would limit themselves to endorsing financial transactions and leave the planning and direction of the Home project to the women. The Board of Control not only refused, but Governor West ordered an investigation to determine whether there was sufficient demand for the Home's services. When West added insult to injury by telling the women of the Industrial Christian Home Association that their leadership was no longer needed, he infuriated Newman and the Utah women she represented.

Never one to turn the other cheek, Angie Newman appealed to the Congressmen who had listened sympathetically to her testimony at the hearings. Then she wrote directly to President Grover Cleveland. She asked him to stop West's interference. She wanted West to acknowledge that the Home should be under the direction of the female Industrial Christian Home Association, not the male Board of Control. "President Cleveland," she wrote, "this enterprise is *woman's* work for her suffering sex. . . . To have the enterprise entirely withdrawn from those who originated it and won the victory is certainly not *just*." "We trust you to save us from defeat," she concluded, adding impatiently that he must do so quickly, before "[Mormon women] who wearily *wait* for our ministry grow sick at heart and fall by the way."[85]

In the meantime, the Industrial Christian Home opened in December of 1886, and the conflict over financial power soon turned into deep disagreement over the philosophy of the institution. During the first nine months of its operation, 154 women and children asked to enter the institution. All but a relative handful were refused admission because the Board of Control, led by West, favored a narrow interpretation of the language of the legislation, which provided that entrance to the Home be limited to "women who renounce polygamy and [to] their children of tender age." To the delight of watchful Mormon commentators, West interpreted the phrase to exclude many first wives, children of polygamists apart from their mothers, and women and children not currently involved in plural marriages but who home mission women believed might prove susceptible to inducements to enter polygamy.[86] West's position, which limited admittance to repentant plural wives and their children, infuriated the women of the Home Association, who held that almost every woman in Utah was a potential victim of polygamy.

The quarrel between the women of the Association and the men of the Board raged throughout the first year of the Home operation. To the amusement of Mormons eager to discredit the Home— and to Mormon and Gentile readers who followed the battles in local papers—rhetorical jibes escalated. At one point, an exasperated Angie Newman went so far as to question the propriety of the men's behavior, telling them that "it is folly to entertain the thought that an institution for treatment of women and children of diseased minds and bodies should be under the official care of men."[87] In essence, the men did not share either the urgency women felt for the establishment of charities or the relatively inclusive conception of "female victims" the women held. For their part, the women believed that West's strict interpretation would "cripple" the institution; they interpreted his behavior as a threat to the spirit of Protestant women's sympathy for female victims they wanted the Home to symbolize.[88]

When President Cleveland did not come to its aid (he referred the letter to the Secretary of the Interior), the Home Association sent Newman back to Washington to seek legislation to restore its control over the Home project.[89] In 1888, the women came close to winning their point. By that time, the Board of Control was ready to submit its first annual report to Congress, and its exasperated members wanted nothing more than to wash their hands of the whole operation. Apparently deciding that supervising the Industrial Christian Home was more trouble than it was worth, the Board recommended that its administrative and policy-making functions be turned over to the women's Home Association and requested that Congress pass legislation to enlarge the admission policies of the Home.[90]

By this time, however, the Industrial Christian Home had become something of a laughingstock in Salt Lake City. The battle between the Home Association and the Board had made sensational copy for rival local newspapers. One Mormon editor accused Newman of having gained government support by "false pretenses, by wilful lying, and by the manufacture and utterance of prurient and filthy stories."[91] Newspaper coverage like this helped to discredit Home Association claims that the institution was managed by "kind-hearted Christian women" out of sympathy for "those women who feel themselves wronged and oppressed by polygamy."[92]

Yet the women's association, still determined to make their project a home mission showplace, tried to convince Congress that the construction of a grand new building might solve the Home's problems. Congress, which remained eager to show off its oppo-

Industrial Christian Home, Salt Lake City. This grand building, paid for by the federal government, opened in 1889.
(*Courtesy of the Utah State Historical Society*)

sition to polygamy, approved this plan and provided an increased appropriation of $50,000 for building construction; but once again insisted that the women be supervised by male officials.[93] This time the Utah Commission, a group of federal appointees sent to the territory several years earlier, was appointed to carry out this task. Although the women worked much more smoothly with the Utah Commission than they had with the Board of Control, their lavish new institution attracted few residents after it opened in 1889.

While the women scrambled to find enough residents to fill their grand building, they learned of yet another threat to the institution. A group of prominent Gentile men, some of whom had helped found the Home Association, had organized themselves into a "syndicate" dedicated to what the women believed was an "attempt to wrest the home from the designs of its founders."[94] Congress was considering a bill to fund a federal office building in Salt Lake City, and the syndicate suggested that legislators could save money by simply expropriating the Industrial Home building.[95]

Most of the syndicate members lived, or owned businesses, on the East Side; they hoped to make a tidy real estate profit by rerouting city traffic in that direction.[96] The scheme ultimately failed; but while it was debated a number of its proponents sought to advance their cause by publicizing the "failure" of the Industrial Home project.[97] As the women put it, "the promoters of the scheme represented that the home was a failure because of the fewness of the inmates, omitting the fact that there were needy inmates, both women and children, continuously applying for admission."[98] To home mission women in Salt Lake City, even a few needy women seemed enough to justify the continuation of the Home. To them, as to their counterparts in other western cities, female victims had a symbolic significance far exceeding their actual numbers.

Like the San Francisco Chinese Mission Home and the Denver Cottage Home, the Industrial Christian Home reveals the dynamics of the search for female moral authority adapted to a particular western city. In particular, the besieged Industrial Christian Home Association illustrates the political dilemma Protestant women faced. Federal government support, unprecedented for a refuge planned by women for women, had come only at the cost of losing control of the enterprise to men who did not share home mission women's vision of its significance. The result was a protracted battle for control of the institution that exposed the fault lines between Protestant women and men in Salt Lake City.

By the late nineteenth century, middle-class women had stretched the republican formulation of true womanhood into a new shape: no longer willing to value submission or to limit their activities to their domestic circles, they sought to impose the Victorian female values of piety and purity on American society in general. Because these values were adapted from mainstream Victorian gender roles, they allowed home mission women a fighting chance to manipulate men. What good Victorian man could object to women who spoke for the purity of Victorian womanhood? Protestant women missionaries built their case around the concept of "woman's work for woman," depicting themselves as pious wives and mothers hoping to extend the Christian home to victimized women everywhere.

This search for female moral authority, a nationwide phenomenon, took on special urgency when home mission women in western cities ran into the resistance of male community leaders. In the case of the eastern-based Connecticut Indian Association, women's anger at men was muted. Among home mission women in San Francisco, Denver, and Salt Lake City, however, social fluidity, highly visible male institutions, and a virtual absence of charitable networks sharpened tension between women and men. In these cities, Protestant women's attempts to inject their concerns into the community issues of their day form a significant—and as yet little understood—part of the process of western community development.

Thus, in the early years of home mission work, middle-class women's search for female moral authority in the American West was expressed largely as tension between women and men. Conceived in Victorian gender roles, nurtured by Victorian women's culture, and exacerbated by the conditions of western cities, this tension was institutionalized in the creation of rescue homes. These home mission projects displayed Protestant women's outrage at male-dominated social orders and their belief that women knew a better way. Rescue home founders started with high hopes: they would house and care for women overlooked or victimized by men; they would provide residents with education, domesticity, and even a chance for professional training. But as the institutions developed, middle-class women expressed their quest for authority less often in relation to men and more often in relations with rescue home residents. Before we can investigate those relations, however, we need to turn from the institutional origins of the search for female moral authority to its ideological underpinnings.

2

The Ideology of Female Moral Authority, 1874–1900

"The purpose of our organization," wrote Winifred Spaulding in 1892, "is to educate the girls to that sturdy independence of spirit that can say no—[to educate them] to that lofty ideal of purity and virtue that shall lead them to reject vice, in however alluring a form it may present itself." Spaulding, the Colorado superintendent of the Young Woman's Christian Temperance Union, elaborated in a lengthy article linking the lofty ideal she mentioned with the concept of the Christian home. "It takes a woman to make a home," she told her readers, "and I believe and every true woman believes, that the making of a christian home is the highest sphere of woman." In the 1890s, any middle-class Victorian, male or female, might have made such a statement. It was entirely conventional to speak of true women and Christian homes in the same breath, assuming any reader would recognize the connection.

But Spaulding, a home mission woman, went further. Because of the "sad and lamentable fact that there are not enough good men to 'go round,' " she warned young women that "every marriage does not mean a home, and it is a mockery to call [some of] them homes." Since comments like these might well seem startling, she added that "I would not have you think we are opposing marriage [since] it would do no good if we did, except individually." Nevertheless, she believed that it was "better to live alone and unloved a thousand years" than to live in an impure home. "If it is a sacrifice to forego the society of young men of doubtful character," she advised, "then let us make the sacrifice for the good of the world, our sisters." There was, she believed, an alternative. In her opinion, "noble minded girls who preferred to support themselves and make their homes with other girls . . . [have proven that] homes can be made by women alone."[1]

Spaulding's outspoken rhetoric provides the strand we need to unravel the twisted threads of the ideology of female moral authority spun by home mission women in the American West. Taking for granted the "separate spheres" middle-class Victorians assigned to men and women, home mission women worked within the assumptions and through the networks of Victorian women's culture. Starting from two conventional values of true womanhood—piety and purity—and the equally conventional notion of the Christian home, they used Victorian women's identification with morality to press for authority in American society. In the process, they stretched these conventions almost beyond recognition. In home mission usage, "the Christian home" was identified with the moral authority of women rather than the patriarchal control of men; the term implied criticism of male domination in families. The Victorian female values of piety and purity became tools to carve a particular form of women's emancipation, one that, in some cases, even included woman suffrage. Missionary women's appeals to the values of true womanhood and to the Christian home allowed them to attract an enormous following among middle-class women. Because they derived new meaning from old terms rather than rejecting the terms altogether, they were also in a position to sway unwary conventionalists.

But, despite home mission redefinitions, reliance on "the Christian home" created enduring political and institutional dilemmas for the search for female moral authority. Because they believed that women's moral influence stemmed from their positions as wives and mothers, home mission women had to argue for expanding women's authority in family life without endangering the family as a social institution. As we shall see, they carried off this balancing act partly by directing their sharpest critiques at families outside Victorian middle-class culture. Over the long run, this tactic would dilute their criticism of the middle-class Protestant men who had so excited their ire in western cities. In the meantime, their concern about female victimization led them to carry on their campaign to strengthen female moral authority largely through the lives of women, ironically exempting men of all classes and cultures from the process of change. Rescue homes, the most characteristic of home mission projects, ultimately placed more emphasis on changing the lives of the women who entered them than on challenging the power of men.

The Moral Leverage of "the Christian Home"

Paeans to home and family were rhetorical staples of Victorian middle-class discourse, but no single group—except, perhaps, the national Woman's Christian Temperance Union—invoked the image of "the Christian home" as frequently as home mission women.[2] In order to understand the ideology of female moral authority, we have to probe the meaning of "the Christian home" not as it appears to us today, but as it was used in late–nineteenth-century Victorian women's culture.

The journey to this understanding has been a long one, because historians, along with other modern readers, tend to be misled by the seeming conventionality of the phrase. For decades scholars considered the Victorian rhetoric of home and family little more than an expression of sanctimonious sentimentality.[3] Beginning in the 1960s, however, social historians took a second look at Victorian familial rhetoric. Starting from two shared assumptions— that family ideology mirrored reality and that the Christian home was a bastion of male power—historians reached two different conclusions. Some scholars, mostly males, glorified the self-contained "haven" of the Victorian family and lamented its later demise.[4] Pioneering feminist scholars disagreed. In their eyes, the Victorian Christian home was a truss binding women's lives in a narrow circle of domestic patterns.[5]

Although both these interpretations were an advance over the sentimentality thesis, they made it difficult to understand why Victorian women as well as men promoted "the Christian home" with obvious enthusiasm. Recent historians of the family offer one solution to this puzzle. Comparing the Victorian family to its traditional predecessor rather than to its modern successor, they analyzed the late–eighteenth-century transition from colonial to Victorian marriage. The shift, they argued, increased the status of women because Victorians expected their unions to be mutually pleasurable, based on affection between spouses, and dependent on women as child-rearers.[6]

Another group of feminist scholars offers a different, but not unrelated, explanation. Seeking to understand Victorian women as they understood themselves, they probed the ways women used the values of true womanhood to extend their influence over community life through quasi-domestic activities, from school teaching to "social housekeeping." A growing body of evidence suggests that Victorian female reformers fought against male privilege even as they defended the Christian home. Women prison reformers refused to entrust women prisoners to male guardians and insisted on opening separate women's prisons modeled on the family; women temperance workers mounted a critique of male authority through their "home protection" rhetoric; and female moral reformers from the mid–nineteenth century into the Progressive era criticized male sexual license as a threat to the home.[7]

These new perspectives point the way to understanding the conception of the Christian home advanced by Protestant women in the West. Mission women's rhetorical devotion to the Christian home reflected their acceptance of the ideal of Victorian marriage, an ideal that differed significantly from its traditionally patriarchal colonial predecessor. Victorian unions were based on attraction between prospective spouses rather than guided by parental arrangement: in them, at least according to the ideal, women played the role of nurturant mothers and moral guardians. In contrast to the ethic of female submission that characterized traditional marriages, Victorian marriages offered a vision of romantic affection between husbands and wives, with wives assigned unprecedented responsibilities as mothers and moral arbiters.

Yet, as feminist historians have pointed out, gender inequality thrived within the ideal of Victorian marriage, for Victorian wives gained affection and moral influence at the cost of legal and economic powerlessness.[8] According to the ideal, husbands were assigned economic responsibility for the family. Wives were expected to be economic dependents, a status that sharply limited women's alternatives inside and outside of marriage. Often deprived of formal control over their own property, throughout the nineteenth century, married women had to fight for such basic rights as the legal guardianship of their own children.[9]

According to the ideal, husbands were expected to bow to their wives' gentle moral guidance, even in such matters as sexuality. Many Victorian men did regard sexual self-control as one indication of middle-class social status; accordingly, some historians believe that men's actual self-restraint can be deduced from the steady decline in the fertility rate of married women in the nineteenth century.[10] But Victorian women knew that a strong countertradition of male sexual privilege lay just beneath the surface of public protestations of self-restraint: indeed, their uncertainty that their much-praised moral influence was sufficient to offset men's sexual prerogatives, much less their economic power, was one reason they fought to turn their private moral influence into public moral authority.

Throughout the nineteenth century, Victorian reformers waxed eloquent about the need to protect "the Christian home." Yet its many complex elements made "the Christian home," like most cultural symbols, an elastic concept that meant different things to different people. Many Victorians, including the male clergymen who led so many moral reform drives, saw their task as one of protecting women by shoring up male authority in the household.[11]

Home mission women, however, made use of the rhetoric of the Christian home in a different way. Tapping into the popular symbol—and thus gaining access to the middle-class audiences it guaranteed—they subverted its conventional meaning in their work. Aware that most middle-class women had few economic alternatives to marriage, home mission women were reluctant to criticize the institution of the family head-on.[12] Instead, they used their position as sexually pure moral guardians of the home to put forth a different image of family life. They envisioned a Christian home centered around the moral authority of the wife rather than the patriarchal control of the husband. Their rhetorical devotion to the Christian home was both heartfelt and strategic, a way of turning the Christian home, an image of powerful symbolic significance for Victorian culture, into a symbol of female moral authority. Thus, Protestant women engaged in a delicate balancing act. On the one hand, they defended the Christian home at every opportunity; on the other, they put forth an image of it pruned of patriarchal power. Home mission women revealed their thinking in their criticism of men, their attitudes toward divorce, and their advice to young women.

Missionary women's depictions of ideal Christian homes were accompanied by a bold critique of male behavior in the family. As we will see in more detail in the last sections of this chapter, they found fault with husbands who offered inadequate financial support; who failed to consult their wives about decisions; or who did not restrain their sexual drives or their taste for alcohol, opium, or gambling. Most frequently of all, however, they castigated husbands who sought to compel obedience from their wives. Their catalogue of criticisms shows how far they had come from their early–nineteenth-century roots; to late–nineteenth-century home mission women, female "submission" was no longer a mark of true womanhood.[13]

Their critique of husbandly behavior led them to wrestle with the issue of divorce. When they considered divorce in theoretical terms, their attitudes toward it were conditioned by their assumption that women's economic support as well as their influence over society stemmed from their roles as wives. Consequently, they interpreted the dramatic late–nineteenth-century increase in divorce largely in terms of the plight of wives deserted by their husbands. Along with many other women in the nineteenth century, they tried to ensure that husbands would live up to their economic responsibilities by calling for standardized divorce laws that would eliminate so-called easy divorce states and territories, the most notorious of which were in the American West.[14]

They did not, however, believe in continuing a marriage at any cost. As Winifred Spaulding once noted, "it is a platitude to say that marriage is a divine institution—the institution may be divine enough, but it is sometimes difficult to see what there is divine about the marriage."[15] Thus, while in theory Protestant women hoped to reduce women's vulnerability to divorce by their husbands, the net effect of much of their rescue home work was to break up unions that contrasted with their ideals.[16] The central aim of the Industrial Christian Home in Salt Lake City was to enable Mormon plural wives to become financially independent so they could leave polygamy behind. Because home mission women saw Mormon husbands as the personification of patriarchal tyranny, they found the idea of women's remaining in polygamous marriages intolerable, even though the major alternative, working for wages, challenged the middle-class convention of female economic dependence. In San Francisco, Chinese Mission Home personnel led numerous Chinese immigrant women through the legal process of divorcing men the missionaries referred to as "alleged" husbands because they failed to live up to home mission standards. Even the matrons of Denver's Cottage Home for unmarried mothers did not generally encourage young women to marry the men who had made them pregnant, though they often tried to make the men contribute to their financial support.

Home mission women also gave revealing advice to young women considering entering marriage. Although they encouraged all women to revere the Christian home, they advised some women to delay marriage. Home mission women routinely made such suggestions to those whose professional careers they sponsored. Before the Omaha Indian woman Susan LaFlesche entered medical school, for example, the Connecticut branch of the Women's National Indian Association asked her to promise that she would use her skills in full-time practice for at least a few years before marrying.[17] When, several years later, news of her marriage reached the Association, its members consoled themselves by commenting that "since her health and home restrictions do not permit of her longer engaging in active medical practice, we must bury regret at our loss and trust that her bright, intelligent spirit will shed its light upon the new life and surroundings opening before her."[18]

Rescue home matrons were in a similar situation. Aspiring missionary matrons were well aware that readiness to defend the Christian home was a primary job qualification for rescue home employment. Yet the matrons, most of whom lived as well as worked in rescue homes, were usually single—or, less frequently, widowed—women devoted to careers in missionary work. As such, they occupied a somewhat marginal place in a Victorian gender system that idealized married women.[19] Their marginality did not seem to diminish their devotion to domesticity or to the Christian home—indeed, most saw it as a panacea, which prompts speculation that their lack of experience with the daily constraints of Victorian marriage colored their judgment. Notwithstanding their rhetoric, however, they remained unmarried, and they had the support of home mission women in doing so.

Thus, home mission women's theoretical commitment to marriage contrasted with their realistic assessment of many specific cases. Given mission women's apprehensions about so many of the actual or potential marriages they encountered, it is little wonder that Winifred Spaulding could advise young women to build homes with other women "rather than take the job of reforming a sower of wild oats."[20] Spaulding's comment is perhaps the most direct statement of a message implicit in other home mission writings: women together could make a home, while a woman and a man "of doubtful character" could not, because patriarchal behavior was a primary threat to Protestant women's conception of the Christian home.

Yet, remarkable as it was, the home mission critique of patriarchy encountered some thorny problems. Winifred Spaulding's recommendation that women delay marriage until men consented to defer to female moral guidance worked better in theory than in practice. In fact, most of the women who supported home mission projects were middle-aged women who were themselves dependent on marriage for economic support. Noticeably reluctant to bring their criticism of men into their own homes, they made room for significant exceptions. As Spaulding's co-worker Mrs. E. R. Reynolds, explained, a little defensively, "We who have noble husbands, God-fearing fathers, and pure sons and brothers know the world is not all bad."[21]

Home mission women showed much less restraint about criticizing men in other women's families. Yet, even here, they channeled their criticism according to the terms they knew best: if the Christian home was a good thing, and in it the Christian husband bowed to the moral authority of the true woman, the source of the trouble must be non-Christian families.[22] In focusing on non-Christian families, home mission women concentrated their ire on groups who presented highly visible challenges to Victorian female values. Because these groups were not Protestant, they were considered impious. Because they did not share the Victorian reverence for female purity, they were considered "immoral."

One of home mission women's favorite strategies was to contrast an idealized Christian gentleman with his non-Christian counterpart. Take, for example, the case of Ann Eliza Young, estranged wife of polygamous Mormon leader Brigham Young. Soon after her separation, Ann Eliza explained to the receptive female audience of the *Anti-Polygamy Standard* the difference between Mormon and Christian marriages.[23] Christian husbands, she had learned after divorcing Brigham Young, took pride in their wives, treated them with daily respect and courtesy, cared for them when they were ill, and missed them during temporary absences from home. Young's implied comparison lambasted Mormon men while setting ideal standards for Christian husbands. But if Young expected that all Christian husbands would live up to the standards she broadcast, she was mistaken. Her subsequent marriage to Moses Denning, a wealthy temperance advocate from Manistee, Michigan, ended in unhappiness and divorce when she accused him of being "a man of unreasonable passion and lust."[24] Her story only emphasizes the gap between home mission rhetoric and the reality of Victorian marriage. But despite Young's sobering experience, ideals, not realities, formed the basis of the rhetoric of Protestant women in the West. Home mission women held tightly to a vision of the Christian home as the bulwark of female moral authority.

The Link to Women's Emancipation

Implicit in the home mission concept of the Christian home was a deep concern for improving the status of women. Yet the link between the search for female moral authority and women's emancipation has been easy to overlook. The reason is a simple one: home mission concern for women did not translate directly into calls for woman suffrage, the issue most historians use as a litmus test for nineteenth-century feminism. For missionary women in the

West, woman suffrage was a secondary issue: as we will see, their responses to it were conditioned by their other goals. First, however, we must consider three issues that loomed larger to them than woman suffrage. Protestant women in the West hoped to expand women's sphere by promoting higher education for women and supporting women professionals. They hoped to fortify female purity by eliminating the double sexual standard. Finally, they hoped to enlarge the influence of female piety in Protestant churches.

Home mission women were an active part of a century-long fight for women's education. Early in the century, middle-class and élite women called for female seminaries by arguing that, as mothers of the infant republic, they should be prepared to educate their children to be responsible citizens.[25] In the post–Civil War era, women fought for access to colleges rather than to seminaries. Still, as the biographies of home mission women illustrate, college-educated women remained rarities in the 1870s and 1880s. It was the daughters and granddaughters of home mission women who would find higher education a realistic possibility. Meanwhile, home mission women envied the opportunities of younger women and supported the cause of women's education.

As mission women saw it, formal education was important for all women, but especially so for the women who were the targets of home mission projects. Chinese Mission Home workers in San Francisco, for example, hoped that each Chinese immigrant woman they schooled might become "the keystone in the arch that will lift thousands of her race from misery and degradation." The Mission Home staff wanted each woman to be "educated to know that she is neither a slave or a toy; that her social surroundings do not condemn her to a useless life [or deny her] the means of independence."[26]

Despite missionaries' devotion to homemaking, the education they envisioned for rescue home residents was not entirely limited to domestic training. Some plans were vocational. At the Salt Lake Industrial Christian Home for Mormon women, for example, founders hatched a scheme to provide the "industrial skills" of stenography and typewriting, an ambitious undertaking in the 1880s, when women were just beginning to make inroads in office work.

Other plans included professional education. At the Chinese Mission Home, missionaries selected promising students and underwrote their schooling in teaching, social work, and medicine.

In this case-by-case manner, home mission women used their influence to support women professionals. Connecticut women took great pride in Omaha Indian Susan LaFlesche's achievements in medicine; San Francisco women lauded the Chinese Mission Home residents who completed kindergarten training courses; Denver temperance women insisted that the twelve-member medical staff of their Cottage Home for unmarried mothers be at least half women. Home missionaries' support for female professionalism was reinforced by their belief that western cities suffered from the lack of female guidance; when they could, they tried to turn female professionals into female public officials. In Denver, for example, the Colorado Woman's Christian Temperance Union demanded that city officials appoint a police matron; the woman eventually chosen was Sadie Likens, a temperance union member who was for a short time matron at the Denver Cottage Home. After 1893, when the passage of a Colorado suffrage measure strengthened its hand, the Union kept careful track of the number of Colorado women holding public office.

At the same time, home mission women challenged the double standard of sexual behavior. Angry that Victorians held women to an ideal of purity while turning their back on men's lapses from the supposedly parallel ideal of self-restraint, rescue home workers identified unrestrained male lust as a primary threat to women. Like female moral reformers of the antebellum years and social purity advocates of their own time, home mission women advocated a single standard of moral behavior that would hold men to the strict code of chastity required of middle-class Victorian women. The goal of a single standard stood behind home mission campaigns to raise the age of consent, to rescue Chinese prostitutes and imprison their procurers, and to outlaw polygamy among Mormons and American Indians. As historians of women have noted, these demands were not so much attempts to repress sexuality as they were attempts to control male sexual behavior and limit the vulnerability of women to sexual abuse.[27]

Missionary women insisted that until a single standard was

adopted, women must be absolved from responsibility for their participation in deeds for which men were not punished by courts or by public opinion. One case in particular indicates just how far the women would go to defend female innocence. In 1895, the women of the Colorado Woman's Christian Temperance Union came to the defense of Maria Barberi, a fifteen-year-old girl who had been sentenced to death in New York State for the murder of her "faithless seducer." Although no one denied that Barberi had killed the man, Union women regarded her as "guilty of little more than justifiable homicide" because she had committed the act after he had first seduced her, then abandoned her, and finally refused, despite her urgent pleadings, to marry her. Their condemnation of the court system that convicted Barberi was even more revealing than their defense of her motive. They repeated the caustic comment of a sympathetic male critic that "she was arrested by a male officer, locked in prison by a male jailer, watched by a male guard, prosecuted by a male lawyer, convicted by a male jury, under a law passed by a male legislature, approved by a male Governor, and all elected by male voters."[28] In the Union's opinion, Barberi provided the perfect example of an innocent woman victimized by a legal system that itself embodied the double standard of morality that reinforced male sexual privilege.

Home mission women believed that their concern for women's status was a logical outgrowth of their position as Protestant women of the late nineteenth century. Their convictions were rooted in a highly selective interpretation of Christian history and civilization. Surveying the past, home mission women saw most of human history as a dark story of vice and degradation. They noted that Biblical women like Miriam, Deborah, and Esther were bright spots during Old Testament times, but they believed that women's status had been generally low until "Christ came to emancipate woman [and] lifted the curse that had lain upon her for centuries." They read so much potential into the dawn of Christianity that they believed "it was the object of Christianity to exalt [women]." Soon after Christ's death, however, Christian example—and women's hopes—had been swallowed by vice and degradation. After centuries of what they deemed Catholic embarrassment, it had

become the special task of nineteenth-century civilization to re-
cover for women their lost position in history and point the way
toward progress and Christian perfectibility.[29]

Thus, home mission women developed among themselves a version of history in which women's emancipation was the logical
outcome of Christianization. In ideological terms, their interpretation added Christ's sanction to the search for female moral authority undertaken by Protestant mission workers. The Colorado
Woman's Christian Temperance Union, for example, aimed at
nothing less than becoming a "co-worker with God." Strengthened
by this association with divinity, missionary women challenged
traditional strongholds of Christian misogyny. Alice Hatfield of
the Chinese Mission Home told San Francisco mission women that
"Paul's admonition to wives to learn 'spiritual things of their *own
husbands*' is reversed," suggesting that husbands should learn from
their wives instead.[30]

This aggressive ideology steeled home mission women for the
difficult battles they had to fight with Victorian churchmen, who
did not share their interpretation of female piety. After post–Civil
War Protestant women carved out an arena of relative autonomy
in denominational women's missionary societies, they pushed for
greater recognition from general church authorities. In September
1887, they won their first victory when antipolygamist Angie Newman was elected as a delegate to the Methodist Church's General
Conference in 1888. Newman's election by Nebraska churchgoers
was immediately followed by the election of four other women,
most of whom, like Newman, owed their prominence to their work
in women's mission organizations. Mission women's delight at this
unprecedented recognition of churchwomen was cut short, however, when the Conference refused to seat them on the grounds
that, as women, they did not fit the definition of "laymen"
delegates.[31]

Angered by this exclusion, Newman and other Methodist
women, acting, they said, on behalf of *"all* women of *all* the
churches," formed the New Century Club, dedicated to securing
women's representation in church governance councils and to encouraging "the ever-expanding radius of woman's spiritual activities."[32] James M. Buckley, a Methodist church official, responded
at once, charging that the angry women were not, as they pre-

tended to be, pious women deserving recognition for service, but rather radical suffragists trying to achieve their aims in a covert way.[33] Although Buckley's perception that the women were advocating radical change was entirely correct, his depiction of them as suffragists was misguided. Home mission women did not necessarily set their sights on suffrage; they had other goals in mind that would have been just as unacceptable to church leaders. A correspondent who interviewed the women denied seating at the 1892 Methodist Conference reported that one woman "had divulged that there is a movement among the women of the church for 'ordination' outside the church authorities." He went on to note that "about 200 women are studying Greek and otherwise preparing in scripture study" to be ready for such an event.[34]

Although Newman and home mission women like her believed that Christian scripture supported their demands for participation in church governance, church fathers were just as certain that authority rested with their side. During the representation conflict, the *Christian Advocate* reported the activities of the women as if they were absurdities. One reporter, for example, covered Newman's 1892 welcoming speech to Methodist Conference delegates visiting Nebraska. The reporter wrote, probably accurately, that Newman "suggested that this quadrennial body will never become perfect until the delegates, like Adam in Eden, awake to find Eve sitting by their sides." He could not resist adding, however, that then "[she] congratulated herself on the fact that Lucifer, who introduced the first apple of discord, was not a woman."[35] A dozen more years would pass before women were seated as delegates to the Methodist Conference.

Nineteenth-century Protestant churchmen had a long way to go before they were ready to grant female moral authority, much less equality. Yet James Buckley, the churchman who opposed Newman's election and who edited the *Christian Advocate's* coverage of her speech, prided himself on his support of women's home mission work.[36] Buckley had missed the point of home mission women's transposition of the rhetoric of the Christian home. To him, and no doubt to many other Protestant churchmen, dedication to "the Christian home" implied male rather than female authority. The semantic looseness of the term "the Christian home" allowed him to support the work of home mission women while entirely rejecting its ideological base. As long as men who held such opinions played the dominant role in church politics, the concept of the Christian home would be a slender reed upon which to rest the home mission belief that Protestant Christianity marked the dawn of female emancipation.

The Uses of Woman Suffrage

Home mission workers pictured the emancipation of women as a matter of promoting women's education, supporting women professionals, eliminating the double sexual standard, and strengthening the position of women within the church. They were uncertain about the need for woman suffrage, but their ambivalence should not be taken to mean that they were apolitical. Without concrete political power, they relied on female influence; nonetheless, nineteenth-century women believed they should have a voice in government.[37] Home mission women strongly supported specific political reforms—from the Dawes Act mandating Indian policy reform, to antipolygamy legislation—and they tried, sometimes successfully, to influence legislative bodies. Under these circumstances, their attitudes toward woman suffrage, the reform advanced by women's rights advocates of their day, deserve close scrutiny. As it turned out, home mission women's attitudes toward suffrage, like their concepts of women's emancipation, were shaped by their search for female moral authority: home mission women supported suffrage when it seemed achievable and would help them spread their vision of female values; they opposed it when it did not.

The Colorado Woman's Christian Temperance Union supported woman suffrage in the 1880s and 1890s.[38] The first president of the group, Mary Shields, was a state suffrage lecturer adopted by the Temperance Union; in later years, Union members boasted that they had been so effective in mobilizing suffrage sentiment that a separate suffrage organization had been unnecessary until shortly before passage of the state law in 1893.[39] During the campaign, some Union members demanded woman suffrage as a simple matter of equal justice. Nonetheless, a close look at the Temperance

Union reveals that abstract equality was not the central motivation for Union support.[40]

The group's underlying attitudes came to the surface soon after the passage of the state woman suffrage law. When the 1895 election, the first in which women voted, did not bring prohibition to Colorado, the Union President lamented that "the time was when I said I was proud to be a woman and to live in Colorado. Now I am all at sea. I don't want to move out, neither do I want to stay, unless woman will put herself on record at the ballot-box as the bitter and everlasting enemy of the liquor traffic."[41] Five years later, the editor of the *WCTU Messenger* reflected that "if we had it all to live over again . . . we would say . . . that only upon the ground of the absolute right of it can the claim for suffrage be successfully maintained. We are sorry to apologize [for] our better estimate of the womanhood of Colorado."[42] For these officials as well as other members, the absolute right of suffrage was not enough to sustain their hopes. They had supported suffrage in order to advance a particular vision of women as advocates of purity, piety, and moral reform; it was, to use Frances Willard's well-known term, a ballot for "home protection."

The women who sponsored the San Francisco Chinese Mission Home never raised the issue of woman suffrage in their meetings. Mission Home supporters left no records about their opinions on the matter, but it is possible to speculate a bit about their situation. In the 1870s, they were trying to protect Chinese prostitutes in a political climate dominated by an aggressive anti-Chinese movement. Since Chinese immigrants themselves were ineligible to vote, a woman suffrage measure would have offered little concrete benefit to the immigrant women who came in contact with rescue workers. It also would have been difficult to pass. Unlike Colorado temperance women, who had joined a reform-oriented coalition that enhanced their chances of passing a woman suffrage measure, San Francisco women were cut off from local reformers by their advocacy of the Chinese.[43] For these reasons, suffrage was so far from the grasp of home mission women in California that it could hardly have seemed a practical tool for advancing female values.

The issue of woman suffrage proved problematic for the Women's National Indian Association. The question was raised obliquely in 1888, when the group's national officers decided to align themselves with the National Council of Women.[44] An umbrella group of late–nineteenth-century women's organizations, the National Council of Women had, at the urging of temperance leader Frances Willard, taken a prosuffrage stance. Indian Association member Elizabeth Crannell, a longtime rival of Association president Amelia Quinton, saw the alignment as the perfect opportunity to challenge Quinton's claim to leadership. Although the Indian Association's 1888 annual convention ratified its officers' decision to join the National Council, Crannell and her supporters raised vocal objections at the sessions. They based their argument on three points: that the national officers should have consulted advisory board members before taking any action; that entrance into the Council would identify the Indian Association with suffragism and prohibition; and that the Association should limit its concerns to Indian reform alone.[45] Pressured by Crannell's refusal to concede defeat, national officers asked each auxiliary to reconsider its support for the alignment, and shortly afterwards, they withdrew their affiliation from the National Council of Women.

It is difficult to determine how large a role the issue of woman suffrage played in this reversal. National officers seem to have given in to Crannell to maintain organizational harmony, but some delegates were clearly unwilling to be affiliated with woman suffragists. Connecticut branch president Sara Kinney wrote to a friend that she would "advise [the Connecticut group's] withdrawal from the National Indian Association rather than endorse the action [of affiliation]," but her motive seems to have been her belief that the branch should limit itself strictly to Indian reform.[46] The significant point is that woman suffrage became troublesome only when Crannell refused to accept the convention's decision. Only on rethinking the matter in light of the distinct possibility that continued controversy might embarrass the group did the Association withdraw. Woman suffrage in and of itself was less controversial than its potential to cause public embarrassment. The Association was not so much antisuffrage as it was single-issue.

Suffrage was a much more troubling issue for the Industrial Christian Home Association of Utah. In the Mormon domain, home mission workers had to deal with a very delicate situation, for Utah was one of a handful of western territories in which women could already vote. Mormon women had gained the vote in 1870, when the largely Mormon territorial legislature granted woman suffrage, perhaps hoping to expand Mormon numbers in the face of an expected anti-Mormon assault. In the process, the legislature thumbed its nose at a handful of Congressmen and suffragists who had predicted that Utah women would surely outlaw polygamy when given a chance to do so. The issue of polygamy never appeared at the polls, and the "failure" of Mormon women to outlaw the controversial marriage system embarrassed suffragists and home mission workers.[47] The problem was especially acute for home mission workers, whose campaign against polygamy rested on the assumption that women, being advocates of female purity, were natural enemies of polygamy.

The first women's anti-polygamy organization, Salt Lake's Ladies' Anti-Polygamy Society, struggled with the question in 1883 and emerged finally and firmly in favor of woman suffrage.[48] By the time Angie Newman formed the Industrial Christian Home Association, however, home mission women were willing to endorse legislation, sponsored by antipolygamist Congressmen, that included a provision for the disfranchisement of all women in Utah. Many Utah Gentiles latched onto the proposal with enthusiasm in hopes of diminishing the size of the Mormon electorate and thus increasing the chances for a non-Mormon victory at the polls. The attitudes of home mission women, however, were more complex. Newman, who became a strong supporter of disfranchisement, refused to repudiate woman suffrage in general. Instead, she argued that disfranchisement of women was a short-term strategic necessity for the anomalous situation in Utah. Agreeing with a Methodist bishop who had commented that, in Utah, "woman's suffrage means only woman's suffering," she argued paradoxically that it was necessary to disfranchise women in order to raise their status by eliminating polygamy.[49]

In sum, each home mission group had its own set of particulars to consider when confronting the issue of woman suffrage. In Colorado, where it seemed likely that woman suffrage would provide a useful tool for demonstrating female values and strengthening female moral authority, home mission women grasped it eagerly. In California and Connecticut, where the costs in public hostility and embarrassment seemed high, mission women avoided woman suffrage. In Utah, where the existence of woman suffrage seemed to collide with the home mission concept of female morality, missionaries abandoned it. For home mission women, then, woman suffrage was a secondary issue, judged by whether or not it would help them achieve their own vision of the emancipation of women, formulated as a search for female moral authority.

The Boundaries of Morality

The search for female moral authority, then, was a drive for the emancipation of women that assumed the primacy of Victorian female values and was sharply critical of male privilege. It had another element, too: the assertion that most "impure" women were the innocent victims of male aggression who, if protected from further harm and guided by home mission women, would speedily regain their supposedly natural qualities of piety and purity.

This home mission belief in a shared female morality stretched the usual boundaries of class and race, illustrating the capacity of Victorian women's culture to allow middle-class Protestant women to declare their identification with women victims everywhere. Mission workers expressed with great clarity their anger at male abuse of "unfortunate women" of all sorts; lending support to the claim made by one worker at the Chinese Mission Home that "we are united in that tenderest of ties, a common sympathy for the oppressed of our own sex."[50]

Yet the home mission conception of female morality implied boundaries of its own. Home mission women knew that since their influence in Victorian culture was ultimately tied to their supposed moral purity, the loss of purity would undercut their claims to social authority. Under these circumstances, announcing common cause with "impure" women was a perilous endeavor. In the matter of reaching out to women outside of Victorian middle-class culture, as in the matter of criticizing men, home mission aims were molded by the concept of the Christian home. As long as unfortunate women could be described as non-Christian, mission women could prescribe Christianity as a solution to their problems; in missionary eyes, conversion was so profound a transformation as to explain away earlier, supposedly immoral behavior.

Thus, while Protestant women entered into "woman's work for woman" with sincere concern for the women they hoped to welcome to their rescue homes, it was a concern already shaped by confidence in their own advantages, and that concern was combined with a determination to retain a line between moral and immoral women, to ensure their own status. Still, their critique of male dominance led them to draw this line differently than most conventional nineteenth-century Americans; they included as moral, women who could by any stretch of the missionaries' already elastic rhetoric be seen as victims of male privilege or as likely converts to "the Christian home." The best way to grasp how missionary women drew and redrew the boundaries of morality is to examine their stereotyped images of Chinese prostitutes, Indian women, unmarried mothers, and polygamous Mormon wives. Brought to life as individual histories of unfortunate women in the plethora of annual reports, publicity pamphlets, and novels issued by home mission organizations, these images, which did not necessarily reflect reality, do illuminate the ideology of mission women.

Strikingly similar themes emerge from home mission women's descriptions of four very different populations in four distinct western locations. Focusing on groups whose behavior clashed with Victorian reverence for female purity and piety, missionaries warned of households unworthy of the name "Christian home," of domiciles distorted into prison workhouses by husbands who treated wives as inferiors. In describing these households, missionaries railed against the major threats to female moral authority: male sexual license and patriarchal control in the family. At the same time, they cut out the rhetorical patterns that would imprint relations between home mission women and rescue home residents.

Home Mission Images: Chinese Women

The women who established the San Francisco Chinese Mission Home laid out one such set of images of women victims. Once committed to the cause of Chinese immigrant women, San Francisco mission women rushed to learn more about them. They consulted missionaries who had worked in China; they conducted

English classes for young immigrant children; they listened to stories of deception or abduction told by women who entered the Mission Home; they even sent "house-to-house visitors" Emma Cable and Mrs. Mansie Condit to visit Chinese merchants' wives in their homes. From these encounters, they developed three images of the situation of Chinese women: the girl with bound feet, the carefully guarded merchant's wife, and the Chinese slave girl.

To mission workers, the practice of foot binding was a dramatic symbol of the restrictions on young girls in Chinese culture. "They are very tiny shoes," wrote missionary teacher Mary Baskin, "but capable of containing whole years of pain and suffering."[51] Baskin and her co-workers Condit and Cable wheedled, cajoled, and even bribed parents into promising not to bind their daughters' feet. Although their own devotion to female purity might logically have made them more understanding, mission workers challenged Chinese mothers who pleaded that bound feet were a symbol of virtue indispensable to finding a worthy husband. They steadfastly ignored those who pointed out that, as a social custom, bound feet were comparable to the tight-laced corsets so fashionable among Victorian women. Foot binding was much less common among Chinese immigrants to the United States than it had been in China, but mission women paid close attention to every example they encountered. In one case, they purchased the tiny shoes a couple had intended for their daughter and displayed them prominently in the Mission Home as mute testimony to the horrors Home residents would escape, a sort of trophy from their battle for women's freedom.[52]

Mission workers' distress about the binding of young girls' feet was echoed in their criticism of the restricted lives of Chinese merchants' wives. Married to relatively well-to-do men, merchants' wives were the closest Chinese equivalent to the middle-class white women who filled the ranks of home mission organizations, yet it was the differences in their situations that struck the latter. Protestant women described the lives of merchants' wives as extreme examples of domestic confinement. Mission workers reported that Chinese women were so hemmed in by cultural prescriptions and by their own bound feet that "very few of them are allowed to go on the streets, and the vast majority never leave their rooms."[53] Some immigrant merchants had more than one wife, and in these cases, mission women described households contaminated by "the dark coils of that hydra-headed monster polygamy" and threatened by the explosive undercurrents of jealousy mission women believed were the inevitable outcome of polygamous marriages.[54] As they saw it, Chinese merchants' wives were surrounded by competitors for their husbands' attention and confined within households that made a mockery of the word "home."

But if missionaries worried about girls with bound feet and merchants' wives, they were much more agitated about the condition of Chinese immigrant prostitutes. Consequently, one especially powerful image—that of the "Chinese slave girl"—permeated the writing and reports of mission workers. Although the term *slave* derived part of its force from allusion to American slavery, Chinese "slavery" was based on gender, not race. Accordingly, the slave girl image served as a symbol of female powerlessness that mission women used to describe a variety of situations.[55] Most frequently, they applied the term *slave* to young Chinese girls who had been sold, either by unscrupulous dealers or by poverty-stricken parents; brought by their owners to the United States; and used as servants ("domestic slaves") or, after reaching a certain age, as prostitutes. Ignoring evidence that some Chinese women entered prostitution knowingly, mission workers always described them as powerless victims of evil men, women who had been "decoyed from their native land by false promises and misrepresentations."[56]

The "slave" image had other connotations as well. Mission women believed that the Chinese sanctioned "the traffic in women," the buying and selling, not only of children and prostitutes, but also of wives. Protestant women whose own Victorian gender system made them the economic dependents of their husbands were nevertheless eager to stamp out connections between marriage and economic exchange in other women's lives. Indeed, Protestant women had trouble distinguishing between prostitutes and secondary wives, because they believed that secondary wives could be purchased "in what may aptly be called an open slave market."[57] Their confusion reflects the fact that many Chinese prostitutes aspired to become—as some did—secondary wives; it also reveals their judgment that the marriage customs of turn-of-the-century China, which granted secondary wives some recognition, were illegitimate. Yet mission women extended similar disapproval to monogamous Chinese marriages, believing that the culturally sanctioned pattern of giving gifts for brides was evidence that these marriages, too, rested on the traffic in women. In a comment that diverts attention from the economic underpinnings of Victorian marriages by focusing on the more extreme situation in China, missionary Mansie Condit noted that "[among Chinese immigrants] sacred love has been basely bought and sold ... wives are grown traffic ... marriage is a trade."[58] In the minds of home mission women, marriage without love was hardly marriage at all, for an unloved wife was merely a domestic servant.

Images of girls with bound feet, carefully guarded merchants' wives, and Chinese slave girls expressed home mission women's anger about female powerlessness as exemplified in domestic confinement, sexual exploitation, and the treatment of women as property. At the same time, they provided home mission women with a kind of shorthand to describe a typical pattern of life for Chinese women. As Protestant mission workers saw it, Chinese daughters were born into patriarchal households, systematically taught their inferiority to men, and kept totally at the mercy of their parents, who could choose to sell them into prostitution or to marry them (for a price) to men they did not know. Home mission women believed that women raised under such conditions were destined to become slaves to their husbands. Mrs. E. V. Robbins provided the obligatory connection between social conditioning and religion when she commented that "the inferior place which woman holds among these heathen, and the custom of buying and selling women and female children, is owing to the place that their religious system assigns to woman. . . . She lives on a lower plane and is an inferior creature."[59]

These images of Chinese women illustrate the home mission critique of patriarchy; they also display the assumption of Anglo-Saxon superiority that underlay the racial hierarchy of Victorian America. Yet historians who have tried to characterize the racial attitude of mission workers toward the Chinese have discovered the complexities of making judgments about them. The missionary image of the "Chinese slave girl" bore strong resemblance to racist stereotypes politicians used to galvanize support for immigration restriction and to heighten racism and xenophobia, but it is too easy to lay the blame for this similarity at the feet of home mission women. Just as the image of the Christian home carried different meaning for Protestant women than it did for Protestant men, so the image of the "Chinese slave girl" carried different meanings for female mission workers than it did for racist politicians. More concerned with female powerlessness than with unlimited immigration, home mission women did not favor immigration restriction.[60]

Historians have found it curiously difficult to realize the extent to which missionary women fought against the victimization of Chinese immigrant women. Until very recently, some scholars focused on mission workers' insensitivity to Chinese culture, while others tried to rescue Chinese American history from sensationalism by shifting attention away from the prostitution in Chinese American communities.[61] Both approaches minimized the fact that Protestant women recognized and condemned both patriarchal control, a prominent feature of traditional Chinese families; and male sexual license, a prerequisite for the system of prostitution that exploited large numbers of Chinese immigrant women. Only in the past decade have scholars of Chinese American women initiated a searching analysis of power dynamics based on gender. As their research shows, many Chinese immigrant women were indeed the victims of exploitative sexual and labor practices.[62] Whatever their ideological limitations, mission workers should be remembered for their insistence on battling against this exploitation.

Still, it is only a small step from criticizing "heathen" cultures for their treatment of women to condemning "heathen" cultures in general, and it was a step some home mission women took. House-to-house visitor Emma Cable, for instance, was fond of describing her work with Chinese immigrant women as a process of "undermining."[63] Although Cable intended to imply that she was excavating for gold, her metaphor holds another meaning, that of weakening the foundations of Chinese culture. To the extent that the survival of Chinese immigrant communities depended on the forms of women's subordination illuminated by the ideology of female moral authority—and sometimes beyond that extent— home mission women found them indefensible.

Assuming the superiority of Protestant Victorian culture, San Francisco women attracted support for their Chinese Mission

Home by publicizing images of Chinese immigrant women that served as symbols of female powerlessness. The emphasis on the ill-treatment of women in Chinese culture expressed sharp criticism of male dominance. It also seemed to Protestant women to invite contrast with the treatment of women in Victorian America, and the consequent idealization of Protestant women glossed over the extent to which the male domination and female victimization Victorian women saw as endemic to Chinese culture also existed in their own.

Home Mission Images: Indian Women

Protestant workers thinking of Indian women also focused on what seemed to them the poor condition of Indian home life and bad treatment of Indian wives. In the late nineteenth century, the Women's National Indian Association's annual reports and its publication the *Indian's Friend* analyzed the position of women in Indian societies. In these pages, home mission writers reduced vast differences between tribes to a single "Indian" culture and relied on two powerful images to symbolize that culture's shortcomings: the Indian woman as drudge and the Indian woman as maltreated wife.

Ever since colonial times, white observers who believed women were required to perform a disproportionate amount of tribal labor had described Indian women as "drudges."[64] Frequently they illustrated their words with pictures of women weighed down by the burdens of carrying tepees or laboring in the fields, activities that seemed, particularly to nineteenth-century middle-class Americans, to be *de facto* proof of female subordination in native society.[65] Victorian observers making comments about Indian women were inclined to shake their heads in disapproval and count their blessings as members of a superior society. Similar descriptions of Indians were used by late–nineteenth-century home mission women, but, as in the case of the image of the "Chinese slave girl," they were shaped into a critique of female powerlessness that supported the ideology of female moral authority.

The home mission pattern emerges most clearly in the image of the maltreated wife, which encompassed a life history Protestant women thought was typical for Indian women. According to home mission women, Indian girls, who were the absolute property of their fathers, were married as children to partners chosen by their parents. Although native groups sanctioned a number of different marriage practices, many of which involved gift exchanges between families, mission women insisted that "the selling of young girls for wives . . . and the plurality of wives [are] allowed in nearly all the tribes."[66] Once married, an Indian wife was at the mercy of her husband, who felt no obligation to support her and could cast her casually aside if he tired of her. Home mission writers lingered over incidents in which Indian men learned to show strength by cultivating a "harsh, stern, cruel manner towards all women."[67] Worse yet, as the Indian woman grew old and feeble, she would be left by the tribe to die alone.

The image of the maltreated Indian wife held such power for home mission women that they stretched it to include even the Navaho, a tribe in which women enjoyed relatively high status. Protestant women were aware that Navaho women were property owners and family heads, but they were unable to see these positions as indicators of authority. Wrapped up in their own notions, home mission women did not recognize sources of women's power apart from the Victorian ideals of female moral purity and the Christian home. Thus missionaries saw Navaho women's ownership of property as a thinly disguised handicap that tied women to work in the fields.[68] They ignored Navaho women's familial power, but noticed the selling of girls into marriage, the existence of polygamy, and wives' casual willingness to cast aside their husbands. Noting that Navaho women were the strongest defenders of native religious traditions, Protestant women described Navaho homes as threats to Christian moral development. In the process they drew a distinction between themselves and traditionalist Navaho women, who then appeared irredeemably "immoral" by contrast.

The women of the Women's National Indian Association relied on images of Indian women as drudges and as maltreated wives to symbolize their status in all Indian societies. They argued that Indian tribes did not lead "men to respect womanhood." They complained that Indian home life was so deficient that some tribal languages contained no word for "home" at all. As Connecticut branch president Sara Kinney put it, "in the native order of society, the home, as we understand it, cannot exist."[69]

Their comments illustrate one of the major limitations of the ideology of female moral authority: Protestant women believed so completely that woman's status depended on her role as wife and mother that they found it difficult to understand cultures in which women's influence emanated from other sources. They were confused by unfamiliar formulations of motherhood and mystified by groups who did not emphasize the stability and security of lifelong marriage bonds. Modern students of Indian tribes have noted that Indian women sometimes enjoyed freedoms nineteenth-century white women did not: including land ownership, independent control over property, and the opportunity to play culturally powerful roles in old age. Furthermore, though tribal women did work in the fields, their labor brought them some recognition for their crucial economic contributions.[70]

When home mission women interpreted women's agricultural labor as drudgery, they failed to understand the social power it could help women attain. When they described the marriage customs of Indians as "selling women for wives," they ignored the mutual obligations tribal marriage practices often entailed. When they advocated the imposition of ironclad marriage laws and family-based land allotments that merged husband's and wife's property, they helped to make Indian women economically dependent on their husbands.[71]

Even when faced with contrary evidence, home mission women did not change their view of Indian women as overworked and maltreated. Their depictions of Indian women were developed decades before the modern notion of cultural relativism would focus the prism of judgment away from tribal cultures and back onto missionaries themselves. Yet even in the 1880s and 1890s, a few Victorian women lived with Indian tribes long enough to see beyond home mission stereotypes. Thus one Hampton teacher who visited the Plains tribes stated with some surprise that "contrary to my expectation, I find the women cheerful, happy and independent." She added, "from what I have seen thus far, I prefer the lot of the woman to that of the man."[72] Alice Fletcher, the reformer whose work among the Omaha drew the attention of the

Connecticut Indian Association to the tribe, also noticed some of the limitations of home mission images. Looking back on her work as a government allotment agent, Fletcher remembered the difficulty she encountered in trying to convince Indians that the land allotments of married couples should be one unified parcel. "I was," she said, "more than once interrupted by the remark that our laws showed that 'the white man had neither love nor respect for his women.' "[73] Assessing the results of missionary work and government allotment politics, Fletcher worried that Indian women had been told to give up their healthy outdoor work and had lost control over their property. Fletcher was able to achieve a cultural distance that most home mission women, preoccupied as they were with threats to female moral authority, could not.[74]

Home Mission Images: Unmarried Mothers

Home mission women broadcast images of Chinese and Indian women that reflected the stereotypes self-satisfied Victorians used to assure themselves of Anglo-Saxon superiority. It is significant, however, that missionary women applied similar themes of female victimization, patriarchal control, and male sexual license to the largely white populations of unmarried mothers and Mormon women.

In Denver, the women of the Colorado Woman's Christian Temperance Union relied on a composite image to describe the unmarried mothers who inhabited their Colorado Cottage Home. Their image of the betrayed and helpless young girl owed something to the theme of seduction and abandonment that was the basis of so many Victorian novels and melodramas. It also echoed the popular reform stereotypes of prostitutes as seduced and victimized "fallen" women and working girls as "friendless" orphaned innocents adrift in the city.[75]

At the Denver Cottage Home, reformers drew the line between moral and immoral women with great reluctance, labelling as "immoral" only the very few young women they encountered who flatly rejected their offers of sympathy and aid. Perhaps because the great bulk of Colorado Cottage Home residents were white women about a generation younger than most home mission women, reformers found it especially easy to see them as surrogate daughters in need of protection.[76] Accordingly, missionary matrons struggled to absolve unmarried mothers of blame for actions that would, in the eyes of more conventional Victorians, assure them of pariah status. Seeing themselves as surrogate mothers (a pose that heightened their maternal solicitude), reformers argued that, as all women were naturally pure, those who had "fallen" must be victims rather than perpetrators.

Consequently, Temperance Union women described unmarried mothers as young women who had been "betrayed," either by negligent parents or by "faithless seducers."[77] They characterized the typical unmarried mother as "motherless, weak and untaught—not wicked."[78] Yet while mission workers liked to emphasize cases of orphans (girls who had grown up without any mother at all), the Colorado Cottage Home housed many women who had been raised in two-parent homes. In these cases, home mission women blamed mothers for having raised daughters too ignorant or too weak to resist temptation. In the "mother's meetings" they sponsored for preventive purposes, temperance workers listed the plethora of influences, from highly seasoned foods and skating rinks, to "ignorance upon sexual subjects," that could result in a girl's downfall.[79] As mission women saw it, careful and vigilant mothering after the middle-class model was the cornerstone of virtue for young women. The missionary conception of adolescence as a stage marked by precious innocence reflected their Victorian vision of a young womanhood that should end in triumphant entrance into marriage and the formation of a Christian home.[80] Slipping awkwardly over the fact that many unmarried mothers came from homes that were at least nominally Protestant, reformers described their charges in ways that fit the Christian versus non-Christian dichotomy they had developed: they prescribed Christian conversion under the guidance of the surrogate mother matrons at the Colorado Cottage Home as the best way to "exorcise" loss of moral purity.   .

Yet because home mission women reasoned that even the best-brought-up girl might be betrayed by a male seducer, their class-based criticism of inadequate mothers was muted by comparison with their criticism of men. While the Union would not go quite so far as to condone unmarried motherhood, they stoutly asserted that since men were not punished for sexual libertinism, the girls and women who were their victims were "more sinned against than sinning." Thus the image of the betrayed girl expressed home mission women's anger at the double standard of sexual behavior. Rescue workers described the fathers of their clients' children as "destroyers of womanhood" who failed to respect female virtue and who deserted girls after they became pregnant, thus failing to live up to their husbandly responsibilities. Perhaps reflecting their own awareness of women's economic vulnerability, missionaries were particularly angry at men who had promised marriage as an enticement to sexual activity and then "betrayed" women by backing out when pregnancy resulted. In the rhetoric of home mission women, unmarried mothers were "sacrificed beings" who were, in an oft-quoted phrase of Frances Willard's, "not fallen but knocked down."[81]

Home Mission Images: Mormon Women

The victimization Protestant women saw among unmarried mothers allowed them to extend the boundaries of true womanhood to include "fallen" but repentant women a generation younger than themselves. Mormon women, however, posed a bigger problem, for in this case the subjects of mission concern were white women of about the same age and background as Protestant home mission women; leaving religion the only significant demarcation between the reformers and the reformed. In a century when religious conversion and reconversion were commonplace, home mission women found it terribly easy to imagine themselves in the same situation as Mormon women, and while their heightened sense of identification intensified their anger at Mormon men, it also increased their willingness to label some Mormon women "immoral."

By the time Angie Newman began to agitate for the creation of an Industrial Christian Home, she had a large assortment of condemnations of Mormon practice at her disposal.[82] Mormonism and its polygamous marriage system had been the subject of a loosely coordinated but widespread attack by novelists, home mission workers, Protestant clergy, Salt Lake City Gentiles, and apostate

Mormons since the 1850s. Historians who analyzed the earliest of these materials interpreted anti-Mormon rhetoric as a kind of proto-pornography, filled with images of cruelty and sexual libertinism half-consciously intended to titillate readers.[83] Such an interpretation, however, is of limited use in understanding the antipolygamy literature written by Protestant women who protested against polygamy in the 1870s.

Evangelical women writers took as their paramount theme polygamy as contaminator of the home and as degradation for women. In their novels and "heart-histories," they fought against polygamy with deep urgency rooted in their conviction that Mormonism was a deliberate step downward on the ladder of civilization. As one writer expressed it, "it has been Mormon policy to degrade... [woman] to the position she occupied among barbaric nations in the dark ages, before the light of civilization raised her to be what God intended at the creation, man's equal, companion and helpmate, not his beast of burden nor his slave."[84] This language, which echoed the racialist assumptions applied to Chinese and Indian women, shows both the attempt of Protestant women to distance themselves from Mormon women and the extent to which hierarchies of morality were intertwined with hierarchies of race in Victorian America.

Mission women relied on three images to symbolize the plight of Mormon women: that of the wronged first wife, the deluded plural wife, and the besieged young girl. The image of the wronged first wife figured in many anti-Mormon novels, formed a recurring theme in the women's publication the *Anti-Polygamy Standard*, and appeared in several editions of the life story of apostate Mormon Fanny Stenhouse.[85] In its most common form, the story of the wronged first wife is told by a virtuous woman married to a good man who converts to Mormonism and moves his family to Salt Lake City. Once in the Mormon stronghold, the good woman, who had either been ignorant of the existence of polygamy or unable to believe that her husband would "live up to his privileges" by taking additional wives, finds herself and her husband pressured by community and church authorities to enter polygamy. When the pressure proves too much and her husband inevitably gives way, he is transformed into an unrecognizable demon ruled by lust, and jealousy and domestic discord pull apart the once-happy

This drawing appeared in Fanny Stenhouse's autobiographical account,
"Tell It All": The Story of a Life's Experience in Mormonism, *published
in 1874. Over the caption "Too True!" it depicts Stenhouse's horrified
reaction on learning that the Mormon faith, to which she and her husband
were converts, sanctioned polygamy.*

home. In typically melodramatic Victorian fashion, the loyal first
wife, who has been reduced to little more than a servant as the
husband transferred his attentions to younger later wives, suc-
cumbs to insanity or to pure sorrow, a sacrifice to the evils of
polygamy.

In describing the wronged first wife, home mission women revealed their own fears about Victorian marriages, including their
fear that unrestrained male lust loomed just beneath the surface
of middle-class self-control. Illustrated by vignettes of the domestic
drudgery, desertion, or even death that could result from the loss
of self-restraint, these stories served as an eloquent appeal to evangelical women to eradicate polygamy. Angie Newman relied on
the image of the wronged first wife when she told the Senate
Committee considering funding the Industrial Christian Home
about Mrs. Orson Pratt, the first wife of a well-known Mormon
official. Mrs. Pratt's marriage, Newman said, "had been one of
exceptional domestic unity" until her husband was persuaded to
take another wife and "we see this devoted husband and father

This drawing, which also appeared in Stenhouse's Tell It All, *is entitled "The Crisis of a Life—Entering into Polygamy." It shows an intimidated Stenhouse (at right center) giving formal consent to polygamy by placing her husband's hand in that of his second wife in a wedding ceremony performed by Mormon leader Brigham Young (at right).*

transformed into a fiend."[86] Taken as it was to represent the double standard of sexuality come to life, Mormon polygamy was extremely threatening to evangelical women.

While not as common in home mission usage, two other images provide clues to the concerns of Protestant women in Salt Lake City. Home mission women were on the whole much less generous to secondary wives than to their wronged first-married sisters. The reasons for this lack of sympathy are plain. First, secondary wives tended to be seen as threats to the moral authority of first wives. Second, in the case of Mormon women who were, after all, not so very different from Protestant women, home mission women felt a particularly sharp need to heighten their own moral standing by painting plural wives as women of dubious virtue. Still, if polygamy was, as home mission women insisted, an "offense against womanhood," then all women, including secondary wives, were potential victims.[87] This victimization was easiest for missionaries to describe when plural wives bore some resemblance to unmarried mothers or to Chinese immigrant women; that is, they could be described as "untaught" because they grew up in Mormon homes, or when they had been deceived by men who did not tell them they were to be secondary wives.

Only on rare occasions did home mission concern extend to secondary wives who did not fit into these patterns. One such case was that of Ann Eliza Young, plural wife of Mormon church leader Brigham Young. Ann Eliza's much-publicized autobiography, *Wife No. 19*, made it clear that she entered polygamy knowingly, if not calculatingly; yet she received strong support from Protestant women when she decided to divorce Brigham Young.[88] Ann Eliza appears to have been an exception because the story she told played on one of the unacknowledged fears of Protestant women involved in Victorian marriages in which they were economically dependent on their husbands: Young described her well-to-do husband as a man who refused to support her and left her without companionship for long periods of time. Young's picture confirmed the anti-Mormon belief that Mormon husbands often left plural wives to provide for themselves and their children, a theme home mission women illustrated with stories of women left to their own devices and living in desperate poverty. Echoing the image of the Indian woman as drudge, mission women represented the typical polygamous wife as overworked and the typical Mormon husband as reluctant to support his wives.[89]

Salt Lake City home mission women showed more sympathy for women who fit yet another stereotypical image: that of the young girl induced to enter polygamy by a much older Mormon man. Missionary women believed that every Mormon man had at his command many stratagems to compel an innocent young girl to become a plural wife. He could, home mission women reported, tell her that polygamy was a necessary proof of her devotion to her faith, for if raised in a Mormon household she had been taught that her "only chance of salvation . . . was as a satellite to add glory to some male saint."[90] He could threaten her or her parents with economic reprisals serious enough to bankrupt them. He could entice her with promises of high status and influence over other women. He could even deceive her by promising that she was to be the only wife. Using these themes, home mission women contrasted the image of an innocent young girl with the image of an evil Mormon man motivated by lust and greed for power over women. This theme, illustrated by Angie Newman's comment that "[in Utah] there is not a law against seduction, adultery, incest, bigamy, polygamy, or any sexual vice whatever," helped persuade the United States Senate to grant funding for the Industrial Christian Home.[91] Mission stories relied on hints of incest or the seduction of young girls for much of their impact; they echoed the image of the betrayed girl advanced by the Colorado Woman's Christian Temperance Union.

These images of the wronged first wife, the deluded plural wife, and the besieged young girl formed the core of Protestant women's descriptions of their Mormon counterparts. Jennie Froiseth, editor of the *Anti-Polygamy Standard*, spelled out the big picture in the article "The Home and Mormonism."[92] Froiseth argued that Mormonism led directly to the disintegration of the home as Christian women knew it. She complained that Mormon men did not support their wives economically, that they trampled women's rights by demanding large families, and that they were allowed by Utah's loose system of divorce to cast wives off at will. Since some evidence suggests that in Utah more divorces were asked for by— and granted to—women than men, this last complaint reveals more about home mission ideology than about conditions for Mormon women in nineteenth-century Utah.[93] Froiseth's analysis illuminates some of the fears of Protestant women whose own marriages were based on the shaky foundations of romantic love and female economic dependence. Yet, relying on the major distinction between the two groups of women, Froiseth ascribed all evidence of female powerlessness directly to the Mormon religion. In a remarkable instance of wishful thinking, she went so far as to argue that Mormons, but not Protestants, believed women were cursed by Eve's behavior. As a result, she stated, Mormons thought that "woman should be completely subject to man, under his foot, that he should rule over her."[94]

Because they considered Mormon women (like unmarried mothers, Chinese prostitutes, and Indian women) to be so powerless, Protestant women believed that they had the right to speak for them in the name of empowering women. In the case of Mormonism, however, Mormon women leaders, who resented home mission women's characterizations, made their anger public. In the rhetorical skirmish that resulted, Mormon women tried to claim for themselves the mantle of true womanhood and Victorian self-restraint. In mass meetings called for the purpose, they defended polygamy by arguing that it had been commanded by God and that it was the only family system that safely contained men's sexual urges. They insisted that polygamy avoided the vices of Victorian society—prostitution and illegitimacy—by enveloping men's sexual desires safely within a family structure. In polygamy, they argued, men were held responsible for their behavior, and women were protected from nasty secrets or diseases.[95] In other words, they saw polygamy as a solution to the problem of the double standard of sexual behavior. Where home mission women would eradicate the double standard by insisting that men meet the code of chastity demanded of women, Mormon women would institutionalize the double standard of behavior but hold men responsible for the consequences of their sexual activity.[96]

When Mormon women leaders began to take their interpretation of morality and their support of polygamy public, the spirit of the sisterhood of all women that home mission women had proudly proclaimed quickly evaporated. Home mission women character-ized Mormon women leaders as hypocritical fanatics, and took pains to discredit their opinions. Angie Newman's response to one mass meeting Mormon women held to protest antipolygamy leg-islation is typical in this regard. Because she was a "Christian wife and mother," Newman believed she could speak "in behalf of the Christian homes of this Republic" to "repudiate the oft-repeated charge . . . that the lasciviousness of the age is due to monogamous or Christian marriage." Stung to the quick at the public evidence of women who did not fit her universal definition of pure wom-anhood, Newman condemned the Mormon women who had spo-ken out, describing them as women who were dishonorable enough to "stand before a public audience and vindicate their illicit alli-ances."[97] In calling polygamous marriages "illicit alliances" and casting aspersions on the women who lived in them, Newman drew the moral line ensuring her own status as a moral guardian of Victorian society.

As we have seen, Newman even supported disfranchising Mor-mon women. Mormon women had not organized to fight for suf-frage before its inception in 1870, but they fought hard to keep it when congressional antipolygamy legislation threatened it in the 1880s. When it became apparent that antipolygamy legislation would be enforced, Mormon women pleaded with home mission workers not to break up their families, pointing out that the legislation would result in moral stigma for them and illegitimacy for their children. They appealed to home mission women to understand that they loved their husbands. As one put it, "if we are slaves, let us serve the masters we love and who love us; bondage on such terms is tolerable."[98]

In making their protests, Mormon women leaders complained that Protestant women had compromised home mission values by discarding ideals of sisterhood, ridiculing other women's religious devotion, and—even more unthinkable—supporting laws that cast women out of their families. Surely, they insisted, Protestant women could understand female devotion to the family. To Protestant women, however, it was not "the family" in general that served the interests of women, but a particular version of the Christian family characterized by respect for female moral authority. Because Mormon families seemed to them to threaten, rather than support, female moral authority, home mission women considered them so dangerous that they deserved dismantling.

To home mission women in the West, the ideology of female moral authority held such explanatory power that it fit an almost limitless variety of cases, from Mormons in Salt Lake City, to Chinese immigrants in San Francisco. Relying on claims of an innate and universal female morality to justify their "rescue" of women victims, home mission women developed a sharp critique of male privilege, in the process drawing a boundary of morality for women that was more inclusive than the narrow one preached by more conventional middle-class Victorians. Yet even as we note their relative inclusiveness, we should pay close attention to the women they placed outside that boundary—Mormon women leaders who defended polygamy, Chinese mothers in San Francisco who bound their daughters' feet, Navaho women who defended native rituals, and working-class girls in Denver who flaunted rather than apologized for premarital sexuality. As disparate as these four groups were, they agreed on one thing—that the Protestant missionary women who offered "aid" in the name of "woman's work for woman" did not speak for them.

***

Between 1870 and 1900, the ideology of female moral authority flourished among home mission women. Every feature of this ideology—its identification with powerless women, its criticism of male behavior, and its prescription for women's emancipation—had roots in the assumptions and values of Victorian women's culture. By publicizing sensationalized images of victimized women, home mission women lashed out against male sexual license and patriarchal control in families. Partly because of these images, home mission women envisioned themselves as moral maternalists reaching out to desperate, powerless women. They offered a typically Victorian solution to the problem of female victimization: the emancipation of women through the extension of the Christian home.

Rescue homes were inspired by and designed to replicate the concept of the Christian home advanced by home mission women. They provided a space in which both matrons and their charges were safe from male family dominance: they were homes made by women alone. Mission women hoped that rescue homes would demonstrate the validity of their assumption that at heart all women shared the Victorian female values of purity and piety. In actual practice, however, these home mission images came face to face with the needs, perceptions, and competing cultural values of the women who entered rescue homes. Thus, during the more than fifty years in which rescue homes operated in the West, their story was as much one of relations between women as of Victorian women's anger at men.

SYSTEMS
OF
SOCIAL CONTROL
AND RELATIONS
AMONG WOMEN

3

Some Women's Culture and Other Women's Needs: Motivations, Maternalism, and the Language of Gratitude

In November of 1927, sixteen-year-old Chin Leen decided to take a chance. A rescue party of home mission women had approached her as she sat alone in a car in Reno, Nevada, waiting for her husband, Frank Wong. The missionaries told Chin Leen that her wealthy forty-year-old husband didn't love her, that he had only married her to smuggle her into the country and sell her into prostitution. Chin Leen didn't believe them, but she had not been happy with Frank Wong. Without informing him, she stepped into the car driven by mission women and went with them to the Chinese Mission Home in San Francisco.[1]

By the time the rescue party reached San Francisco, Chin Leen had become a sensation. Under headlines such as "China Girl 'Kidnapped' From Mate," reporters accused mission women of carrying her "screaming and struggling" from her Reno home, forcing her into a waiting automobile, and transporting her across the state line into California.[2] Frank Wong's vocal complaints rallied a number of white officials to his defense on the grounds that he was a respectable married man. With public feeling running high, the would-be rescuers found it necessary to justify their actions.

The women of the Chinese Mission Home had become involved in the case by the Chinese couple who had brought Chin Leen into the United States and arranged for her marriage to Frank Wong. Belatedly reconsidering their actions, the couple told mission women that they feared Frank Wong would mistreat Chin Leen, perhaps even sell her into prostitution.[3] Whatever the motives of the couple may have been (they may merely have wished to cause trouble for Wong), the women of the Chinese Mission Home had interpreted their story as a plea to help a typical "Chinese slave girl" and rushed to Reno to find her.

After Chin Leen was ensconced in the Chinese Mission Home, mission workers dealt with Frank Wong and his supporters from a safe distance. They rejected Wong's assurances that he had no intention of selling his wife and refused his requests to visit Chin Leen. They turned a deaf ear to his promises to buy her luxuries, provide her with an education, move to San Francisco, and let her come and go freely if she would return to him.[4] Mission workers had ample legal justification for their position, because Chin Leen had been brought into the country illegally and married while under the age of consent. It was not legality, however, that weighed most heavily on their minds. As Home superintendent Donaldina Cameron explained to Wong's supporter the Reverend W. M. Case, "there is one vital element . . . which it seems to me everyone, except those connected with our Mission Home is overlooking, and that is, [Chin Leen's] own right to make decisions. It was by her own choice that she left Mr. [Wong]."[5] Cameron told Frank Wong that "even if [Chin Leen] were legally admitted to the U.S., and legally married, [her] decision [to leave him] in itself would be decisive."[6]

And Chin Leen was unwilling to return to her husband. At the urging of mission women, she told her side of the story to newspaper reporters. She said nothing about fearing sale into prostitution. Instead, she explained that her husband had not treated her with the respect she deserved. He had not, she complained, introduced her to his son, nor had he thrown the customary wedding feast in her honor.[7]

Throughout the history of rescue home operations, from the 1870s through the 1920s, women like Chin Leen faced predicaments that hinged on the factors of choice and control central to understanding life in institutions created by home mission women. Historians who have investigated welfare institutions offer two quite different stories of institutional life, both drawn from the motivations of reformers. One of these stories, the liberal historians' tale of selfless reformers dedicating their lives to the downtrodden, emphasizes choice. The other, the radical historians' account of rigid Victorians imposing middle-class values on powerless members of disadvantaged groups, emphasizes control.[8] The reality is more complicated than either story would suggest.

To understand rescue home life, we have to look, not only at the motivations of reformers, but also at the motivations of the women who entered the institutions. For rescue home entrants, there were many constraints on choice, some mandated by reformers and others by forces outside the rescue homes. There were also many forms of control, not all of which were rooted in the middle-class values of reformers. Rescue home entrants faced overlapping systems of social control in which the factor of class interacted with the factors of race, culture, and gender to shape the alternatives available to any given individual.

To home mission women immersed in the ideology of female moral authority, the factor of gender seemed primary. Schooled in the assumptions of Victorian women's culture, Protestant women believed that all women shared values of purity and piety that could form a bridge between the most privileged and the most desperate of their sex. Home mission women illustrated their belief with the stereotyped images of female victims published in annual reports; they institutionalized it in all-female rescue homes.

Home mission women drew on rich ideological resources, and they held the power to shape institutional structures. Yet the survival of rescue homes depended as much on the residents as on missionaries. And here is where the story takes some revealing turns. Chin Leen was not dragged kicking and screaming into the Chinese Mission Home; she chose to go there and did not regret her decision. Yet her reason for doing so—her husband's failure to fulfill the customary Chinese requirements for marriage—was not the one mission women imagined. Chin Leen was rescued from unhappy circumstances; not, as mission women would have it, from "moral degradation." Her decision to enter the Chinese Mission Home highlights some of the ways the search for female moral authority both provided for, and constrained, relations between home mission women and rescue home residents. It is to the dynamics of those relationships as they emerged in rescue homes that we will turn now.

The Structure of Rescue Home Life

Because home mission women held the power to shape the institutional patterns of their relationships with residents, we have to begin by examining the ways missionaries built Victorian female values into rescue home life. The evidence here is abundant: even the term *rescue home*, used to describe all the institutions considered in this study and many others as well, had ideological import. It conveyed the two goals Protestant women had for home mission projects: on the one hand, they wanted to "rescue" women who had been the victims of male abuse; on the other, they wanted to inculcate in all women their particular concept of the Christian "home." Home mission women believed that their institutions would separate women victims from the men who preyed on them, providing space for the supposedly natural virtues of true womanhood—purity and piety—to emerge.

Each of the three rescue homes was established and supported by an organization of Protestant middle-class women. Only the Industrial Christian Home in Salt Lake City secured government funding; the other two homes gained independence from male control by surviving on shoestring budgets comprised mostly of contributions from members moved by sad stories of the lives of rescue home residents. Each institution was supervised by a select committee or supervisory board specially appointed for the task. Although the supervisory boards visited the rescue homes on a regular basis, they employed live-in staff members to take day-to-day responsibility. The staff's mission home matron, a Protestant

The Colorado Cottage Home, located at 427 Fairfax Street in southeast Denver from 1906 to 1939.
(*Courtesy of Western Historical Collections, Norlin Library, University of Colorado, Boulder*)

woman carefully selected to oversee the process of nurturing Victorian female values, was the center of institutional life.

Rescue home matrons differed from their supervisory board employers in their professionalism and in their educational experiences. Matrons were, in a sense, the embodiment of the home mission belief in the need for women professionals. Most had acquired some specialized training to prepare them for their posts. Margaret Culbertson of the Chinese Mission Home and Mrs. A. L. Ryer of the Industrial Christian Home were teachers. Harriet Phillips, one of the earliest matrons at the Chinese Mission Home, had been trained as a missionary. Ruth Wood of the Industrial Christian Home and Waleska Watson of the Colorado Cottage Home were physicians.[9] And there was another significant difference between matrons and sponsors: matrons were almost always single, or sometimes widowed, women, while the overwhelming majority of rescue home supporters were married women.

In practice, matrons' single status and their professionalism com-

The Chinese Mission Home, 920 Sacramento Street, just up the hill from Chinatown, San Francisco. The mission was housed in this building from 1893 until 1906, when it was destroyed by the great San Francisco earthquake and fire. Mission Home personnel were never entirely happy with its post-earthquake replacement, which they considered too institutional to be truly homelike.

(*Courtesy of Pacific Books, Palo Alto, California*)

bined (not always smoothly) with their advocacy of the Christian home to offer a striking example to the women with whom they came in contact. Donaldina Cameron, matron of the Chinese Mission Home from 1900 to 1934, is one example. The youngest daughter of Scottish sheep ranchers Allan and Isabella Cameron, Donaldina Cameron was born in 1869, two years before her parents moved to California. Despite her mother's death in 1874 and her father's precarious health and financial condition, young Donaldina was pampered and loved by her elder sisters; her close-knit family provided a secure emotional base. Because her father's death cut off her plans to attend Normal School, she entered into evangelical work with less preparation than most rescue home matrons. In 1895, twenty-five years old and looking for distraction from a broken engagement, she volunteered to assist matron Margaret Culbertson at the Chinese Mission Home. Culbertson, who was in ill health, needed all the help Cameron could offer, and more. After Culbertson's death in 1897, Cameron filled much of the resulting void; by 1900, she had been appointed superintendent of the home, a position she made into a lifelong career. Although Cameron was engaged twice more, she never married. It is hard to escape the conclusion that she was ambivalent about becoming a wife—she broke one engagement in favor of continuing her work, and another ended when her fiancé, a much older widower who was an enthusiastic mission supporter, died before the ceremony had been planned. Although she was both deeply religious and fond of children, it was not these characteristics that most people noticed—it was her steely determination, her adventurousness, and her flirtatious charm that drew comment.[10]

Yet Cameron and other rescue home matrons were selected and approved by supervisory boards for their maternal characteristics and their dedication to the Christian home. Idealized by supervisory boards as motherly figures with "generous humane heart[s] that give [them] . . . power over these women and children," matrons were expected to symbolize the values home mission women idealized for all Protestant women: purity, piety, and a peculiarly Victorian concept of female moral authority.[11]

Home mission women built support for these values into the institutional routine of rescue home operations. Female purity was ensured by drawing strict boundaries between rescue homes and their surrounding urban communities. Closed doors seemed like mere common sense to home mission women who believed that their charges were the innocent victims of predatory men; missionaries maintained that structured isolation protected home residents. Thus, in Denver, Cottage Home officials built their second Home building far away from the main residential area in a place where pregnant girls and women could exercise outdoors without being recognized by passersby. Fearful that public knowledge of a pregnancy would ruin a woman's reputation for life, they guarded the names of residents carefully.[12] In San Francisco, where tong members and local white gangs frequently threatened Chinese Mission Home residents, officials saw every venture outside their institution as potentially dangerous. Residents of the Home were never allowed outside the institution without escorts; even at church services, they were hidden from public view behind a screen.[13]

Each of the homes had trusted women doorkeepers whose job it was to screen visitors—men in particular—and keep them away from the women within.[14] Contact with people outside the homes was limited to those approved by mission home workers: schoolteachers, employers judged suitable for hiring domestic servants, and young men of "good" character who had been scrutinized by staff members. Cautious missionaries refused to allow residents at the Industrial Christian Home in Salt Lake City to hold a social for their old friends.[15] Matrons at the Colorado Cottage Home and the Chinese Mission Home read all incoming and outgoing mail, and at the latter home, at least, they confiscated mail they thought would prove detrimental to the residents' journey toward Victorian morality.[16]

The extent of the separation between the rescue homes and the wider community is suggested by the fact that both matrons and residents referred to residents as "inmates." Yet we should not be too quick to assume that if residents were inmates, missionaries were jailers; for Victorians often spoke of the "inmates" of private homes, even their own homes, as well as the inmates of prisons or other institutions.[17] At least in part, the harshness of the term reflected the sharp boundaries middle-class Victorians drew around "private" homes to set them off from the "public" world of business and politics.[18]

Within the rescue homes, missionaries encouraged female piety by continually attempting to convert residents to Protestant Christianity. Church services at the Denver Cottage Home and the Salt Lake City Industrial Christian Home were carefully nondenominational, but managers at all three institutions assumed that "the management of the Home shall be thoroughly christian in its character and influence."[19] Morning and evening prayers, with more extended sessions on weekends, were the rule. Protestantism permeated educational and social activities, too. At the San Francisco Chinese Mission Home, managers were pleased to note that "the girls in the Home sing and repeat more Scripture than some children who have been brought up in Christian homes."[20] Training in scripture was such a fundamental part of residents' education that managers cancelled an arrangement with the Board of Education to provide a teacher for the Home because "the staff felt that she did not give the religious influence necessary," even though the decision meant that they had to finance a replacement themselves.[21] At the Denver Cottage Home, too, missionaries were determined that "the Bible shall be deeply implanted within [residents'] minds" in case they were "ever again surrounded with heathen influence."[22]

Even the breaks in the routine of the homes were designed to serve as object lessons in Protestant Christianity. Matrons marked Christian holidays with gift-giving, prayer services, and special meals attended by mission organization leaders. At Easter in 1906, for example, Cottage Home residents planned a recital at which one of the residents, an American Indian, sang for assembled home mission women. She and the other residents were hidden from view behind a curtain, but reports of the event emphasized that it was a family-like holiday enjoyed by all. At Christmas in 1922, residents prepared and ate a turkey dinner, received personal visits from the Home's spiritual adviser, and were given candy and handkerchiefs from the supervisory board.[23]

Missionaries embedded their emphasis on purity and piety in schedules packed with activity. The routine of constant busyness was designed to develop residents' character according to Victorian precepts; missionaries believed that it also kept residents from becoming depressed or missing old friends and acquaintances. In all three cities, matrons would have approved of the comment of San Francisco matron Frances Thompson that "there are no idle hands here even down to the littlest."[24]

At the Chinese Mission Home in San Francisco, the day began with 7:00 A.M. prayers, followed by breakfast, an hour of housework, morning and afternoon school classes, dinner, a 7:00 P.M. prayer meeting, a study session, and then lights out. Each resident cleaned her own room and did her own laundry in addition to the shared household tasks. Pairs of women were assigned each day to special tasks—cooking the Chinese and American meals, perhaps, or caring for the few babies in residence at any one time, a favorite assignment. Because most matrons did not speak Chinese, the staff depended on trusted residents to translate. Some residents assisted in rescue work, litigation, and the critical initial encounters with new entrants. Others recited lessons for visitors or performed skits at the monthly board meetings held at the Home.[25]

At Salt Lake City's Industrial Christian Home for Mormon

wives, each resident was responsible for her own room, her laundry, and her children, and each was expected to join in the work of the larger household as well. Besides cooking and cleaning, the work of the Home included a great deal of laundry and sewing. The scope of this activity is suggested by a report on the first ten months of rescue home operation. Matron Ruth Wood reported that during this period, residents had darned 310 pairs of stockings, mended 259 outfits, cut and fit 159 articles of clothing, and sewed 415 new garments. In addition, they had spent 154 days in laundry work and had, in one especially busy month, baked 264 loaves of bread.[26]

Even in Denver, where the tasks of Colorado Cottage Home residents might reasonably have been limited by their pregnancies, residents were kept busy. Those whose health permitted were expected to practice either cooking, laundering, or housekeeping in hopes they might find employment as domestics after their babies were born. Home residents rose at seven and began a daily round of assigned tasks followed by nightly prayer sessions. They attended weekly devotional classes, they planned receptions and meetings for the Home board, and they helped the matron hold down expenses by raising chickens.[27]

As these descriptions suggest, most of the tasks actually carried on in rescue homes were domestic chores of various kinds, though the Chinese Mission Home, which housed a number of children, also offered classroom education to its charges. The chore-filled routine kept residents occupied while it helped cost-conscious missionary boards hold expenses down. Given the limited range of occupations available to nineteenth-century women wage workers, training in housework reflected matrons' hopes of providing residents with a means of self-support.

Rescue home matrons did not, however, rely solely on housework to provide economic independence. At two of the institutions, the Industrial Christian Home and the Chinese Mission Home, Protestant women tried to develop "industrial" training programs as well. In Salt Lake City, missionaries recognized that residents would have to become self-supporting to leave their husbands behind. Accordingly, the founders of the Industrial Christian Home planned to offer residents training for positions as typists, stenographers, and silk-reelers as well as domestic service; they hoped to establish an employment bureau to find positions for trained graduates.[28] Financial pressures, lack of qualified teachers, and the small number of women who entered the Home led to the failure of these hopes. Instead, the matron secured laundry and sewing work for residents in the Home; she also arranged to care for children so some mothers could work as servants outside the Home.[29] The result can be seen in the final inventories of Home possessions. By the time the Home closed in 1893, all the equipment it had to turn over to the new owners was one sewing machine, one clothes wringer, four flatirons, one ironing board, and one range.[30] The grand intentions of the founders to prepare women for financial self-sufficiency had been reduced to the performance of domestic chores for small wages. Yet missionaries had not exactly imposed these tedious and ill-paid tasks on reluctant "inmates." Because matrons at the Industrial Christian Home, as in other rescue homes, set aside a part of the earnings for individual residents, the women who entered the Industrial Home continually pressured matrons for more paid work.[31]

In San Francisco, too, staff workers at the Chinese Mission Home engaged in a long struggle to provide training in "industrial skills." Time and again, their hopes were dashed by lack of money to buy equipment or pay teachers. Not until 1918 did they find a financial donor whose largesse enabled them to begin their work in systematic fashion.[32] They concentrated on sewing, teaching residents to make articles for sale in mission buildings and Chinatown shops. Among the products were coats, table linens, baby clothes, sachets, samplers, rag rugs, and cookbooks.[33]

In the summertime, Chinese Mission Home residents earned money doing contract work for California fruit growers. The work was arduous: in 1919, residents picked 300 tons of prunes in six weeks, a schedule that allowed little time for relaxation and undermined missionaries' attempts to turn these excursions into outdoor "vacations" by scheduling ball games, song fests, and short trips away from the work camp. Even the backbreaking labor of fruit picking had its compensations, though. At the Chinese Mission Home, too, residents' earnings were carefully put away for individuals, and the chance to earn money proved so enticing that the residents who could not go on the trips reportedly suffered from keen disappointment.[34]

The Chinese Mission Home's "industrial" sewing program in the early 1920s.
(*Courtesy of Cameron House*)

In both San Francisco and Salt Lake City, missionaries' plans to prepare rescue home residents for self-support ultimately amounted to little more than training in underpaid occupations. There was, however, an important exception to this general picture: the Chinese Mission Home sent some residents outside the institution for higher education. Over the years, a few dozen Chinese immigrant women studied to become professionals in business, mission work, medicine, or teaching. Since this kind of schooling was extremely difficult for Chinese immigrant women to gain in American society without white sponsorship, it was more significant than its small numbers would indicate.[35] Like the ambitious but ultimately disappointing "industrial" work programs, the professional schooling reflects missionaries' determination to prepare their charges for self-sufficiency even at the cost of chal-

Residents of the Chinese Mission Home picking prunes for California fruit growers in the Santa Clara Valley, summer of 1917.
(*Courtesy of Cameron House*)

lenging the Victorian middle-class ideal of female economic dependence.

In each of the rescue homes, home mission women institution-alized their search for female moral authority by isolating residents from the outside world to ensure their purity, surrounding them with Protestantism to encourage piety, and immersing them in a busy daily routine. Trumpeted by home mission reports and pub-licity, this exacting routine is the most conspicuous aspect of in-stitutional life. Even a glance at the structure of rescue home activities suggests the extent of control matrons held over the daily lives of residents. Such a look, however, takes in only one side of the story. Before we can go on to examine the relations between matrons and residents in the institutions, we have to probe a less visible matter—the needs and desires of the women who entered rescue homes.

Residents' Motivations

Determining the real motivations of rescue home residents is a challenging task. To carry it out, historians have to become skilled at seeing through the veils of home mission ideology that color the inmate histories and annual reports issued by rescue homes. Building on images of defenseless Mormon wives, Chinese prostitutes, and unmarried mothers, rescue home workers depicted residents as victims of male lust and patriarchal control. Hoping to justify their programs in evangelical terms, they described residents as morally degraded women whom rescue home matrons could transform into model Protestant wives and mothers. Partly because these rhetorical veils are so thick, historians have found the records of welfare institutions more useful for understanding reformers than residents: historians have used these records, in the main, to critique reformers' middle-class biases.[36]

But for voluntary rescue homes, unlike the coercive prisons or state reformatories on which the most convincing of these critiques are based, the question of residents' motivations is essential.[37] It will not do to accept either the home mission portrayal of residents as "degraded" women who chose to embrace Christianity, or the scholars' depiction of them as helpless victims of middle-class moralists. Mission workers hoped to convert residents to Protestantism, but they knew that the survival of rescue homes depended on attracting women by providing services desirable to them. The women who entered rescue homes had their own reasons for doing so, reasons that rarely had much to do with the home mission ideology of Christian womanhood. The real history of rescue home life lies in the negotiation of conflicts between matrons' ideology and residents' needs. Despite differences between the perceptions of matrons and residents, accommodations were possible, because, when considered in the context of the whole society rather than that of the institution alone, rescue homes provided for the unmet needs of many women.

The women who entered rescue homes hoped to extricate themselves from difficult straits. Poverty, illness, and condemnation from their families or the surrounding society limited their choices for improving their situations on their own. For poor women, women without families to fall back on, and women who wanted to escape prostitution or unhappy home lives, rescue homes offered an alternative, a way they might get back on their feet so they could get an education, find a husband, or secure a job. The decision to enter a rescue home did not necessarily imply acceptance of the home mission ideology of female moral authority. Still, many women—including abused wives, "owned" prostitutes, abandoned unmarried mothers, and Mormon women replaced in their husbands' affections by newer wives—sought to escape the constraints of socially enforced female powerlessness. Residents of all three rescue homes sought relief from temporary embarrassment or powerlessness. Like Chin Leen, they lived in a world with many constraints and few opportunities; they calculated their advantages and took their chances where they found them.

Salt Lake City

The women who entered the Industrial Christian Home in Salt Lake City decided to do so in the context of bitter feeling between the local Mormon majority and Protestant home mission workers. As the political tide began to turn against Mormon civic government in the 1880s, Mormons held fast to those elements of their culture, polygamy among them, that distinguished them from other Americans. For most Mormon women, the need to protect their threatened culture prevented the full flowering of a Mormon version of the search for female moral authority: Mormons acknowledged, even enforced, differences between men and women, but carefully prevented them from developing into political divisions.[38] By the 1880s, Mormon women leaders defended themselves from anti-Mormon attack by arguing that they embodied all the values of true womanhood—purity, piety, domesticity, and submission. They made the most of this effective tactic, emphasizing the similarities between Victorian and Mormon female roles. Yet, despite these claims, the gender system of Mormon culture was distinct from that of Victorian women's culture. Mormonism retained the value of female submission home mission women were struggling to discard; further, polygamy institutionalized the double standard of sexuality Protestant women challenged.[39]

Afraid that a successful Industrial Home project would endanger

Mormon cultural cohesion, Mormon leaders tried to dissuade women from entering the Home when it opened in 1886. The editor of the Mormon *Woman's Exponent* called on women to demonstrate their love for their husbands and to honor their religion by refusing to enter the institution.[40] Opinion makers at the *Deseret News* pointed out that the Home was supported by the same Congress that was threatening Mormons with antipolygamy legislation. Editors warned that the institution was "the velvet glove" covering the "iron fist" of legislators hostile to Mormonism. Repeating the verse "Come into my parlor, said the spider to the fly," they accused women who considered entering the Home of helping Protestants break up Mormon families.[41] Outwardly confident that they would succeed in these efforts at discouragement, Mormon women leaders defiantly told Congressmen that their followers would refuse to accept charity at the hands of their enemies.[42]

Yet these attempts to discredit the Home in the eyes of potential residents were not immediately successful. Despite editorial warnings, 154 women and children applied to the Industrial Christian Home in the first nine months after it opened. Due in part to the conflict between the women managers of the Home and the male Board of Control assigned to it by the government, only thirty-three of these applicants were admitted. Over the next few years, applications slowed to a trickle as managers fought Board members for control of the institution and Mormons took advantage of the divisions to embarrass them. By the time the Home closed its doors in 1893, a total of only 150 residents had been received into the Home: an average of about twenty women and children at any given time.[43]

Although case files of the institution do not survive, hints about the women who resided in the Home can be found in local newspapers, government documents, and investigation reports. These sources reveal a somewhat different picture than the home mission images of wronged first wives, besieged young girls, and deluded wives. Many of the women who originally applied for admission had only tangential connections to polygamous marriages. Due to the strict policies of the male Board of Control, all those actually admitted to the Home were plural wives, some with children; they were also likely to be financially desperate or physically ill. The local Gentile paper, the *Salt Lake Tribune*, featured the stories of two such women.[44] One, who had left her husband on learning of the existence of an unsuspected second wife, was pregnant when she entered the Home. The other, who had been deserted by her husband for a younger woman, was a seventy-four-year-old Danish woman in a "sick and helpless" condition. An 1887 investigation of the Home provided further information about the backgrounds of residents. One woman, Tomnida Sorenson, contrasted the comforts of the Home with the discomforts of her previous impoverished "home in the country." Another, Mrs. Almeda Chatterton, a former resident who worked as a domestic while her three children remained in the Home for their schooling, remarked that she "could not earn that amount under other circumstances if encumbered with children."[45]

Because they were willing to renounce their polygamous marriages, these women gained entrance to the Industrial Christian Home denied to other women by the Board of Control's strict admission policies.[46] As was true of many of the rejected applicants, however, their most desperate need was not for moral "improvement," but for food, lodging, employment, or schooling for their children. Some who sought to enter the Home found the promises of financial independence advertised by the Industrial Christian Home more attractive than their major alternative—dependence on charity dispensed by Mormon church leaders. Others, however, could not hold jobs because of physical incapacities. So many of the Home residents required medical care that the Home Association authorized the payment of a medical bonus to matron Dr. Ruth Wood after hearing her report on the first year's work.[47]

Some residents needed the Home's shelter so badly that, once in the institution, they did all they could to remain there. One woman, Mrs. Hicks, incensed home mission women by refusing to leave when missionaries discovered that she had entered the Home on false pretenses (she was a bigamist). Matron Wood tried in vain to find employment for her, then offered to pay for her board elsewhere, but was unable to dislodge her until she was finally committed to the county poorhouse.[48] The same tenacity characterized some other residents as well. Those in the Home when it closed in 1893 proved almost impossible to relocate. Once, in a last-ditch attempt to convince Congress of the continued need for the Home, Association president Jeannette Ferry threatened to return the Home building to the Government with the residents still inside it.[49]

Thus, it appears that the Industrial Christian Home, born of home mission workers' desire to rescue women from polygamy, more closely met the needs of women whom a variety of circumstances had reduced to poverty or illness. All indications are that the Home housed few residents who fit the image of the "wronged first wives" for whom home mission women expressed such sympathy. In the end, Home residents provided little material with which to sustain even the illusion of "woman's work for woman" in the name of female purity and piety; as one disappointed supporter commented, "at present [the Home] is but a roaring farce, a county poor house."[50] As we will see, Salt Lake City matrons' inability to encompass residents' actual needs under the ideological categories of female moral authority set the Industrial Christian Home apart from rescue homes in Denver and San Francisco.

Denver

In Denver, too, financial need drew women into the Colorado Cottage Home. Girls who had lost one or both parents and young women who lost their jobs because of pregnancy were especially likely to need Cottage Home services. The Home's 1915 report can serve as evidence of this. In that year, thirty-three women were admitted, thirty-two of whom were white and one of whom was black. Twelve came from families with both parents living, and twenty-one came from homes in which one or both parents were dead. All but three of the residents professed some sort of religion, almost all Protestant, and most had worked for wages outside their homes. The group included five teachers, five students, one nurse, one telephone operator, and sixteen domestic servants.[51]

Such a list of characteristics would place most of the Cottage Home residents within the working class, a group historians have paid much attention to of late. Constructing a model of working-class culture, historians have suggested that its gender system differed significantly from that of the middle classes.[52] Working-class people, the argument runs, did not have the luxury of making the rigid moral judgments that underlay the middle-class Victorian enshrinement of female purity. Indeed, there is considerable evidence that for working-class women, sexual bartering was valued as a survival skill rather than despised as "immorality."[53] Yet working-class women whose pregnancies marked their failures at turning socially tolerated sexual bargaining into socially acceptable marriage could be subjected to severe social sanctions. Many of the capsule histories of Cottage Home residents published in the *WCTU Messenger* tell of women whose pregnancies created a crisis that interrupted plans to marry their suitors.[54] In the absence of marriage, pregnant women confronted a grim list of alternatives: ranging from abortion, infanticide, or suicide, to facing head-on the derision of their working-class communities.[55]

Middle-class Victorians were hardly inclined to be more tolerant. To them, there was something basically immoral in the very milieu of working-class life: there was genuine surprise in the tone of a Cottage Home matron who commented that "most of [the residents] come from good industrious families [and are] fairly educated . . . nearly all of them having filled honorable positions."[56] Yet for many of the women who entered the Colorado Cottage Home, the (temporary) pious moralism of Protestant home mission women was a less frightening prospect than the intolerance of their own working-class communities.

Even within the supposedly less judgmental working classes, social stigma was attached to unmarried pregnancy. Women who wanted to marry feared that pregnancy would make them unacceptable in the eyes of prospective husbands and in-laws.[57] Humiliation of a different kind loomed large for women whose parents saw their behavior as a threat to their own aspirations to social mobility.[58] Even in families where parents offered financial and emotional assistance, daughters might find the idea of remaining at home to bear their babies unthinkable. Mission officials lamented that some young women hinted darkly at "the sweet refuge from shame and sorrow" that death might provide.[59] Social opprobrium led many young women to try to conceal their condition by entering the Colorado Cottage Home; to them, the need for a private hideaway was paramount.

Other women turned to the Home for shelter and medical care

when pregnancies lost them their jobs and left them without financial resources. One such woman wrote to a Cottage Home board member asking admittance, saying, "I have no father or mother. I came out west to make my own living when sixteen. I am now nineteen and in dreadful trouble."[60] In Denver, where the female work force quadrupled in the 1880s, many young women might well have found themselves in similar positions.[61] Home officials thought that cases where girls were "betrayed" by members of their own families were "unusual," but they mentioned many cases where girls had fallen victim to men who lived in the same household; including employers of domestic servants, and Protestant pastors.[62]

The Colorado Cottage Home prided itself on never turning away a prospective resident because she could not afford to pay for her care. Scattered statistics indicate that, while a percentage (varying from one-third to one-half) of those admitted were able to pay the sum asked for their board, most could afford to pay only a part of the fee or none of it at all. In these cases, apparently mostly of self-supporting women, Home officials exacted promises to pay when able and admitted the women immediately. Financial support from biological fathers was rarely forthcoming. Although Home officials tried to track the men down, matrons complained that "a very large per cent of the men immediately leave for parts unknown, deserting the girl to bear the suffering, the shame, and the expense alone."[63] Fearful that legal proceedings would make the names of unmarried mothers public, missionaries rarely took fathers to court.[64] Thus, in 1917, of forty-six women admitted, only two received financial support from the men involved.[65] Many residents found themselves without family resources, without financial help from the biological fathers of their babies, and unable to continue at their jobs. Institutions like the Colorado Cottage Home filled the gap by providing economic assistance.

At the same time, residents' need for privacy was congruent with the very different needs and programs of home mission women. The Protestant founders of the Cottage Home, worried that their goal of reclaiming "betrayed girls" challenged conventional middle-class morality, conducted their rescue home in an atmosphere of near secrecy. They never advertised publicly for residents; they avoided publishing the life stories that most homes used to drum up public support for rescue work; and they did not allow visitors to meet residents even when they attended receptions held at the Home.[66] Most of the women who found their way to the Cottage Home came there by word of mouth, on recommendation from friends or doctors, and they were welcomed by missionaries who saw them as "betrayed" girls in need of protection.

Cottage Home residents' origins and motives changed very little over the years between the founding of the Home in 1886 and its closing in 1931. The annual number of admissions, which ranged from a low of thirty-two in 1894 to a high of eighty-eight in 1923, followed an erratic pattern of ups and downs, except for a general rise in the 1920s that may have been attributable to the effects of rising challenges to Victorian morality in that decade. The Home housed more women in the 1920s than it had in the 1890s, but those who came entered for the same reasons. Whether or not they saw themselves as "betrayed girls" (and current studies of working-class culture would suggest that many did not), they endured the rhetoric of home mission women in order to get shelter, medical care, and protection from public scrutiny otherwise unavailable to them. At the Cottage Home in Denver, unlike the Industrial Christian Home in Salt Lake City, the needs of residents were different from, but not incompatible with, the ideology of matrons.

San Francisco

Just as the Mormon community in Salt Lake City and the working-class community in Denver had gender systems distinct from that of middle-class Victorians, so did the Chinese immigrant community in San Francisco. The particular set of gender distinctions taught to most immigrants in their Chinese homeland had roots in family arrangements historians usually label "traditional" and see as nearly the opposite of Victorian patterns.

Traditional Chinese families focused their energies on raising male heirs to carry on the lineage.[67] Given this goal, parents considered young girls less important than young boys from birth. Especially—but not only—in impoverished families, daughters might be sold to pay debts or expected to demonstrate their filial piety by working for wages. At marriage, the full weight of this gender system descended on young women. Matches were generally arranged by go-betweens, with little personal contact between prospective mates. Young couples lived with the husbands' parents; and young brides tried to please not only their husbands but also their in-laws. In and of themselves, they had little status until they produced male heirs; until then, they were expected to serve their mothers-in-law.

The subordination of young wives was ensured by a series of social sanctions. Wives who did not produce male heirs might find their husbands taking concubines; there was a thriving business of prostitution that produced concubines to choose from.[68] Wives who did not behave according to custom might be divorced and sent back to their own families in disgrace.[69] Even young wives' most forceful weapon—committing suicide as a protest against bad treatment—brought social judgment on their in-laws only at the cost of their own lives.[70] Yet women who adapted to the constraints this traditional patriarchal system placed on newly married women could look forward to having significant social status later in their lives. As mothers and mothers-in-law, they might wield considerable authority within the patrilineal family.[71]

By the late nineteenth century, when Chinese immigration to the United States was in full swing, this traditional system of patriarchal control had already lost some of its power over young women in China. In Kwangtung, the home of most Chinese immigrants to America, some young women employed in the sericulture industry mounted a "marriage resistance" movement and chose to live in all-women's houses rather than with parents or in-laws.[72] Their relative freedom was based on a combination of economic circumstances that allowed them to support themselves outside of marriage.

Most of the Chinese women who immigrated to America were less fortunate. Only a few married Chinese women traveled to America; partly because in-laws expected young wives to remain in China, and partly because United States immigration policies made it difficult for them to enter the country.[73] Most of the female immigrants were impoverished young women who eluded immigration restrictions to seek economic security. Some had been promised lucrative jobs in the United States; others had been promised wealthy husbands.

Women were only a tiny part of the Chinese immigrant population: as late as 1890, there were twenty-two Chinese men for every Chinese woman in California.[74] The highly skewed sex ratio of immigrant Chinatowns increased the vulnerability of Chinese immigrant women to sexual exploitation, even as it offered opportunities for the immigrant women who could find a way to take advantage of them. Both the skewed sex ratio and the absence of established in-laws created unusual opportunities for immigrant prostitutes to marry and leave prostitution behind.[75] In immigrant Chinatowns, then, women measured their opportunities against the constraints of the traditional Chinese gender system as well as the racial hierarchy of American society. The stakes were high, and the choices all problematic. The Chinese Mission Home offered one possibility, and for several groups of immigrant women, it proved an attractive one.

Between 1874 and 1880, most of the entrants to the Chinese Mission Home were prostitutes who sought the protection of Home officials in order to marry. Since most Chinese prostitutes were either endentured to or "owned" by vice operators, leaving prostitution for marriage meant finding a way to escape their owners' control.[76] Faced with this difficulty, many suitors who were unable to pay the large fees demanded by owners to release prostitutes brought the women to the Chinese Mission Home. In return for an agreement that the prospective husband would pay for her board and that the woman would remain in the Home for a set period of time (at first, six months; later, a year), the Mission Home extended its protection to the couple. While the woman remained in the Home, mission workers tried to convert her to Christianity and instruct her in Victorian gender roles; at the end of her stay, her fiancé paid for a formal marriage ceremony. Because mission workers, as white middle-class citizens, could demand police protection if the woman's previous "owners" threatened to harm the couple, many Chinese immigrants, especially those without the protection of large clans of their own, found the Mission Home useful.[77]

In the 1880s and 1890s, San Francisco Protestant women began to engage in more aggressive "rescue" work. Acting on cryptic messages sent by prostitutes or on appeals from Chinese observers, they invoked the aid of a few sympathetic policemen to rescue prostitutes directly from brothels.[78] In the twentieth century, widely publicized photographs portrayed Mission Home superintendent Donaldina Cameron and policemen, hatchets in hand, standing outside a Chinese brothel, about to raid the premises in search of a particular prostitute. Women who had contacted the Mission themselves usually welcomed the rescuing parties. But for those whose rescues had been arranged by third parties, the arrival of the group sometimes created panic. Many vice operators had convinced prostitutes that Home inmates were poisoned, tortured, or imprisoned.[79] In these cases, Mission officials tried to persuade the frightened women to enter the Mission Home, but as long as the women were of age, mission workers were powerless to take them if they refused.

Case files suggest that many of the rescued entrants of the Home regarded prostitution as a means of finding a husband or making a financial start in the United States, an opportunity that would enable them to lead a better life or to support a poverty-stricken family at home. Their employment as sexual "slaves"—the fact that so troubled mission women—did not in itself lead them to request help; for the most part, they contacted missionaries only when they felt that their owners had treated them particularly badly. One woman, Nellie Tong, wrote to matron Donaldina Cameron in 1922 that "my master [is] forcing me to give him five thousand dollars, or he will sale me to some one else." Because the sale seemed to mean that she would be "condemned to slavery all my life," she asked Cameron to "help me from destitution and . . . the misery and agony of shameful life."[80] Another woman, Li Hah, ran to the Home after quarreling with her employer because she had "demanded as she had many times before an accounting of how much money she had earned" but was not given the information she sought.[81] These two women, like the immigrant prostitutes brought to the Home by prospective husbands, saw prostitution as an unpleasant but temporary necessity rather than a lifelong moral shame; they appealed to the Home for help when it seemed that their avenues of escape or financial gain were cut off.

Besides prostitutes, three other groups of women entered the Chinese Mission Home: abused women, "U.S. boarders," and children. Many women came to the Home to escape ill-treatment in their marriages. Mrs. Tom She Been, the second wife of a Chinese doctor, arrived at the Home "badly bruised from a beating" by her husband. She remained at the Home until her husband came "many times to apologize to [mission workers] and beg her forgiveness." She returned to her own house only after the secretary of the Chinese Consul asked her husband to treat her better.[82] One woman fled to the Home after her husband treated her "cruelly" because she sang "Jesus Loves Me," a song taught to her by Protestant visitors that "so offended her master that he was about to take her to China."[83] Apparently unwilling to play the subservient role of the Chinese daughter-in-law that would have been demanded of her in her homeland, she entered the Mission Home.

Most of the prostitutes and unhappy wives who entered the institution chose to do so, but two other groups of residents— United States "boarders" and children—had little choice about coming to the Chinese Mission Home. United States boarders were Chinese women stopped by customs officials and boarded in the Mission Home at federal expense while immigration officials considered their cases. After the passage of the Chinese Exclusion Act in 1882, only women who could claim to be wives of merchants were allowed to enter the country or to remain in it; immigration officials considered most other women "immoral" and deported them.[84] Although many detained women resisted entering the Mission Home, few maintained their objections for long. Until the opening of the Angel Island Immigration Station in 1910, boarding at the Mission Home saved women lengthy incarceration in the crowded and unsanitary mail dock area used for receiving immigrants. Furthermore, women under threat of deportation stood to benefit from the efforts of Mission officials on their behalf. If Mission Home workers testified to the women's good character, immigration officials might expedite delays or postpone deportations, sometimes indefinitely.[85]

Many of the children who entered the Chinese Mission Home had been taken from their homes by child protective agencies or, after the turn of the century, the juvenile court. Both groups had the legal power to remove children from abusive homes or supposedly "immoral" atmospheres. A child protection officer brought one eleven-year-old child, Chin Mui, to the Home after she had been blinded by ill-treatment at the hands of a woman with whom her father had left her.[86] The juvenile court sent Chinese girls charged with vagrancy, immorality, or disobedience to the rescue home. A substantial number of parents brought adolescent daughters to the Home and asked Mission officials to teach them discipline or, sometimes, to provide educations for them.

Some juveniles, however, came all by themselves. One fifteen-year-old, Amy Chan, went to the Home when her father started planning to return to China, a decision Chan feared would lead him to arrange a marriage for her. Chan's older sister had been married to a man who abused her, so Chan, who had heard of the Mission Home from a woman who used to visit her sister, entered it determined to avoid marriage and to secure an education.[87] For Chan, the Mission Home provided a haven available in the all-female homes of women "marriage resisters" in China but nearly impossible to find in America, where the skewed sexual ratio of Chinese immigrant society and the lack of economic alternatives for immigrant women pushed women toward marriage.

The wide variety of services offered by the Chinese Mission Home attracted large numbers of women. By the late 1880s, the Mission housed an average of fifty residents a year; by 1900, the numbers were in the eighties. Over the sixty years of the Home's existence, the resident population changed. The number of prostitutes brought by hopeful suitors declined in the 1890s, while the number of girls sent to the Home by the juvenile court rose in the twentieth century. Although "rescue" work with prostitutes continued throughout the period, proportionally more children entered the Home during the late nineteenth and early twentieth centuries.[88]

Yet, throughout the period, the Mission Home rested its public reputation on cases in which Protestant women dramatically rescued women they saw as "Chinese slave girls" from moral degradation at the hands of male procurers. Mission women regarded residents as trophies in a tug-of-war between vigilant Protestant women determined to eliminate sexual slavery and Chinese organizations that thrived on the profits of prostitution. The mission

In this staged photograph, Donaldina Cameron, her assistant Ida Lee, and two policeman demonstrate the "rescue" of a prostitute from the Siberia Club in Chinatown in the early 1920s. The rescue scene illustrates the single-sided public image cultivated by the Chinese Mission Home, which actually housed a wide variety of residents.

(Courtesy of Cameron House)

stance reflected the ideology of female moral authority rather than the actual motivations of residents, which were, as we have seen, far more diverse than home mission imagery would suggest.

But in San Francisco, as in Denver, the needs and desires of residents could be reconciled, however awkwardly, with the preconceptions of mission women. Chin Leen was not the "slave girl" that mission women believed she was, but she found the Chinese Mission Home useful. In separating from her husband, she freed herself to take another chance at balancing the precarious mix of exploitation and opportunity that marked the shifting gender system in San Francisco's turn-of-the-century Chinatown. Just as important, Mission Home women (hampered, perhaps, by their inability to speak Chinese and the difficulty of comprehending the nuances of an unfamiliar culture) found no reason to doubt that she wanted what they most hoped to provide—training in purity and piety administered by a motherly matron in the name of Victorian female moral authority.

Relationships Between Matrons and Residents

The survival of rescue homes, then, depended on establishing some correspondence between the ideology of home missionaries and the needs and desires of home residents. In Salt Lake City, residents and matrons were unable to do this, and their difficulties sealed the fate of the short-lived institution. Their failure is intriguing because the gender systems of Mormon and Victorian America differed more in degree than in kind; the actual correspondence between the two groups of women was greater than in the other two homes. So what went wrong at the Industrial Christian Home?

Residents and matrons at the Salt Lake City Home expressed their difficulties in the language of the search for female moral authority. In April of 1887, Miranda Boss, a resident of the Home, complained to a Mormon newspaper reporter that she was overworked, forced to serve matron Wood, and forbidden to leave the institution or to take her children away from it. Because her charges echoed Mormon suspicions that the Home was a thinly disguised prison, the Mormon-owned *Salt Lake Herald* printed her statement along with an endorsement from Georgia Snow, an unsuccessful candidate for the position of Industrial Home matron.[89] The Boss revelations created a furor in Salt Lake City and prompted the government-appointed Board of Control to launch a full investigation. The Board subsequently interviewed residents about their experiences in the Home. A record of their testimony published in the non-Mormon *Salt Lake Tribune* revealed that Boss and one other woman, a Home employee, were highly critical of the Home, but three other residents held more favorable opinions.[90]

As all the residents agreed that the Home was more comfortable than the homes they had left behind, Wood's "cruelty" was not a matter of physical deprivation. Rather, residents resented Wood's tendency to correct their behavior. The investigators quoted Boss as saying, "I have no fault to find with the food, the beds nor nothing; only Dr. Wood's talk."[91] Boss charged that Wood had scolded her for disobeying Home rules, disapproved of her enthusiasm for the minstrel theater, and complained about the way she disciplined her children. On the last point, Boss admitted under questioning that when Wood told Boss not to take her children away, she meant that the children would be worse off with Boss than in the Home, a comment that seemed to impugn Boss's abilities as a mother.

In essence, this conflict revolved around the question of who would exercise female moral authority—that is, who would play the role of mother—in the rescue home. In Salt Lake City, where Mormon and Gentile women had long argued about which group had the greatest claim to the mantle of true womanhood, both residents and matrons expected to wield ultimate authority within the all-female institution. To Boss, the conclusion was obvious: "Mrs. Dr. Wood did not belong here and never did . . . she was not here to be waited on like a lady, she was here to wait on the inmates, and not the inmates on her."[92]

The Home's Board of Control dismissed the suggestion that matrons should wait on inmates and exonerated Wood, but the conflict suggests just how difficult it would prove to translate the ideal of sisterhood professed by missionaries into institutional form. Raised in Victorian culture and taught to emulate home mission ideals, matrons envisioned motherhood as the ideal position from which to turn influence into authority. But in a rescue home designed to fit the image of the monogamous Christian home, there was no space for more than one mother, and those who were not "the mother" were all too easily considered to be "the children." Matron Wood revealed her assumptions on this point in an exchange with Georgia Snow, the woman who had brought Boss's complaints to public attention. According to a reporter who observed the interchange, Wood "asked [Snow] if she wished to consider herself a polygamous child of tender years and an applicant for admission to the Home," suggesting that if Snow did so, Wood would have the authority to change her behavior.[93] Neither Snow nor Boss was willing to submit to Wood's authority. As their resistance suggests, the conflict over who would be the mother and who would be the child reached its height in the Industrial Christian Home because the residents were grown women, many of whom had children themselves. Although Wood herself was exonerated, the Industrial Home, already hampered by disagreements between its middle-class female and male managers, never recovered from the Boss investigation. The Salt Lake City institution attracted only tiny numbers of residents in its final years of operation.

By contrast, in long-lived rescue homes, matrons managed to avoid the conflicts that polarized matrons and residents at the Industrial Christian Home. In San Francisco and Denver, rescue home matrons charted a smoother path. The first matron of the Chinese Mission Home in San Francisco, Harriet Phillips, took the opposite approach from that of matron Wood in Salt Lake City. Unwilling to confront residents openly, she did the housework herself rather than try to teach reluctant residents to do it.[94] Judged too compliant by the Home's supervisory board, Phillips was replaced by board member Mrs. E. V. Robbins. Robbins established stricter control over the residents' behavior, but cemented her relations with them partly by acceding to their requests for Chinese food.[95] After reestablishing matronly authority, Robbins was replaced by Margaret Culbertson. Culbertson, who presided over the Home for almost twenty years (from 1878 to 1897), adopted an attitude of maternalism that set the pattern for matron–resident relationships in the Chinese Mission Home for the next half-century.

The maternal approach of Culbertson and her successors was paralleled at the Colorado Cottage Home in Denver. Maternalism worked most effectively when there was a substantial age differ-ence between matrons and residents. Since most of the unmarried mothers who entered the Colorado Cottage Home were young women, matrons easily perceived them as surrogate daughters and treated them as such. In San Francisco, the establishment of ma-ternalism followed shifts in the Home population. Most of the initial entrants were adult women who resisted matrons' attempts to inculcate Christian domesticity. Hoping that younger children would be more malleable, Mission officials quickly set out to in-crease the numbers of "young girls and children" in the Home.[96] After 1880, the proportion of young residents increased dramati-cally as a series of child welfare reform measures enlarged the power of mission workers to draw children into the Home.[97]

As practiced in both Denver and San Francisco, maternalism provided a form of female moral authority that softened the sharp edges of control in the homes. Envisioning themselves as loving mothers to surrogate daughters, maternalist matrons tried to de-velop emotional ties to residents. They did not always succeed. In both Denver and San Francisco, relations between matrons and residents ran the gamut from sharp conflict to warm affection. Sources from the Denver Cottage Home, most of which were sketches of residents circulated in the Temperance Union news-letter, reveal little about the conflicts in that institution, although matrons occasionally mentioned women who left the Home before their babies were born.[98] At the Chinese Mission Home, where case files survive, conflict between matrons and residents can be traced in some detail.

Not surprisingly, conflict was most pronounced when residents were brought to the Chinese Mission Home without their consent. "Rescued" prostitutes who had not themselves requested mission interference often disliked the Home. The worst problems came near the turn of the century when San Francisco police picked up crowds of prostitutes in raids and dumped them in the Home to be held until their trials.[99] Fearful of the influence they might exert on other residents, Mission women kept the newcomers under lock and key in a large room. None of the women thus incarcerated showed any willingness to remain in the institution, and mission-aries soon put an end to cooperating with large-scale police raids. Some prostitutes who had chosen to enter the Home also raised

grievances. Accustomed to making money, disdainful of housework, and as a rule too old for school, they were generally more
critical of the Home than other groups of residents.

Children, too, exercised little choice about entering the Chinese
Mission Home, but their reactions to it varied. Abused children
brought to the institution by the Humane Society reportedly regarded the strenuous Home routine as "light compared with the
burdens [they] had been accustomed to carry."[100] Juveniles brought
to the Home because of their illicit relationships with "undesira-
ble" men were, however, prone to dislike the institution. Some of
them nursed such strong desires to return to their lovers that they
plotted to run away to join them. In the 1920s, all three cases in
which residents actually ran away from the Home fit this description. Even rebellious juveniles, however, admitted that the Home
had its attractions. One of the residents who left wrote to a friend
that her lesson had been "lots of fun" but that she was determined
that "by gosh, I won't let nobody coax me into staying here."[101]

In their reports to the boards, matrons glossed over conflicts
with residents and offered instead a picture of mother-daughter
harmony. In home mission circles, the highest praise any supervisory board could offer a matron was to say that she so gently
guided residents that "she was regarded almost as their own
mother."[102] Many rescue home residents did in fact speak of matrons as mother substitutes. Residents at the Chinese Mission
Home consistently referred to Donaldina Cameron, its matron
from 1900 to 1934, as "Lo Mo," a term gratified mission women
translated as "the mother."[103] One historian has suggested that
the use of the term "Lo Mo" was "expected" of residents, but I
have found no specific evidence to support her claim; indeed,
residents who wrote letters to "Lo Mo dearest" seem to have felt
considerable devotion.[104] Similar tributes delighted Harriet Dunklee, president of the Denver Cottage Home Board from 1904 to
1915. Dunklee cherished the comment of Alice, an American Indian resident of the Home, who told her that "I feel like you are
my mother and I would like to have a good talk with you."[105] We
do not have to accept the missionary claim that a "sweet spirit of
loving confidence" enveloped the Colorado Cottage Home to acknowledge that many home residents responded warmly to the
emotional overtures of matrons.[106] One resident said ardently: "I

kiss you dear Mrs. Dunklee, I love you like you was my sister. You can believe me sure."[107]

Yet even residents who called matrons "mothers" did not necessarily mean the concept of maternal motherhood so dear to the hearts of Victorian women. Indeed, investigation into the matter reveals intriguing subtexts according to cultural background. In many American Indian cultures, a variety of women might be referred to as "mother"; the use of the term did not necessarily imply an exclusive emotional attachment. Among the Chinese, prostitutes called the madams of brothels "lao mama" (mother), a practice that seems to have been retained in the United States. The Mission Home files describe San Francisco female slave owners named "Lowe Mo" and "Lau Mo," and contemporary observers, too, reported that Chinatown prostitutes referred to madams as their mothers.[108] In this case, the term would seem to suggest a relationship based largely on respect and obligation.

For rescue home residents, however, respect and obligation were not trifles. After they left the institutions, many residents wrote to matrons complaining that they missed the care they had received there. Women who left the Colorado Cottage Home found themselves ground down by poor wages, lack of entertainment, and isolation from social life. They wrote to inquire about friends in the Home, to request information about adopted babies, or to ask the Home to help care for children they kept while they earned money to support them. Matron Harriet Dunklee once reported that a former resident had written that "she is very lonely and would like to return to the Home and live with us."[109] A number of women from the Chinese Mission Home had been placed in Protestant households outside San Francisco where they did housework in return for their room and board while attending school. Although Mission officials hoped these placements would assure the women of affectionate familial support while they finished their schooling, comments from the women show that many preferred their lives in the Home to their present situation. One such woman told Cameron that "being out in the world is not like the four protective walls of [the Mission Home]. Give me back those happy days, and I'll give some years of my life for it."[110] Another, who attended school in China, wrote to say, "I am full of worry since I left you. But since I must have an education I must."[111]

Most of the interactions between matrons and residents fell somewhere between the extremes of hushed-up conflict on the one hand, and publicly proclaimed daughterly affection on the other. These interactions reveal how, in long-lived rescue homes, a delicate balance was maintained between the ideology of home mission women and the motivations of residents, skirting the point where persuasion turned into coercion. Believing they knew what was best for home residents, matrons pushed residents to adopt home mission goals. Yet, conceiving of themselves as loving mothers rather than stern disciplinarians, matrons saw residents as wayward daughters in need of Protestant salvation. In both homes, matrons resented charges that they compelled residents to follow the Protestant example against their wills. As Donaldina Cameron explained, "the word compulsory . . . does not convey the true attitude or spirit of guidance given our girls."[112] For the most part, residents expressed genuine gratitude for the services rescue homes provided, but they eluded the transformation home mission women envisioned for them. They observed the outward rituals of purity and piety expected of them in the homes, but in private they responded only selectively to the ideology of female moral authority put before them by Protestant missionaries.

At the Denver Colorado Cottage Home, the issues of choice and control came to a head over the difficult decision of what to do with the babies born in the institution. A Cottage Home official made it clear that authorities understood that, for residents, "parting with [babies] is heart-breaking—the longing for them unspeakable."[113] Yet, she felt that "experience oft repeated" showed that it was better for the child to be placed with foster parents.[114] Accordingly, matrons did all they could to influence young mothers to give up their children. Comments from residents suggest that matrons asked them to consider the future interests of the child, the economic struggle, and the social stigma of illegitimacy. In rare cases, matrons went so far as to suggest that some women were unworthy to raise children.[115]

Most of the women in the Home did, in fact, give up their babies. One who did so defended matrons from charges that they forced their opinions on the mothers. "In my case," she wrote, "while I admit it broke my heart to give up my darling babe no one could have influenced me to do it, not even Mrs. Smith." She continued:

"as far as I am personally concerned I would have taken [my baby] and faced the world and told them she was mine. But I loved her so much that I could never have had anyone [else] point the finger of scorn at her."[116] For this woman, at least, the climate of opinion outside the Home was the critical factor.

In their public statements, Cottage Home officials insisted that "the mother is always permitted to take her child, and encouraged to do so, where she is capable of earning for it."[117] In fact, each year a number of women decided to keep their babies despite the arguments of matrons.[118] One resident who decided to keep her child wrote to a Home official to defend her decision. "Perhaps in years to come," she wrote, "I may regret this and we both may suffer for it, but nothing is harder than giving him away."[119] Whether or not matrons approved of residents' choices, the Home offered concrete assistance to mothers who kept their babies: many of the women boarded their babies at the Cottage Home while they worked for wages outside.

At the San Francisco Chinese Mission Home, matrons confronted the boundary between choice and compulsion when they decided how to deal with individual residents brought to the Home by authorities and left there while their court cases were pending. Since Mission officials believed that every satisfied resident must choose to be in the Home, and since judges frequently took the woman's stated preference into account in deciding where to send her, Mission officials tried to persuade the women brought to them to agree to stay in the Home. In this task, they faced two major obstacles: first, the women often resented the authorities who had taken them from brothels or from their families; and, second, many had been warned by procurers that the Home was a place of confinement where inmates were tortured or poisoned.

Mission officials found that the best way to deal with these fears, which sometimes led entrants to refuse food and drink, was to introduce them to the other residents and encourage them to take part in the Home routine. One such case was that of Ah Fah. Ah Fah, who had been picked up by a juvenile court officer who heard she was a domestic slave, had been purchased—but not physically abused—by her "owner." She was reluctant to enter the Mission Home. Yet, mission workers reported, "two of our dear little girls proved to be missionaries indeed, for they even went to the jail [where she was held pending disposition of her case] and stayed with her all night to win her to the Home. On the way to court they put their arms around her and prevailed."[120] The judge who heard her case sent Ah Fah to the Home after she told him she would prefer to go there.

One indication of the delicate balance between the hopes of mission officials and the desires of residents is the language of gratitude that pervaded residents' letters to matrons. Expressions of gratitude were the currency residents presented to matrons and matrons presented to mission boards as payment for their charitable generosity; both residents and matrons knew that mission supporters expected regular displays of appreciation. Some of the letters written by residents must have been composed in the heads of matrons: they consisted of a series of humble thank-you's to be read aloud on public occasions.[121] However, the bulk of the letters, published and unpublished, reveal that the language of gratitude is more useful as a key to the different perceptions of matrons and residents than as evidence of the firm hand of matrons.

In speaking to mission boards, matrons represented residents as women grateful for the Christian transformation rendered in their lives, but residents ordinarily expressed gratitude for the specific services offered by the institutions. Residents of the Denver Cottage Home voiced appreciation for the private shelter and medical care otherwise unavailable to them. One wrote that "I do not know what poor girls would do if it were not for that Home I think we should kill ourselves."[122] Another, on hearing of newspaper criticism of the Home, wrote to say that "I can't stand to hear anyone even hint at a criticism of Cottage Home and it made me mad." She continued: "I believe that Cottage Home does the very best possible under the circumstances."[123] A number of parents also wrote letters expressing gratitude for the kindnesses shown their daughters in the Home.[124] Residents of the Cottage Home emphasized their need for a place to go during their pregnancies, their need for economic support and medical assistance, and their worry at the lack of suitably private alternatives. Residents at the failed Industrial Christian Home made similar comments, thanking matrons for food, jobs, and shelter. Even Miranda Boss, whose criticisms of the Home matron prompted the public investigation described earlier in this chapter, expressed appreciation for the food and shelter, judging it more comfortable than her previous home.[125]

Residents at the San Francisco Chinese Mission Home thanked Mission officials for a variety of specific services in addition to food and shelter, including protection from abusive families or owners, assistance in returning to China, aid in securing medical and dental care, and help with immigration officials, divorce courts, or creditors. Long-term residents, well schooled in appealing to matrons' sympathies, used the language of gratitude to gain everything from jobs outside the Home to money for advanced schooling. Letters from women sent to college by the Mission Home included repeated assurances of gratitude interspersed with pleas for money, books, new clothes, or other necessities.[126] As at the Denver Cottage Home, some relatives of residents also thanked the Home for its services. One brother of a Home resident told matron Donaldina Cameron, "I am sending you all the thanks my heart can conceive, or my words can express, for the countless troubles and cares my poor sister . . . has caused you."[127]

Although matrons often cited letters from residents as evidence of their transformation into Christian faith and Victorian womanhood, residents' responses to Protestantism were highly selective. In the Colorado Cottage Home, officials reported high numbers of conversions, but their statistics are less impressive than they appear at first glance.[128] Although matrons glossed over the fact, most of the Cottage Home residents came from homes that were nominally Christian in the first place, so their professions of faith were as much a return to the fold as a change of heart. Reports of devotional meetings held in the Home reveal that mission workers, sensing the susceptibility of young women at a crisis in their lives, promised frightened and miserable girls outcast by society that if they would turn to Protestantism, God would forgive their sins. As one sharp-minded convert commented, "it seems too good to be true."[129] While the hope of starting life with a clean slate proved attractive to unmarried mothers, it did not necessarily translate into wholehearted support for Christianity.

In the Chinese Mission Home the numbers of religious conversions were always low, despite the persistent efforts of Mission officials to win residents to Presbyterianism.[130] Officials proudly reported that residents regularly contributed small sums from their tiny savings to mission causes, but most residents stopped short of joining the church. Few were as candid as the young woman who said simply, "it gives me a pain to hear this Jesus Christ stuff," but many gave up all pretense of Christian piety on leaving the Home.[131] One such woman, whom matron Cameron had helped to return to China, told the women at the mission home there that "she did not want to stay with us, she had only told you [Cameron] that she did, because you had treated her well, and she wanted to give you a face."[132]

In long-lived rescue homes, matrons cultivated an attitude of maternalism and sought to reconcile the divergent aims of matrons and residents. Maternalism fostered emotional bonds between matrons and residents even as it reinforced mission women's tendency to treat their charges like children. In these institutions, residents and matrons spoke to each other in a language of gratitude that masked differences and allowed Protestant women to take comfort in home mission imagery. Home mission women believed that their institutions succeeded in transforming morally "degraded" women into exemplars of female purity and piety, the Victorian values that informed rescue home life.

Yet, the women who entered rescue homes were real people rather than home mission images. Despite the institutional power of home mission women, the motivations of residents were crucial to the survival of rescue home operations. Rescue home entrants were neither powerless victims nor entirely free agents; they were women whose choices were constrained by a number of forces. The ideology of home mission women was only one of these forces, and for many rescue home entrants, it was less burdensome than forces outside the rescue homes. Many women entered rescue homes to escape poverty or illness; others sought relief from physical abuse, "ownership" by procurers, or condemnation of their pregnancies. Gender inequality, expressed in the wide variety of gender systems that characterized the Mormon, Chinese immigrant, or working-class cultures of rescue home residents, was a significant constraint on the choices of women outside the rescue homes.

The interaction of these gender systems with Victorian systems of social control propelled many women to see rescue homes as a desirable alternative. For most rescue home residents, the ideology of female moral authority was papered precariously over a list of goals that differed from those of the home mission women. There were, however, a small group of ethnic minority women who enthusiastically adopted the Victorian search for female moral authority. By examining their experiences, we can add yet another dimension to our survey of the systems of social control that affected intercultural relations among women.

4

Home Mission Women, Race, and Culture: The Case of "Native Helpers"

On a visit to the East Coast, Tien Fu Wu, an assistant at the Chinese Mission Home in San Francisco, took time to check in on a former resident, Ah Ho, who was married and living in Boston. As Wu reported to Mission Home matron Donaldina Cameron, she found Ah Ho "thin and frail and well worn out with her nest of babies." Wu informed Cameron that Ah Ho "wept and told me her family troubles, and I tried to comfort her the best way I could."[1] Maddie, another Mission Home resident who accompanied Wu, was also distressed by Ah Ho's condition. Maddie lamented that "it is dreadful how our dear [friend] is hemmed in on all sides . . . she isn't free even in her own home." Ah Ho's husband, she charged, was "stubborn as a mule [and] . . . so Chinesey about letting his wife go out" that it made her "most thankful that I haven't a man to boss me about."[2]

Wu stewed over Ah Ho's predicament all day, and finally returned later that night to confront her husband. "I began to lecture him as if he were my boy," she told Cameron, "[and told him] that he must be more thoughtful and kinder to his wife. . . . I tried hard to impress upon him to be more sensible and considerate of his wife by not having any more children." Although Wu was aware that she was skating on thin ice in lecturing a husband (rather than a young boy), she defended her actions. She told Cameron that "I really didn't care whether it was a delicate situation or not. I feel strongly that poor Ah Ho ought to be protected in some way or another."[3]

Tien Fu Wu was one of a handful of ethnic minority women who had been selected by home mission women to serve as trusted assistants referred to as *native helpers,* a term that suggests the mixture of fascination and condescension with which mission women regarded them. By all accounts the most enthusiastic of home mission converts, native helpers wrapped themselves in the mantle of female moral authority and dedicated themselves to implanting the values of Victorian women's culture in their own communities.

To Protestant home mission women, native helpers were living proof of the transforming power of female moral authority. For this reason, home mission women lavished attention on them, making them the centerpieces of mission public relations efforts by telling and retelling their life stories. Historians have for the most part ignored these relatively abundant historical sources. To those accustomed to late–twentieth-century conventions of race and ethnicity, which focus attention on the members of minority groups who champion ethnic solidarity, such women can only be a bit of an embarrassment, evidence of the power of white efforts to assimilate peoples of other races—in other words, classic Uncle Toms.[4] In terms of these conventions, Tien Fu Wu would have done better to defend Ah Ho and her husband against the incursions of white missionaries than to defend Ah Ho against her husband.

But, as Ah Ho's situation indicates, such an analysis would not take adequate account of power differences based on gender.[5] Although only a small percentage of the ethnic minority women who came into contact with home mission women became native helpers, by exploring the lives of those who did, we can begin to understand the interaction between the ideology of female moral authority and nineteenth-century ideas about race and culture.

Home Mission Women and Nineteenth-Century Ideas About Race and Culture

Modern scholars of race relations usually distinguish between race, a biological classification, and culture, a more diffuse set of attitudes, values, and traditions unrelated to biology, closer to what we nowadays term *ethnicity* than to race.[6] But because such a distinction rests on twentieth-century intellectual developments, it is of limited use to historians trying to understand Victorian race relations. To be sure, a handful of nineteenth-century doctors promoted a theory of "scientific racism" that depended largely on a biologically determined concept of race, but such fine distinctions were lost on most nineteenth-century Americans. At least until the first decades of the twentieth century, the concepts we call race and culture were fused in the popular mind, the differences between them only dimly perceived.[7] As late as 1897, one native helper, Omaha Indian Susan LaFlesche, could speak of the different "races" of "Swedes, Irish, Danes, Dutch, and Indians" with none of the confusion such a statement would cause for modern readers.[8]

In late–nineteenth-century America, to conflate race and culture in order to speak of different "races" was not to suggest equality between them; for Victorian evolutionary theory posited a distinct hierarchy of racial development ranging from the "primitive" to the "civilized."[9] Victorians would have said that only the highest group, the "civilized," showed "culture." To them, culture was not a rough synonym for society; rather, to have culture was to display one's standing at the apex of evolution by adhering to Victorian standards of morality. In such a scheme, culture and civilization were assumed to be the sole property of white middle-class Americans; other races, classes, and (what we would call) cultures were considered both morally and physically inferior.[10]

Historians disagree on the extent to which Protestant missionaries adhered to this Victorian racial hierarchy and its accompanying ideology, the set of ideas we have come to call "racialism" to distinguish it from twentieth-century racism. Some historians celebrate the potential for equality in the Protestant belief that people of all colors could—and should—be brought under the umbrella of Christianity; others consider missionaries the shock troops of American ethnocentrism.[11] Both the celebrators and the critics have a point, but neither grasps the central importance of the ideology of female moral authority in shaping the racial attitudes of Protestant missionary women.

What stands out on examination of these racial attitudes is the extent to which home mission women challenged racial biological determinism. This challenge was in large part an outgrowth of missionary experience with native helpers. Because Protestant women were eager to convince Americans that Tien Fu Wu and her peers were models of Victorian morality, they argued that race should be no barrier to educational opportunity or to participation in religious activities.

Home mission challenges to racial biological determinism rested on several justifications—scriptural, environmental, and even evo-lutionary—each intended to prove that nonwhite women could become exemplars of Victorian female values. Determined to show that "mind and morals are not olive, or white, or black," some home mission women chanted the Biblical verse, "He has made of one blood all the nations of the earth."[12] Others stressed that social environment, not biological race, determined individual de-velopment. Taunted by those who believed that Chinese children were incapable of learning, one home mission woman in San Fran-cisco responded with the flat statement that "environment means everything to the children of every race and nation."[13] A writer in the Women's National Indian Association publication the *In-dian's Friend* echoed her when she wrote, "I would beg that in the outset we eliminate the notion . . . that Indian girls differ funda-mentally from the girls of any other race. If we observe a difference it is but the result of their peculiar early environment, the same as appears among those of one family when the brothers and sisters are separated in infancy."[14]

Other home mission women argued that the evolutionary gap between white and Indian cultures was far smaller than more com-placent whites assumed. Sara Kinney, president of the Connecticut

Indian Association, took such a position in her standard speech, "Good Cheer." After describing the Roman ancestors of her white audiences as having "bodies painted blue, their hair long and shaggy, the skins of wild beasts their only covering," she argued that "it is the pessimist, not the Indian, who makes no progress, for blue he was at the beginning and blue he proposes to stay till the end of time, while the Indian, red at the start, is fast changing his color, and in less than a century will be as white as the conquerors of his country."[15] Kinney thus turned the assumptions of most evolutionists on their head, to diminish rather than emphasize differences between whites and Indians. To Kinney, Connecticut Indian Association protégée Susan LaFlesche served as an example of an Indian woman who, in taking on the attributes of Victorian Protestant womanhood, had demonstrated the insignificance of biological race.

The strength of these convictions can be seen in the educational programs of the Chinese Mission Home. Mission Home officials encouraged all residents to excel in their studies; good students who adopted the Victorian values of piety and purity were sent on for advanced schooling. A core of these students became *de facto* ambassadors of integration, because Protestant women fought for their admission to Bible schools and business colleges— in one case, even to Stanford University—composed of predominantly white student bodies.[16]

These challenges to racial determinism put home mission women in an anomalous position *vis-à-vis* their Victorian contemporaries. On the one hand, their defense of Chinese and Indian women set missionaries apart from the general context of late Victorian social thought. The ideology of female moral authority stressed universal bonds between women; expressed in high hopes for native helpers, it nurtured home mission challenges to racial determinism. Perhaps the best measure of the home mission challenge is the vehemence of the opposition it aroused. Missionaries at the Chinese Mission Home, for example, found it impossible to forget one woman who had declined their invitation to attend a meeting with the comment, "I'd rather see all the Chinese women heaped in a pile—*and set fire to.*"[17] They sensed strong intolerance even among "those who call themselves Christians."[18] They never ran out of opponents, from those who advocated Chinese exclusion in the 1880s, to the "buy and employ American" advocates of the 1930s. Yet, despite this opposition, Protestant women maintained their belief in racial malleability. They held to their ideals into the twentieth century, ignoring both the revival of neo-Lamarckian racialism, and the heyday of scientific racism (exemplified by anthropometry, eugenics, and IQ tests) that culminated in the immigration restriction campaigns of the 1920s.[19] During a period when even the most committed assimilationists were beginning to doubt their own assumptions, they forged a link in the chain that connected the racial optimism of antebellum reformers to the egalitarianism of the mid–twentieth-century attack on biological racism.[20]

Yet the same Protestant women who challenged distinctions made according to biological race maintained distinctions according to culture. Native helpers were expected to display Victorian piety and purity, but they were also encouraged to retain ties to the culture of their original communities. In some respects, home missionaries' interest in cultures other than their own approached that of the better-known settlement house workers of the same period. For this reason, it is important to avoid the temptation to lump all the activities of home mission women into the oversimplified category of "assimilation."

At the Chinese Mission Home in San Francisco, for example, missionaries hedged the assimilation of residents by expressing a desire that residents retain what they termed, so revealingly, "all that is *good* of Chinese tradition and custom."[21] They provided Chinese food for residents; they also put together a small museum to display Chinese artifacts. All Home residents took Chinese language classes, even though some of those born in the United States were less than enthusiastic about doing so. "My Chinese lessons are very difficult," wrote one such woman to a friend outside the Home. "I wouldn't take [the class] if it wasn't required."[22]

Furthermore, white officials insisted on retaining Chinese stylistic touches in the clothes Mission Home residents wore, from the dark skirts and white saams they wore every day, to the distinctive collars and fastenings added to their wedding dresses.[23] As a result, one visitor to the Home in 1887 commented that "the only Americanism I could discover was that some of the girls had banged their hair."[24] In 1902, Mrs. E. V. Robbins described the attitude of white mission women during a visit to an official at the

Chinese legation in Washington, D.C. When the minister commented on the "American" clothes worn by Choi Qui, a Home resident brought with the group, missionaries told him (perhaps a little defensively) that she was wearing them for the first time, and "this by the request of the man she is to marry." "We keep them in their own costumes, and supply them with their own food," explained Robbins, "deeming it wise not to detach them from their own people."[25] White officials tried to hold to this plan through the 1920s; as one visitor remarked, matron Donaldina Cameron "keeps her girls in native costume, deploring their preference for leather shoes over their own gay embroidered ones [and only] regretfully indulging them in a change from their own style of hairdressing."[26]

Some white missionaries developed strong personal fascinations for their "adopted" cultures.[27] Sara Kinney, president of the Connecticut Indian Association, referred to herself and the other white members of her group as Connecticut "Indians," a practice that suggests the extent of her personal identification with Indian women as well as her belief that she could speak on their behalf. Kinney was a long-time member of the Daughters of the American Revolution who boasted openly of her Anglo-Saxon heritage, yet she frequently became discouraged with white behavior towards Indians. She once told a correspondent that "the white race seems to be a curse—wherever it goes. Are'nt you about tired o' white folks? I am."[28]

Donaldina Cameron, matron of the Chinese Mission Home, was equally proud of her own Scots ancestry and her dedication to the Chinese, "among whom," she once remarked, "I have lived for twenty five years, and whom as a nation I love."[29] Her delight when Mission Home residents redecorated her rooms in Chinese style overcame her reluctance to accept personal gifts. Years later, a part of her much-loved Chinese print bedspread was framed and displayed on a wall in the Mission Home. Cameron lived in the Mission Home from her mid-twenties until national mission officials forced her to retire after she turned sixty-five. She left then only with a deep sense of personal loss, no longer quite at home in white American society.

Neither the missionary challenge to biological determinism nor matrons' fascination for their "adopted" cultures allowed home

Sara Kinney, president of the Connecticut Indian Association and "mother-in-chief" to Susan LaFlesche, proudly displaying her DAR medals.
(*Courtesy of the Connecticut Daughters of the American Revolution*)

Donaldina Cameron, matron of the Chinese Mission Home from 1900 to 1934, posed here in Chinese dress, demonstrating her nearly lifelong fascination with Chinese culture.

(*Courtesy of George Wilson, Palo Alto, California*)

mission women to overcome all of the racialism inherent in Victorian social thought. Just beneath the surface of their calls for the education and fair treatment of ethnic minority women ran a persistent theme of racialist moral judgment. Nevertheless, the extent to which this racialism was expressed was shaped by the ideology of female moral authority. Protestant women held their Victorian concept of womanhood so dear that they focused their complaints about Chinese culture primarily on its challenges to Victorian female piety and purity.

As we have seen, home mission women used Victorian female values to establish a different boundary of morality than that accepted by most middle-class Victorians. Although they were quick to cast aspersions on women who publicly challenged their goals, in general they relied on depictions of unfortunate women as innocent victims of predatory men to resist the tendency to label women as immoral. Their experience with native helpers concentrated this dynamic by strengthening their belief that most ethnic minority women were natural advocates of purity and piety.

Home mission women had, however, very little equivalent experience with ethnic minority men. When they lapsed into racialist rhetoric, they usually aimed their remarks at minority men. Because their Victorian conception of gender roles led them to see men in general as sexually aggressive creatures in need of female restraint, their complaints about ethnic minority men were reinforced by their gender consciousness. And when moralistic racialism was combined with Victorian assumptions about the nature of men, Protestant women were capable of sounding like the most extreme racists.

Consider, for example, the words of Donaldina Cameron, who, in a moment of exasperation at the tenacity of Chinatown procurers, railed that "the Chinese themselves will never abolish the hateful practice of buying and selling their women like so much merchandise, it is born in their blood, bred in their bone and sanctioned by the government of their native land."[30] Such a statement was hardly typical; Cameron spent most of her life defending Chinese women immigrants from stereotyping, sensationalism, and ideas of racial determinism. It is, however, revealing, because it suggests the limitations of the missionary challenge to biological determinism rooted in the Victorian ideology of female moral authority. Protestant women assumed that just under the surface of every ethnic minority woman was a pure, pious Christian woman waiting to emerge; but they routinely suspected the intentions of ethnic minority men, even those who professed Christian belief. In this sense, the gendered assumptions of Protestant women conditioned them to defend most ethnic minority women but condemn most ethnic minority men.

As the experiences of the three native helpers considered in this chapter will show, some ethnic minority women joined in the condemnations. Because the ideology of female moral authority could be used to challenge the social vulnerability of ethnic minority women, it held great appeal for native helpers. Donaldina Cameron may have been outraged at Chinese immigrant slaveholders, but Tien Fu Wu was so furious with Ah Ho's husband that she swept past Cameron's demurrals and went out of her way to lecture him to respect female purity. Maddie, the Chinese American girl who accompanied her, expressed indignation, too. Revealing the links between home mission ideology and Victorian racial hierarchies, Maddie charged that Ah Ho's husband was too "Chinesey," asked Cameron "never again [to] marry any of our girls to unchristian men," and said she was relieved that she didn't have "a man to boss me about."[31] Despite her complaints, Ah Ho saw a different reason for her husband's behavior. "The American teachers are so kind and want me to go often to church," she wrote to Donaldina Cameron, "but the Chinese people here gossip so much about women going out that my husband does not approve of my going out very much."[32] As her comments suggest, missionaries and native helpers developed a sharp critique of behavior that many Chinese immigrants considered entirely ordinary.

Like the Victorian Protestant women who ran home mission projects, native helpers defended women in the name of Victorian female values. Unlike them, native helpers had to confront in their own lives the conflict between the Victorian ideology of female moral authority and the distinctly different ideals maintained by ethnic minority communities. Before we can explore the dilemmas native helpers faced, however, we need to understand how they became a part of the search for female moral authority in the first place. To do this, we will consider the lives of three such native helpers: Susan LaFlesche, Ah Tsun, and Tien Fu Wu.

Susan LaFlesche and the Connecticut Indian Association

Susan LaFlesche, an Omaha Indian woman, hooked up with home mission women at the suggestion of reformer and anthropologist Alice Fletcher. In 1879, Fletcher met Susan's sister Susette during Susette's eastern speaking tour on behalf of the Ponca Indians. Inspired by this meeting to focus her anthropological research on American Indians, Fletcher conducted research and government service among the Omaha tribe in Nebraska beginning in 1881. The LaFlesche family acted as her hosts on the reservation, and Fletcher developed such a close relationship with them that she regarded Susan's brother Francis, who would later co-author her anthropological studies, as her adopted son.[33] It was Fletcher who told Sara Kinney, president of the Connecticut Indian Association, about young Susan LaFlesche's desire to become a doctor.

Susan LaFlesche was the daughter of the best-known of the Omaha chiefs and his wife, both of whom were closely aligned with Presbyterian missionaries who had worked among the tribe since the 1840s.[34] Regarded by missionaries as among the most "progressive" of Indian tribes, the Omaha was one of the first in which the federal government assigned members individual allotments of farmland.[35] Young Susan grew up in a frame house on an individual plot of land and attended Protestant missionary schools on the reservation until her parents sent her to a ladies' boarding school in New Jersey when she was thirteen. After a short stint as an assistant teacher in a reservation mission school, she enrolled at Hampton Institute, the famous industrial school for blacks, which was then in the midst of an experiment with Indian education.

Over time, the Connecticut Indian Association would build a typically Victorian legend of LaFlesche as an inspiring example of the transformation from primitive life to highest civilization. They were initially attracted to her, however, because she had had so much contact with Victorian culture that she seemed likely to succeed as "Connecticut's first venture in Indian Education."[36] By the time she graduated from Hampton in 1889, the Connecticut Indian Association had agreed to "adopt" her as their Indian daughter and to finance her education at the Woman's Medical College at Philadelphia.

LaFlesche's Hampton graduation speech, entitled "My Childhood and Womanhood," demonstrates how effectively she appealed to the preconceptions of Protestant Victorians. She told her audience that "some people have to wait for their work to be revealed to them, but from the outset the work of an Indian girl is plain before her." She maintained that "we who are educated have to be pioneers of Indian civilization. We have to prepare our people to live in the white man's way, to use the white man's books, and to use his laws if you will only give them to us." She announced her plans to become a physician, telling her audience that, while she expected her work to be difficult, she had discovered that "the shores of success can only be reached by crossing the bridge of faith."[37] Her address neatly combined the themes of dedication to her own people, devotion to Victorian morality, and commitment to Christianity.

The Connecticut Indian Association was particularly pleased by her plans to "go back to her own people as a physician for women and children."[38] Attaching missionary zeal to her professional aspirations, LaFlesche emphasized to the Association that her work as a doctor would help transform her tribe according to the ideal of the Christian home. She wrote to Sara Kinney that "as a physician I can do a great deal more than as a mere teacher, for the home is the foundation of all things for the Indians, and my work I hope will be chiefly in the homes of my people." She told Kinney that she planned "to go into their homes and help the women in their housekeeping, teach them a few practical points about cooking and nursing, and especially about cleanliness."[39]

In return for her dedication to home mission goals and her promise to delay marriage in order to make full use of her medical skills, the Connecticut Indian Association provided LaFlesche with encouragement, financial assistance, and political influence. The group began by persuading a reluctant Commissioner of Indian Affairs to use educational funds intended to place Indian students

In this student pageant held at Hampton Institute, Susan La Flesche (third from left) and the woman next to her represented the "Indians of the Past," and the couple at the far left represented the "Indians of the Present." The student on the far right, the "interpreter," is Charles Picotte, brother of Susan's future husband, Henry Picotte.
(*Courtesy of Hampton University Archives*)

in segregated schools to help underwrite her professional education at the mostly white Philadelphia Woman's Medical College.[40] Because government funds for this mission-inaugurated experiment in integration failed to arrive in time, Sara Kinney paid for La-Flesche's trip to Philadelphia herself.[41] When Susan LaFlesche arrived in Philadelphia in October 1886, trainsick and homesick, she was met by a Connecticut Association official who took her shopping, helped her find lodging, and accompanied her to the college to smooth her entrance into the institution.[42] At the college, she was greeted by Dean Rachel Bodley, already in contact with Association members, who assured her that "we welcome you and are proud of your lineage."[43]

All the members of the Connecticut Indian Association followed LaFlesche's progress avidly, but major responsibility for "mothering" her rested with president Sara Kinney. Kinney, a warm-

hearted woman, corresponded affectionately with both Susan and
her older sister Rosalie, who lived on the Nebraska reservation,
telling them about her own family, offering condolences on the
death of Rosalie's baby and of the sisters' grandmother, and mon-
itoring LaFlesche's academic progress. LaFlesche, who called her
"my dear 'mother-in-chief,' " kept a photograph of Kinney's Connecticut home on her wall and wrote to her of her school
activities.[44]

Although she missed her family and labored, according to Kinney, under academic "disadvantages" in competing with her class-
mates, LaFlesche completed her medical studies successfully and
earned the respect of the students and faculty.[45] Captivated by
medicine, she delighted in the intricacies of her profession and
wrote home enthusiastically of her school experiences. Her letters
suggest that one important part of her studies in Philadelphia was
an introduction to the ways of its Victorian élites. Though she
sometimes worried, "I am afraid I will be too quiet and too dull—
I can't cut up here or sing or dance for the children," she wrote
with pride of her visits to the Academy of Fine Arts and to the
opera. She boasted of acquiring her first bustle and her first pair
of white gloves. She listed the Christmas gifts she received from
her sponsors in Connecticut, including combs and brushes, nail-
brushes, cologne, white ties, a card basket, and books of scripture
and poetry.[46] When not studying medicine or learning the conventions of Philadelphia society, LaFlesche spent her time speaking before missionary gatherings or charity projects. She once
spoke to a group of boy "ragamuffins" collected by an acquain-
tance, reportedly entrancing them by singing "Nearer My God to
Thee."[47] She made frequent visits to the Lincoln School for Indian
children outside Philadelphia, where she encouraged students to
follow in her footsteps.

In March of 1889, Kinney and other Connecticut Association
members watched Susan LaFlesche graduate as the first Indian
woman physician in the United States. Soon afterwards, she em-
barked on a triumphant speaking tour of Association branches,
visiting Hartford, Waterbury, New Britain, Winsted, Norwich, and
Meriden. For each audience she retold the story of her life, her
academic achievements, and her plans to work as a doctor on the
reservation. Her efforts dramatically increased the membership of

the group, and, according to one white observer, she "charmed" her audiences with "her modest ways and her evident earnestness in the work she has chosen."[48]

The Connecticut Indian Association hailed LaFlesche's return to her Nebraska reservation as a triumph for its Indian education program. She had secured an appointment as government school physician, a position not usually granted to an Indian.[49] Again the Connecticut Association offered help: they bought LaFlesche her surgical tools and appointed her the official Association medical missionary to the Omaha, at a salary added to her other earnings.[50] They looked forward to helping her finance her ultimate goal, that of constructing a hospital on the reservation. As for her work as a medical missionary, LaFlesche argued, "I shall have an advantage over a white physician in that I know the language, customs, habits, and manners of living among the Indians."[51] Agreeing with her, the Connecticut Indian Association had come to regard Susan LaFlesche as the pivot of its home mission program for the Omaha.

Ah Tsun, Tien Fu Wu, and the Chinese Mission Home

Like Susan LaFlesche, Ah Tsun was a home mission "success" story, the first in the history of the Chinese Mission Home in San Francisco. Ah Tsun entered the Home in 1877 at the age of sixteen, fleeing from her "owner," who, after bringing her into the country disguised as a boy (a ruse to evade immigration officials), planned to sell her into prostitution. Shortly after entering the Home, she was arrested on charges of grand larceny, a ploy slaveowners used to regain control of prostitutes by convincing police officers that they had stolen clothes or jewelry found in their possession—and regarded by them as legitimate payments or gifts. After two court trials, Ah Tsun was acquitted and released to the custody of the Mission Home.[52]

Ah Tsun was one of only a few residents who stuck out the difficult early years when matrons and the Home routine shifted frequently.[53] Within a year, missionaries regarded her as "the pet of the Home."[54] She touched the hearts of Home board members by announcing at their annual meeting: "I wish to tell you that I love this home, and am happy here. When my time for staying has expired, with your permission, I still wish to remain. I do not wish to marry and leave the Home. I love Jesus and pray to him each day for a clean and new heart."⁵⁵ Although she did, after turning down several proposals, eventually marry and leave the Home, her words were nonetheless prophetic, for she retained strong ties to home mission women.

Her marriage to Chinese Christian Ngo Wing in 1884 evoked a great deal of ambivalence among Mission Home officials who regretted losing her services as Home interpreter, organist, and prayer leader. They reminded themselves, however, that "we cannot travel the road with them [after they leave the Home], nor do they need us, as they need to travel it themselves to their own destination. We can only take the stones of stumbling out of the way, or throw light before them and save them from wandering, or hold them up over some rough places and save them from falling."⁵⁶ Mission women tried to do just that by establishing the new bride in a nearby residence selected so that the handful of "Christian girls who had married from the Home might feel that they were secure from molestation."⁵⁷ In her new home Ah Tsun Wing busied herself with housework, child-rearing, and proselytizing; she reported regularly to mission women on her evangelistic activities.

Neither Wing's Victorian morality nor her mission-selected residence saved her from local toughs who stoned the house during anti-Chinese disturbances in 1885. Although Mission officials tracked down her harassers and told them "that these Chinese women had rights that were as dear as our own, and were entitled to the same protection as American women," they seem to have made little impression on the toughs.⁵⁸ Partly to escape such disturbances, Wing entered a Bible school in Canton, China, where she remained for two years. On her return to San Francisco, she completed her professional education by spending a few months in the Golden Gate Kindergarten Training School.

By now a widow who needed work, Ah Tsun Wing found her best hope of employment within the mission system. She enrolled her children in the Mission's Occidental School for Chinese children (a parallel project operated outside the Mission Home), and began work as a kindergarten teacher, Mission Home assistant, and Sunday school leader. The first native helper to come out of the Chinese Mission Home, she would remain associated with it for more than forty years, from 1894 until her retirement in 1935.[59] Just about the time that Ah Tsun Wing started to work for the Chinese Mission Home, Tien Fu Wu entered the institution. Wu had been brought to the United States as a child of six after her father, reduced to poverty through gambling debts, sold her to an agent. In California, the young girl was transferred from person to person until she ended up in the hands of a woman who abused her with hot iron tongs. When someone reported her condition to Mission workers, they located her and took her to the Mission Home.[60]

Once away from her abusers, Wu was, as she later remembered, a "happy-go-lucky tom boy" who had a tumultuous adolescence in the Mission Home. She remembered years later that on one occasion she held her head out the window of her room in a vain attempt to contract pneumonia and die so that she could return to haunt the matron who had reprimanded her for some minor offense. In her late teens, however, she had a change of heart and converted to Christianity.[61]

Wu attributed her conversion to a single incident that occurred one night as she sat beside matron Donaldina Cameron at the deathbed of Cameron's interpreter Yuen Qui. Wu had volunteered to help Cameron because she was attracted to Yuen Qui, "in spite of the fact" that she was a "quiet student, a seamstress and a reader." Wu remembered that "when Miss Cameron saw [Yuen Qui die], she absolutely broke down. I felt very sorry for her and was convinced of the great loss. So I offered to help her in the rescue work." This decision, she later remarked, saved her from leading a "selfish and worldly life."[62] It was the personal connection she felt with Cameron, based on Cameron's grief at Yuen Qui's death, that laid the basis for Wu's lifelong dedication to home mission work.

By 1905, Wu had completed the course at the Mission Home school to the satisfaction of Mission workers, who reported that she had been "of such assistance as a dear elder daughter may become to the burdened mother of a large family."[63] She was able to continue her education because of a benefactor, Mr. Coleman, who had attended a Philadelphia lecture about the San Francisco rescue work. Coleman visited San Francisco in 1905 and invited

Tien Fu Wu, shown here at age sixteen, sent this photograph to a Chinese Mission Home benefactor.

(*Courtesy of Pacific Books, Palo Alto, California*)

Wu to join a party of evangelical guests at his country house at New Hampshire. After she told him she needed more education to hone her skills as Mission Home interpreter, he offered to pay for further schooling. As a result, she spent four years at the Stevens' School in Germantown, Pennsylvania, and two years at the Toronto Bible School.[64]

In 1911, Wu returned to the Mission Home to work as Donaldina Cameron's helper, a job that involved assisting in rescues and appearing in court as Cameron's interpreter. She saved her salary until she could afford to return to China and search for her long-lost relatives. Unable to locate them, she decided that "I must come back to help Cameron House because they had helped to rear me."[65] Like Ah Tsun Wing, Tien Fu Wu would remain in home mission work until her retirement.

The Dilemma for Native Helpers

For Susan LaFlesche, Ah Tsun Wing, and Tien Fu Wu, the emotional bonds they shared with mission women, the educations they gained, and the praise they received for their exemplary behavior were formative experiences that inspired trust in the benevolence of home mission women. Adopting the central tenets of Victorian women's culture, native helpers dedicated themselves to extending Victorian conceptions of female purity and piety to their own communities. Their task required them to weld the ideology of female moral authority onto their own distinct cultures.

Reminded since childhood that they were examples of the best their peoples had to offer, native helpers saw themselves as cultural spokeswomen. Susan LaFlesche, for example, was one of the first generation of Native Americans to look beyond tribal loyalties to adhere to a concept of "Indians" in general; she never doubted her qualifications to speak for all Indians.[66] A comment made by a white school supervisor about her sister Marguerite applied equally well to Susan in this regard. "She is so sensitive on the Indian question," he wrote, "that she regards every criticism of Indians or Indian customs as a personal insult to her, and so resents it as a general rule."[67] LaFlesche's strong identification with the interests of Indians was matched only by her determination to mold their future along the lines of Victorian morality. She dedicated her life to this process of transformation, all the while insisting, "I have no cause but that of my people."[68]

Yet, even while native helpers pledged themselves to defend their peoples, the universalizing thrust of the ideology of female moral authority distanced them from their own communities by challenging conventional arrangements of gender power in those communities. In the case of San Francisco's Chinatown, Chinese immigrant men who made their money from prostitutes reserved special ire for native helpers, whose work threatened their livelihoods. Since it was part of Wu's job to assist Donaldina Cameron in rescuing prostitutes from San Francisco brothels, she frequently had to face brothel owners in court. After one of these incidents, an angry Chinese man tried to intimidate Wu by writing her a letter that indicates slaveowners' hostility toward her. "Tien Fook, stinking sow," he wrote, "now you are interpreter in the Mission Home and have the backing of the Home so you even dare to arrest a family girl." After accusing her (incorrectly) of being a prostitute, the letter threatened that "you have overreached yourself and in so doing negroes, dogs, and thunder will come after you."[69] Mission women deemed the rest of the letter "too vile to translate."

This viciousness from the men who profited from organized prostitution might have been expected; but criticism was also forthcoming from Chinese immigrants not directly involved with the trade. Thus, after one troubled Chinese woman fled to the Mission Home for assistance, her father-in-law wrote to tell her, "you made a mistake by going to the Mission Home because good women do not enter there. . . . I am afraid that you have surely lost your reputation by going into the Mission Home."[70] Many other immigrants shared his opinion. Chinese Mission workers like Ah Tsun Wing, who taught for many years in the missionary group's Occidental School, had to dissociate the school from the Mission Home for fear that Chinese merchant parents would not let young children attend if missionaries acknowledged the connection between the two.[71]

Attitudes like these cut at the very heart of Protestant mission work. In choosing native helpers, white women assumed that reinforcing Victorian female moral authority was a viable strategy for commanding community respect. But, given the precepts of

From left: Donaldina Cameron, an unidentified assistant, and Tien Fu Wu on the steps of the Chinese Mission Home building.
(*Courtesy of Cameron House*)

the Chinese gender system, Chinese immigrants found it only too easy to discredit native helpers as immoral women who had "overreached" themselves. When Chinese immigrants saw native helpers as threats to (rather than exemplars of) morality, they inadvertently revealed the Victorian bias of the search for female moral authority.

As native helpers were to discover, the lip-service Americans paid to white mission home women was based, not only on claims to female moral authority, but also on the operation of the Victorian racial hierarchy. Although white mission women, too, received threatening letters from Chinese opponents, writers took care to be much more polite in addressing them. Given the white dominance in American society, Chinese vice operators who offended white women risked reprisals from Victorians eager to defend the purity of white womanhood, the cultural symbol used to justify, among other things, the widespread lynching of blacks in the American South. Under these circumstances, slaveowners saved their strongest barbs for Chinese native helpers, and native helpers' determination to fight against prostitution set them apart from a significant segment of their Chinese immigrant communities.

A similar dynamic operated in the case of Susan LaFlesche. In her case it was dedication to temperance, an issue high on the agenda of Victorian Protestant women, that placed her most at odds with her tribal community. LaFlesche's opposition to liquor was both principled and personal. She regretted that the granting of citizenship to the Omaha had given them the right to buy liquor, a right previously limited by government supervision and by tribal police. In her view, the subsequent history of the Omaha was one of degradation. "Intemperance increased," she explained, "until men, women and children drank; men and women died from alcoholism, and little children were seen reeling on the streets of the town; drunken brawls in which men were killed occurred, and no person's life was considered safe."[72] LaFlesche restricted her own movement around the reservation because she feared being molested by drinking parties; she gave shelter to a number of women who feared abuse at the hands of their inebriated husbands. She worried about her brother, who drank more than she thought he should, and her beloved sister, who had been threatened in her own home by a drunken man.[73] After her marriage in 1894, she added her heavy-drinking husband, Henry Picotte, to the list.

Susan LaFlesche Picotte waged a continuous—and often unpopular—battle for temperance that placed her in direct conflict with drinkers and with an opposing faction of white-educated Omaha on the reservation. Dismissing the claims of her opponents that Indians had as much right to drink as white men did, she saw the situation as an emergency. She spoke for politicians who favored prohibiting the sale of liquor to Indians, praised white officials who arrested drunkards and liquor salesmen, and prided herself on having prohibited liquor sales in the newest of the reservation towns.[74] Her actions infuriated the half-blood tribe members who defended white liquor sellers and criticized the harsh treatment Indians received when arrested by government officials.

Picotte was no stranger to factionalism on the reservation, since her "progressive" father, an early advocate of temperance, had long excited controversy among the tribe. She withstood the painful hostility her stand on temperance engendered, because opposition to liquor seemed to her to be a moral necessity. She made her convictions clear when she protested the government's firing of a white official, John Commons, whom she credited with protecting the tribe from whiskey sellers. The inspector who removed Commons had called his defenders factionalists; Picotte retorted that the inspector should have seen "that the so-called 'factional fight' was between Right and Wrong." In a sentence that was perhaps the culmination of her acceptance of white paternalism, she told government officials: "I know that I shall be unpopular for a while with my people, because they will misconstrue my efforts but this is nothing, just so I can help them for their own good."[75]

In San Francisco as in Nebraska, native helpers' determination to help Chinese immigrants "for their own good" caused the rifts between themselves and their communities to widen. Yet their efficacy as agents of community change depended on their holding to home mission goals without losing ties to their own communities. When the gap between the two seemed unbridgeable, native helpers faced difficult choices.

Native helpers at the Chinese Mission Home found little scope to maneuver within their own communities and only minimal op-

Dr. Susan LaFlesche Picotte, Omaha Indian woman, temperance advocate, missionary, and physician.
(*Courtesy of the Nebraska State Historical Society*)

portunities to work in white-owned businesses. Despite their educational achievements, those who sought employment outside the Mission Home faced blatant discrimination. Many white employers took racial boundaries for granted to such an extent that they refused to hire Chinese women regardless of their qualifications. Even those who managed to find jobs found little security in them. One such woman, Ah Tye Leung, a Mission Home interpreter, was appointed Assistant Matron when the Angel Island Immigration Station opened in 1910. Since her appointment put her in a position to intercede between immigration officials and Chinese women immigrants, Home officials were delighted. They optimistically quoted a minister who told them that "if [Leung's appointment] was the only result of the work of the [Chinese Mission Home] Board, it was enough." As they saw it, it was "splendid . . . to know we shall have a dear Christian girl to do this work among heathen women!"[76] Their high hopes, however, evaporated when Leung married a white immigration worker. Both were fired for this affront to white racial sensibilities.[77] As her experience indicates, even the best-prepared native helper was vulnerable to racism of the most arbitrary sort. The female moral authority that had been the backbone of mission training could ensure them neither the respect of their own communities nor acceptance by white Americans.

Faced with obstacles like these, Ah Tsun Wing and Tien Fu Wu chose to remain within the mission system. Their decisions allowed them to retain the emotional bonds they had formed with mission officials and to use their skills in paid employment. While in the Mission Home, they were insulated from the most blatant forms of racism. Nonetheless, they were never allowed to hold substantial authority within that institution either. Tien Fu Wu, for example, worked as "interpreter and general supervisor of girls" at the Chinese Mission Home from 1911 through the 1930s, during which period she was Superintendent Donaldina Cameron's closest confidante. Yet Mission Home residents referred to Wu as "auntie" rather than as "mother," the term used to describe Donaldina Cameron.[78] In a mission system in which authority rested in claims to motherhood, the distinction was significant. It helped to pave the way for another, much more telling, slight.

When Cameron began to think about retirement in 1934, some

Presbyterian officials proposed Wu to be her replacement, but others assumed she would not be interested in the post. Belatedly consulted for her opinion, Wu formally declined consideration, saying that she was not adequately prepared for the job and that she was more interested in assisting Cameron or working with children than in shouldering the supervisory duties of administering the Home. "I am," she wrote, "of the same opinion as I told Miss Cameron before, that an American person should be the head of this work."[79] She based her conclusion in part on her belief that judges were prejudiced against her because she was Chinese, an opinion supported by accounts of her treatment by court officials.[80] Wu's demurral suggests her recognition that, in white-dominated American society, a white woman would hold more influence with the power structure than Wu could command. In the end, the job went to Lorna Logan, a white woman who had begun her work at the Home only two years earlier. Unlike Wu, Logan could not speak Chinese.

Wu recognized—and chafed at—the limitations of her authority within the Mission Home. Her relations with Donaldina Cameron were affectionate, not to say adoring, but she had no such emotional ties to Lorna Logan. To Logan, Wu made her resentment clear. A dozen years later, Logan told Presbyterian officials that "[Wu] has been increasingly unhappy here, partly because we have disagreed on some points of policy, and partly because she feels that she is not given the status she should have."[81]

Wu's resentment was not the only evidence that home mission women slighted Chinese women. Ah Tsun Wing was so routinely grateful to mission workers that her own personality is difficult to unearth from the sources, but she, too, recognized that mission authority was tied up with pretensions to motherhood. On the one occasion when she disagreed with the missionaries in public, she spoke out against those who implied that Chinese women who sold their children were inadequate mothers. "A Chinese mother's love for her child," she insisted, "is as great as any mother's love." She defended "poor mothers with large families [who] are not able to support so many children and [for whom] poverty compels them to give away some."[82]

Personnel folders kept by the Presbyterian mission board suggest that some missionaries regarded Chinese native helpers as domineering and insufficiently educated co-workers.[83] Yet missionaries also praised native helpers' loyalty and recognized that rescue homes could not survive without their assistance. Both Wing and Wu remained within the Mission Home, which continued to be the most attractive alternative for Chinese native helpers caught in a conflict between the ideology of female moral authority and the gender system of Chinese immigrant communities.

Susan LaFlesche Picotte ultimately chose a different path. For most of her adult life, she trusted in the efficacy of white Indian reform and the beneficence of government officials. For a long time, her medical training, her support from the Connecticut Indian Association, and her generally favorable relations with government agencies reinforced her convictions. During her years on the Omaha reservation, she had enjoyed considerable success in cutting through government red tape for individual members of her tribe. Confronted by the tangle of bureaucratic regulations involved in administering the government trust over Indian lands, she had often appealed to government officials to shorten the process. Impressed with her professional status and by her standing as an exemplar of Victorian morality, officials had frequently taken her recommendations into consideration. Yet, late in her life, there were indications that her faith in these avenues of change was diminishing.

Her misgivings were fueled by a personal confrontation with government officials. After her husband's death, she tried to gain control of the inheritance he had left her young sons, only to be told that a distant male relative of her husband, long ago appointed as guardian, would administer the funds. Angered by this injustice, she protested to the Indian Office. "It is strange," she noted, "that I, a mother, and one who has worked hard to support herself and children, and bitterly opposed to whiskey in any form, should be denied the right to care for her children's money." What offended her was that "it should be given into the care of a man who is a hard drinker, and who has seen these children only once in his life, and who resides in another state."[84] Her contention that she deserved special consideration for her Victorian female morality had frequently proved influential, but in this particular battle, she won her point only after sending the Indian Office testimonials to her character from a number of white friends.

Susan LaFlesche Picotte, her mother, Mary Gale LaFlesche, and her two sons, Caryl and Pierre, on the porch of her house in Bancroft, Nebraska. (Courtesy of the Nebraska State Historical Society)

Picotte's doubts grew as her personal supportive contacts with home mission women diminished. Although Picotte had continued to work for the Women's National Indian Association as its medical missionary for several years after returning to the reservation, her dream of building a hospital had never materialized. The Association did not explain their decision to give up the project early in the 1890s, only announcing delays due to "local conditions" and lack of necessary cost estimates.[85] These obstacles might have been overcome if Sara Kinney, whose support for Picotte had been so significant in financing her medical training, had thrown her influence behind the hospital project. During 1890 and 1891, however, Kinney suffered a series of personal tragedies as her mother, her father, and her husband all died.[86] Soon afterwards, she resigned her position as head of the Women's National Indian Association home-building committee and restricted her other activities, although she remained at the helm of the Connecticut Indian Association until her own death many years later. As the years passed, she lost influence within the National Association and had fewer contacts with members of the LaFlesche family. She was replaced on the home-building committee by Mrs. E. P. Gould, who was much more tightfisted with the Omaha tribe than Kinney had been. Gould's resentment at Picotte's delay in paying back a small loan from the committee led to bad feelings.[87]

Susan LaFlesche Picotte's attenuated ties with home mission women and her doubts about her effectiveness in influencing government officials helped prepare her for a turning point in her relationship to her own community. The critical moment came late in 1909, when the Department of the Interior, which contained the Office of Indian Affairs, unveiled a new policy for the Omaha reservation. Without consulting the tribe, the department decided to extend restrictions on Indian land use beyond the twenty-five-year period originally set by legislation; to consolidate the Omaha and Winnebago reservations; and to set up a program in which white farmers would train Indians to use their land more efficiently. As part of the delegation sent by the Omaha to Washington, D.C., to protest the policy, Picotte broke her lifelong habit of defending government policy and lashed out against government officials.

In the process, she experienced the exhilaration of speaking with the unanimous support of her tribe; the factionalism of her temperance campaign seemingly erased. She described her feelings to a friend: "It makes me feel so good to know all the Omahas had so much confidence in me—their choice of me as a delegate was unanimous." "When I [initially] refused," she continued, "they threatened to carry me to [the] train and put me on." In her mind, the tribe's protest was unprecedented. "We are going," she insisted, "to cut loose from government supervision as far as possible."[88] When her old mentor Alice Fletcher, who supported the new policies, cautioned Picotte that her protest had consequences, Picotte dismissed them firmly. "As to my loss of influence at [the] Department," she wrote to Fletcher, "I should most certainly lose my self respect were I to keep still when I thot any thing was going to be done that would be to the detriment of the Omahas. I don't care an iota what the Depart[ment] thinks of me!"[89]

The incident was significant in several respects. The woman who had once encouraged Connecticut Indian Association maternalism by telling its members that "[the Omaha] are now like little children, without father or mother" had decided to join her tribe in arguing that "this condition of being treated as children we want to have nothing to do with," asserting that "the majority of the Omahas are as competent as the same number of white people."[90] Seeing in government policy a "new" condescension, she began to argue for her people as a group instead of as reformed individuals. Although Picotte favored retaining government controls on the sale of Indian lands (she feared their withdrawal would lead to rapacious whites' depriving Indians of their holdings), she wanted Indian land management to begin at once.[91]

Picotte's demands for Indian autonomy in land management spilled over into other areas, too. By 1910, she had begun refusing calls for medical help from white people in order to "save herself" for the Indian work.[92] Furthermore, she reversed her position on the use of peyote. Like most Protestant missionaries, she had originally compared the "mescal bean" to alcohol and had seen its use as immoral. In 1908, shortly after peyote had been introduced to the Omaha, she told a white audience that "we have had much trouble with this [peyote use] . . . and we try to teach the victim that he is deluded."[93] Evidence from later in her life, however, suggests that she changed her mind. When her brother Frank was called on to testify at a government hearing on the influence of peyote, he quoted a letter from Picotte in which she told him that "a strange thing has happened among the Omahas. They have quit drinking, and they have taken a new religion [Peyote Religion]." She reported, "members of that new religion say they will not drink; and the extraordinary part of the thing is that these people pray, and they pray intelligently, they pray to God, they pray to Jesus, and in their prayers they pray for the little ones, and they ask God to bring them up to live sober lives; they ask for help from God."[94]

Susan LaFlesche Picotte, then, faced with the realization that the moral influence of Protestant womanhood was not powerful enough to solve her problems, began to reinforce her ties to the Omaha tribal community. In 1913, she finally succeeded in opening her long-awaited hospital on the reservation, having raised the funds by deftly playing a variety of missionary groups off against each other. Absent from the list was the faltering Connecticut Indian

Susan LaFlesche Picotte (second from left, holding baby), at a meeting of the Peyote Religion. The religion, which advocated temperance and emphasized Indian identity, won LaFlesche's approval in the years just before her death in 1915.
(*Courtesy of the Nebraska State Historical Society*)

Association: in the end, the hospital stood as Susan LaFlesche Picotte's personal declaration of independence.

A look at the lives of Susan LaFlesche Picotte, Ah Tsun Wing, and Tien Fu Wu helps us understand the relationship between the ideology of female moral authority and Victorian racial hierarchies. The universalizing thrust of the Victorian ideology of female moral authority encouraged home mission women to challenge biological determinism as it applied to ethnic minority women. As one member of the Women's National Indian Association explained of Indian women, "these women are our sisters; the color of their skin should not blind us to that fact."[95] In this significant sense, home mission women were antiracists who anticipated the modern distinction between biologically determined race and socially constructed culture.

Home mission convictions allowed for the flowering of relationships between white missionary women and native helpers that sustained women of both groups. Susan LaFlesche Picotte and Sara Kinney enjoyed such a relationship for many years; indeed, its loss seems to have precipitated Picotte's later doubts about home mission work. The ties between Tien Fu Wu and Donaldina Cameron lasted even longer. After working as Cameron's assistant from 1911 until Cameron's retirement in 1934, Wu stayed on at the Mission Home until her own retirement. In 1952, she moved into a cottage next door to Cameron's Palo Alto home, and the two women shared both their daily lives and their memories of rescue work until Cameron's death in 1968.[96] Matrons and native helpers formed bonds between women across socially drawn racial boundaries; these bonds, along with employment in the mission system, shielded trusted assistants from the worst of the racism prevalent in American society outside the institutions.

But the ideology of female moral authority had limitations as well as strengths. Home mission women may have distinguished between race and culture, but they never took the step towards cultural relativism that characterized the work of the twentieth-century anthropologists who set the terms for modern ideals of race relations. Because white missionary women were unable to transcend Victorian "racial" hierarchies, trusted assistants grew into "native helpers" rather than full-fledged colleagues, and never held autonomous authority in mission circles.

Furthermore, while missionaries' experiences with native helpers encouraged them to avoid using racialist rhetoric to describe ethnic minority women, they applied few such restrictions to ethnic minority men. Schooled in the conventions of Victorian assumptions about men and women, home missionaries saw women in general as naturally pure and men in general as naturally aggressive. The home mission challenge to racial determinism was ultimately rooted in a gender determinism expressed in the ideology of female moral authority.

As for native helpers themselves, mediating between the racial hierarchy of the white society on the one hand and the gender hierarchy of their own communities on the other posed an enduring dilemma. To understand their predicament, we have to realize that for female native helpers, gender systems as well as racial hierarchies shaped their experience and affected their choices. To the extent that female moral authority could be used to challenge the social vulnerability of women, it held great appeal to native helpers. Thus, Tien Fu Wu used the Victorian value of female purity to try to protect Ah Ho from unwanted pregnancies, and Susan LaFlesche Picotte advocated temperance to protect Omaha Indian women from abuse at the hands of drunken men.

The dilemmas native helpers faced in their missionary work outside rescue homes remained muted for rescue home residents who lived within institutional walls. When residents prepared to leave the institutions, however, they, too, were pulled between overlapping systems of social control based on class, race, and gender.

5

Homes Outside
the Rescue Homes

On Saturday, April 13, 1878, several home mission women attended a wedding in San Jose, California. The bride, Ah Fah, had resided in the San Francisco Chinese Mission Home for two years. She was employed as a domestic servant; her groom, Ng Noy, was a Chinese Christian who worked in a nearby household. The white women could not understand the words of the ceremony, which was conducted in Chinese by a Presbyterian missionary. They were, however, convinced that this "organization of a home on Christian principles" was "the first step upwards from heathenism to civilization." One of the white guests wrote a lengthy account of the event for a Christian newspaper. She reminded her readers that "at the foundation of all Christian living lies the home," then went on, in terms that echoed newspaper society pages, to describe the prewedding entertainment, the presents, and the appearance of the bride, who dressed in Chinese fashion but carried a bouquet of white roses. On behalf of home mission women, she wished the newly married couple well, trusting, she said, that their "future housekeeping" would "indeed be a *home*-keeping."[1]

From the beginnings of their work in the West, home mission women had invested great symbolic significance in images of "home-keeping." Because they believed that "Christian homes" were the fountainhead of women's influence in society, they adapted Victorian ideals into a model for rescue home life. Within the rescue homes, they envisioned the "Christian home" as a bastion of female moral authority—a leap of faith that was possible because, after all, rescue homes were homes without husbands; to echo Winifred Spaulding's words, they were homes made by women alone.

Inside the institutions, home mission women tried to pattern residents' behavior according to Victorian female values. They did so in the virtual absence of male authority and with minimal contact with the communities from which rescue home residents originated. This relative insulation, however, ended abruptly when rescue home residents reentered the world outside the institutions. Once outside, residents, whose motivations had always differed from those imagined by home mission women, pursued their goals in the wake of an enormous gap between the ideal homes of missionary lore and real-life households embedded in the diverse gender systems, racial hierarchies, and class structures of late–nineteenth-century communities.

Ah Fah experienced the gulf between the two firsthand. On April 20, 1879, she and her husband became the first Chinese members of the Presbyterian Church near their home, an act that led home mission women to praise their model Christian marriage.[2] Yet, the young immigrant couple found it hard to establish an economic foothold. In these years of economic depression and anti-Chinese sentiment, Ng Noy was often out of work, so Ah Fah supported them by taking in hand sewing.[3] Her wage work flew in the face of home mission assumptions that, while single women might be self-sufficient, wives should be economically dependent on their husbands; furthermore, it left her little time to attend mission meetings or church services. Searching for an explanation, disappointed mission women blamed Ah Fah's predicament, not on poverty or prejudice, but on "her husband's influence." "Though a professing Christian," one visitor from the Chinese Mission Home commented, "[he] is still a Chinaman, with all a Chinaman's deeply-rooted prejudices in favor of women leading secluded lives, with not too much education or freedom of any sort."[4]

While in the Chinese Mission Home, missionaries had praised

Ah Fah as "sprightly, tidy, quick to learn housework, sewing, fancy work, and books."[5] None of these attributes, however, gave her the moral authority mission women envisaged. Three years after her marriage, a visitor from the Chinese Mission Home found her "in an ill humor," complaining that learning English had done her no good because she would soon have to accompany her husband to China. In China, Ah Fah would be expected to live with Ng Noy's mother, who disliked her because she had no children.[6] In China, home mission ideals would clash with a gender system in which female authority rested with mothers-in-law rather than young wives. For Ah Fah, mission ideals were tenuous enough in American society, for, once outside the rescue home, she was caught in the middle of a conflict between her husband, who had pressured her to limit activities outside their household, and mission women, who criticized her for taking on the economic burden of supporting her husband.

Yet, it is too simple to say that because life outside the rescue homes rarely lived up to mission expectations, the search for female moral authority was a practical failure for rescue home residents. In fact, the tension among home mission ideals, gender systems, racial hierarchies, and economic pressures pulled departing residents in diverse ways. The patterns of this interaction can be traced most clearly in courtship, marriage, and domestic service, the three aspects of life outside the rescue homes that missionaries correlated to the "Christian home." In the case of the Chinese Mission Home, where the sources are rich enough to explore in some depth the experiences of married home residents, the clash between the ideology of female moral authority and the more traditional gender system of Chinese immigrants set the stage for the emergence of one theme of a distinctive Chinese American gender system.

The Significance of Marriage

In Salt Lake City, all the residents of the Industrial Christian Home had already been married, and missionaries avoided the potentially scandalous issue of remarriage, concentrating instead on finding residents jobs in domestic service. In Denver and in San Francisco, however, most residents were young unmarried women, and in these two cities both residents and matrons saw marriage as a fitting culmination to rescue home life. For matrons, the marriages of residents provided an ideological litmus test for rescue home operations: they used the contrast between the presumably miserable relationships residents left behind and the Protestant marriages they eventually formed to measure institutional success. Home mission women hoped that departing residents would create Christian homes in which they would preside as wives and mothers respected and honored by kindly Protestant husbands.

Whether or not they shared matrons' ideological perspectives, marriage was important to rescue home residents, too. To them, marriage was a critical means of acquiring economic support and social status; furthermore, it provided an arena in which they might play the socially valued and sometimes powerful role of mother. Thus, many women entered the San Francisco Chinese Mission Home to obtain mission protection for marriages that would take them away from prostitution. Others traveled long distances to enter the Denver Cottage Home in hopes of keeping unplanned pregnancies from interfering with their prospects for marriage.

Courtship: The Search for the Elusive Christian Gentleman

As residents prepared to leave the rescue homes, the problem of finding husbands loomed large. Home mission women offered a rather elusive solution: they tried to ensure the happiness of residents by persuading them to marry men who adopted the role of the Christian gentleman. Such paragons, they believed, would not only forgive their wives for past indiscretions, but would also restrain their own sexual desires, care for wives kindly, support them in comfort, and—most important—bow to their moral authority. Missionaries depicted the Christian gentleman, or, as one worker at the Cottage Home referred to him, the "Knight of the New Chivalry," in stark opposition to the "seducers," "betrayers," and "procurers" women left behind when they entered the rescue homes.[7]

The model husband was brought to life in mission newsletters, which published countless tales of happily married ex-residents.

Women at Denver's Colorado Cottage Home told a typical story. While visiting an outlying town, Denver Temperance Union president Antoinette Hawley stopped at the home of a happily married woman who, much to Hawley's surprise, confessed that she had once been a Cottage Home resident. After leaving the Home, she took a job as a secretary. When her boss proposed marriage, she tearfully refused, telling him of her earlier pregnancy. Her fiancé, true to the hopes of mission women, responded by saying, "my love, my past is not even as white as yours; be my wife, and help me to be as good a man as you are a woman."[8] Missionaries saw such a husband as a paragon partly because he accepted their assertion that a woman's early "fall" was not a lifelong shame; furthermore, he agreed to defer to his fiancée's greater "goodness." In stories like these, matrons equated images of victimized but morally pure women and forgiving Christian husbands with social reality, promising that if rescue home residents chose truly good—and Christian—men, all would be well.

Yet, even among the men in the white middle-class communities from which most home mission women came, men who played the role of the Christian gentleman were more likely to demand propriety than to offer forgiveness. In the first years of home mission work in the West, Protestant women recognized men's reluctance to support charity for women and children as they struggled to overcome the roadblocks men put in the way of the establishment of rescue homes for women. Yet, once home mission women began to focus more attention on the residents within rescue homes than on the men without, missionaries swallowed some of their misgivings about middle-class Protestant men. Slowly but surely, they stretched the exceptions they had once made for their own husbands and a few favored mission supporters. Eventually, matrons routinely commended middle-class Christian gentlemen as suitors to residents.

Matrons' counsel was more idealistic than realistic, but it was not entirely utopian. The role of the Christian gentleman appealed to many white middle-class men of the period, as adherence to its tenets might yield social status and social esteem within Victorian culture.[9] Within American society at large, however, Christian gentlemen competed for influence with men who eschewed Victorian self-restraint and played the role of the sexually aggressive male.[10] The double standard of sexuality continued to thrive; indeed, it appears that the role of the sexually aggressive male gained popularity in the late nineteenth century. And, since neither Colorado's working-class culture nor San Francisco's Chinese immigrant culture offered substantial rewards to men who fit Victorian ideals of self-restraint, rescue home residents seeking husbands were caught in a conflict between home mission ideals and opposing patterns of gender relations.

Residents of the Colorado Cottage Home for unmarried mothers in Denver faced the conflict when they decided whether to tell prospective husbands about their previous pregnancies. Middle-class home mission women, angry that Victorians censured women rather than men for illicit sexual behavior, used rescue homes to shield women from "the scorn of the world" while they tried to establish a single standard of morality for men and women.[11] Most women who left the Home, however, went back to working-class communities in which female marriageability might have survived illicit sexual activity but was decidedly threatened by previous pregnancies. "Shall I tell him? Can I tell him? How will he take it?" wrote one resident of the Cottage Home, summarizing the quandary such women faced.[12]

One Cottage Home resident recounted what happened to her when she told the young man she loved about her pregnancy because her "conscience would not let [her] marry" otherwise. "He was very much upset about it," she reported, "and decided that he considered me not fit to become his wife, so I am going to keep up my work of nursing in the hospital."[13] In this case, mission workers' description of her as "one of the finest girls we ever had in the Home" may have meant that this young woman aspired to—or had roots in—the middle class; it is even possible that her fiancé's rejection showed his own pretensions to the role of Christian gentleman as he (but not mission women) understood it. Whatever their specific situation, however, it is hardly surprising that many Cottage Home residents opted to keep their pregnancies a secret from prospective beaux. As long as home mission women were unable to change the attitudes of men like these, the Colorado Cottage Home could offer residents little more than concealment and temporary refuge. Without the power to enforce restrictions on male sexuality—and with little opportunity to exert any influence over residents' prospective husbands—Colorado Cottage Home matrons sang the praises of Christian men, but could do little more than hope that men (of any class) would live up to their expectations.

The conflict between home mission expectations and community mores affected Susan LaFlesche, too. Despite her commitment to home mission ideology, LaFlesche felt little romantic interest in men who fit the role of the Christian gentleman. During her school years at the Hampton Institute, she was attracted to Thomas Ikinicapi, a young Sioux Indian from the Cheyenne River reservation. Although her teachers suggested (not very subtly) that their star pupil should develop an interest in the more respectable Charles Doxson, LaFlesche dismissed him from consideration. She knew that Doxson "is a splendid Indian and all that, and he is very noble," but she preferred Ikinicapi, whom she described as *"without exception* the handsomest Indian I ever saw."[14]

During her first year at medical school in Philadelphia, La-Flesche struggled to justify her affection for Ikinicapi to her family and to reconcile it with her own pretensions to moral influence. After she traveled to Hampton to see Ikinicapi during her first Christmas vacation, an alarmed teacher intervened. Relying on the language of female moral authority, the teacher told LaFlesche that while it was a good sign that the clearly "inferior" Ikinicapi seemed to "respect" LaFlesche, both would be better off with a platonic friendship in which LaFlesche could "help" Ikinicapi as a friend, rather than in the "deep waters" of romance. "She said," reported LaFlesche to her sister, "that I was too good for any of them."[15] LaFlesche vacillated between her desire to have a "good influence" over Ikinicapi and her knowledge that "he is very handsome and one of the kind girls like and he would not have to go far to get anyone"; she reported to her sister that she was "a little afraid it is 'Deep Waters' with him."[16] Heavily pressured by friends and family, however, she ended the relationship.

LaFlesche kept her feelings for Ikinicapi a secret from the home mission women who sponsored her medical training in Philadelphia. She had promised them not to marry for several years as an assurance that she would use her hard-won professional skills to help her tribe, and she kept her promise. Her attraction to men who did not meet mission ideals resembled that of many rescue home residents, but, because her professional training as a doctor allowed her to be self-supporting, she had an economic alternative to marriage that was beyond the reach of most rescue home residents. She took consolation from this fact when she dismissed another potential boyfriend, telling her sister, "I haven't any time or patience for such things nowadays—Doctors don't have much time *you know,* so he will have to keep his place."[17]

When LaFlesche did marry, she chose a man she was deeply attracted to but whom she perceived to be "utterly unlike" herself.[18] This time, too, her friends and family were dubious, but LaFlesche married Henry Picotte in 1894. Her husband, a Sioux Indian from the Yankton Agency, was popular with the Omaha, among whom he developed a reputation as a storyteller and a drinker. After only eleven years of marriage, he died, succumbing to a lingering illness that may have been related to alcoholism.[19]

Like Susan LaFlesche's teachers, Colorado Cottage Home matrons tried to persuade women to marry Christian gentlemen, but supervision of rescue home residents' courtships reached its height in the San Francisco Chinese Mission Home. Partly because of the enormous gap between Victorian and Chinese gender systems, home mission women in San Francisco were eager to influence residents' choice of husbands. Their determination was obvious even in the earliest years of the Mission Home, when the largest group of residents were prostitutes who approached the Home with suitors in tow. Although Mission workers agreed to these arrangements because they needed to attract enough residents to sustain their operation, they harbored deep reservations about the young men who brought prostitutes to the Home. Whenever they could, missionaries persuaded women to break off these engagements and choose mission-approved husbands instead. Mission officials made so much of the case of Chun Ho—a woman who had, they said, "entered the Home . . . promised . . . in marriage to a Chinese Romanist, but as light came into her mind . . . voluntarily gave him up"—that a group of young women in Ohio offered to contribute to the Home on her behalf.[20] Always ambivalent about their role in facilitating marriages to non-Protestant men, missionaries wanted to abandon the practice from the first, but not until the turn of the century were they able to do so.[21] In the meantime, however, San Francisco Presbyterian women had ex-

A wedding at the Chinese Mission Home, about 1921.
(*Courtesy of Cameron House*)

panded their mission and their rescue work to include neglected or abused children as well as betrothed prostitutes. As these young girls grew into adulthood, they, too, were married, again with considerable intervention by Mission Home workers.

To arrange for the marriages of long-term residents, missionaries chose from the Chinese immigrant men who approached the Mission Home looking for wives. Missionaries seem to have taken for granted that residents would—and should—grow up to marry Chinese men; in only a very few cases did Donaldina Cameron agree to sanction interracial marriages, and then she did so only in private, recognizing, as she told one correspondent, "I must not be publicly connected with this ... as there is such a strong prejudice against Orientals and Americans marrying in the U.S.A."[22]

Chinese immigrant men had several reasons for seeking Mission Home brides. They were handicapped in finding wives by the skewed sex ratio of the Chinese immigrant community in San Francisco. They had few other alternatives. Only the wealthiest of immigrant merchants were in a position to bring brides from China. Few minor merchants had the financial resources to pay for the trip, and those who did had to face hostile immigration officials. Exclusion laws prohibited laborers—the vast majority of immigrants before 1882—from bringing wives into the United States, and California miscegenation statutes prohibited marriage between Chinese immigrants and whites.[23]

For these reasons, there was no shortage of suitors for Mission Home residents. Although many proposals came from men in San Francisco who had seen or heard about particular residents, others came from men at great distances from the Mission Home. One man, for example, asked Home officials to consider finding a wife for a cousin of his who was the owner of a restaurant in New Mexico. The suitor, who was fifty-one years old, had $5,000 in the bank, had never been married, had no formal schooling, and was not a Protestant. He was, he said, willing to accept an older woman.[24] Chinese missions in large cities throughout the country recommended other prospective husbands, and the husbands of former residents suggested still other mates. Mission Home employee Tien Fu Wu was approached by potential suitors even on a trip to Boston. "Everybody is after me for girls," she wrote to Donaldina Cameron back in San Francisco, jokingly adding, "I might as well open a Matrimony Bureau here in the east."[25]

Both matrons and residents expected "the better classes" of Chinese men to recognize the value of educated wives, but men of truly high status in Chinese immigrant communities generally had the wherewithal and the desire to find wives in China.[26] Three groups of Chinese immigrant men showed the most interest in marrying Mission Home residents: those who wanted to marry prostitutes but could not afford to "purchase" them from their "owners," those who owned small (and often precarious) businesses in the United States, and those affiliated with Protestant missions in large cities.

All applicants had to win approval from Mission Home personnel. "He who would win a member of the Mission Home family for his wife," noted one Home official, "must present the very best credentials before he is ever permitted to call upon, or to write to the young lady of his choice."[27] Matrons quizzed applicants about their religious convictions, their financial prospects, and their marital status. Missionaries were especially anxious to weed out men who might have been trying, under the guise of marriage proposals, to reenslave women on behalf of their old "owners."[28] Some men went to great lengths to convince mission workers of their sincerity. One who was well aware that missionaries weeded out applicants who "have any [other] wives, present or prospective," included with his proposal "the intelligence that he had buried his former wife, proof of which might be had by visiting a certain undertaking establishment, name and address given."[29] He was not excessively cautious. Mission officials once held up a pending marriage ceremony when they heard that the bridegroom had been previously married in China.[30]

It was not, however, matrons' careful perusal of suitors that marked mission-arranged unions as unusual, for Chinese parents would also have chosen their daughters' marriage partners had they been in a position to do so. The distinctive aspect was the emphasis home mission women placed on the role of the Christian gentleman when selecting proper husbands for Mission Home residents. They were charmed, for example, by a young businessman, Wong John, who, on receiving permission to correspond with resident Qui Ngun, sent a diamond and sapphire ring with his assurance that "when you look at the white stone in this ring you must know that I mean that for your own pure good life, and when you look at the blue stone it means I will always be true to you." Qui Ngun, who believed that "all happiness and love depend upon having a good hearted faithful husband," accepted Wong John's proposal.[31] This marriage turned out to be both long lasting and happy.

A more typical suitor was Mr. Jung of New Orleans. Initially impressed by Jung's letters, San Francisco women asked a New Orleans contact to investigate his claims. The investigator reported that Mr. Jung's supposedly thriving business was actually a small laundry which he and his late wife had struggled to keep open, sometimes taking their children out of school to help. Although the investigator was dubious about his financial prospects, she recommended Jung on the basis of his well-mannered children and his kindly, considerate character.[32] The comments of other mission workers and Jung's neighbors reinforced her conclusions. One of them praised Jung for nursing his sick wife through her final illness and noted that "he treated and took care of [his] children better than some mothers would do."[33]

Residents' courtships highlight some of the contradictions between the ideal of the Christian gentleman and the husbands who chose rescue home residents for brides. Yet to understand the clash between home mission ideals and community reality, we also need to examine the marriages of rescue home residents. Such a task requires exceptional source material, for we have to go beyond what missionaries reported to their boards about ex-residents to try to trace the residents themselves. Only in the case of the San Francisco Chinese Mission Home, where individual case files survive, did this prove possible. Using that material, we can explore in some detail the conflict between gender systems faced by women who married from that institution.

Marriage: Gender Systems in Conflict Among Mission-Educated Chinese American Women

Given the relatively small population of Chinese immigrant women in San Francisco, the number of women who married from the Chinese Mission Home is impressive.[34] Mission Home workers claimed that by 1888, only fourteen years after the establishment of the institution, fifty-five Home residents had been married; by 1901, they took credit for 160 such marriages.[35] No comparable summary figures are available for the twentieth century, but extrapolating from the average number of marriages recorded in scattered yearly statistics, as many as 266 Chinese women may have married after residing in the Home in the period between 1874 and 1928.[36]

The public—and some of the private—documentation of these marriages illustrates the Victorian ideal put forth by home mission women. One critically ill ex-resident in Philadelphia described her marriage in a letter to Mission Home superintendent Donaldina Cameron. "My husband has been nursing me day and night," she reported; "he even gave up his restaurant to another party to look after, so he can nurse me, altho, our restaurant is the largest one in town." She went on to say: "he treats me like a real Christian.

I regret very much that Heaven doesn't give me longer time to be with him. Yet, I thank God and you [Cameron] that we have had one another for more than ten years. As husband and wife we are most satisfied."[37]

When we look behind the rhetorical curtain of Victorianism, the most striking thing about mission-arranged marriages is that they put immigrant women at a particular level of the emerging social structure of American Chinatowns. While scholars and officials dominated the social structure in China, merchants dominated the social structure in immigrant Chinatowns. Although the wealthiest of these merchants disdained immigrant women, Mission Home brides were in demand among less prosperous merchants, some of whom were destined to rise in importance as immigrant communities came to depend on them for goods, services, and community leadership.[38] Although historians have largely ignored the immigrant marriages of this period, commonly referred to as the "bachelor" years of San Francisco's Chinatown, mission marriages merit careful attention.[39] By pairing promising Chinese merchants with young women inculcated with Victorian family ideology, mission-arranged marriages established a core of middle-class Protestant Chinese American families in San Francisco and half a dozen other cities.

Some Mission Home husbands achieved considerable prominence. One example was Ng Poon Chew, the husband of Mission Home resident Chun Fa. Chun Fa had been brought to the Home at age six when a Chinese informant told San Francisco juvenile authorities that she was suffering regular beatings at the hands of the woman who had purchased her. She married Ng, who had made his start in California as a domestic servant, attended a Christian mission school, and had taken a degree in theology from the San Francisco Theological Seminary. After several years of conducting mission work with Chinese immigrants in southern California, Ng returned to San Francisco to edit the *Chung Sai Yat Po,* an influential daily paper that catered to Chinatown merchants. The Ngs prided themselves on being the first Chinese American family to live in their Oakland neighborhood. They had five children. Of their four daughters, Mansie, named for a Presbyterian missionary, became a piano teacher; Caroline graduated from the University of California and became a social worker; Rose studied at Mills College and worked for the San Francisco Chinese YWCA; and Effie became the first Chinese American woman to be accepted as a (kindergarten) teacher by the Oakland Board of Education. Their son, Edward, achieved notice as the first Chinese American man to be commissioned by the Army in World War I.[40]

Outside San Francisco, too, Mission Home marriages contributed to the development of Chinese American middle classes. Presbyterian Mission Home workers received marriage inquires from Chinese immigrant men all over the country and used them to establish mission-influenced satellite communities in several major cities. Small groups of Mission Home brides gathered in Los Angeles, Philadelphia, New Orleans, Portland, Minneapolis, Boston, and Chicago. The Philadelphia community, for example, took root when Qui Ngun married Wong John in the late 1890s. In 1901, another Mission Home resident, Choi Qui, traveled to Philadelphia and married Wong John's cousin Wong Moy. At the beginning of their married life, Choi Qui and her husband set up housekeeping with the older couple. In 1915, Mission Home resident Jean Leen married Won Fore in the same city. When mission helper Tien Fu Wu brought Jean Leen to Philadelphia for her wedding, she used the occasion to visit all the other ex-Home residents in the area. A few years later, Mission Home officials sent Augusta Chan to be a household helper to Qui Ngun. In 1922, Qui Ngun's daughter Eliza sent a wedding invitation to "grandma" Donaldina Cameron, superintendent of the Presbyterian Mission Home.[41]

Not all mission marriages proved to be financially comfortable. Even fewer mirrored the Victorian ideals of matrons. Nonetheless, for a variety of reasons, mission-arranged marriages seem to have met some of the needs of Chinese immigrant women. As we have seen, many prostitutes initially entered the Mission Home hoping to gain protection from their previous "owners" so they could marry young men of their choice. Other young women found that mission-arranged marriages spared them the worst ravages of hardworking poverty by uniting them with men with promising economic prospects. For Rose Chan, marriage to the part owner of a Prescott, Arizona, restaurant promised freedom from the debts she had incurred after the death of her first husband.[42] Still others sought mission-arranged marriages to escape deportation. Foong

Lon was brought into the United States to entertain at the Panama–Pacific Exposition of 1915. She remained in the country only because mission officials got permission for her to marry a Christian widower with two young boys.[43] The appeal of mission marriages is suggested by the fact that the number of marriages far exceeded the number of baptisms among Mission Home residents. By 1901, for example, Mission Home officials claimed 160 marriages, but only 100 baptisms.[44]

In fact, the prospect of mission marriages proved so attractive that some already married women came to the Mission Home in search of new husbands. Some of these women had been the victims of men who had deceived them into technical marriage ceremonies to smuggle them into the country. Others had been married quite legitimately in China but wanted to leave incompatible mates. One such woman wrote to Donaldina Cameron in 1923 to ask her to "let me enter your Home and study English [because] I am going to divorce with my husband for the sake of free from repression." "I understand," she explained, "that you as a Superintendent of the Home, always give aid to those who suffer from ill-treatment at home."[45]

Mission workers, who were horrified by the deceptions and ideologically prepared to label traditional Chinese marriages illegitimate because they did not display female moral authority, helped some women secure annulments or divorces. In at least a handful of these cases, missionaries arranged for new husbands as well.[46] Occasional facilitation of second marriages persisted despite the fact that it exposed the Mission Home to sharp criticism from white Americans outside the Home. Missionaries tried to justify their behavior in terms acceptable to the public, but at least one lawyer who opposed a divorce proceeding initiated by a Mission Home resident could not restrain his sarcasm. When the divorce was declared final, he commented acidly that "the cute little defendant is now at liberty to marry whosomever the good lord may direct across her path."[47]

In much larger numbers than those who sought new husbands, married women approached the Chinese Mission Home to jockey for position *vis-à-vis* their current husbands. Unhappy Chinese immigrant wives repeatedly asked workers at the institution to intervene on their behalf. In the early years of the Home, matrons were cautious about acknowledging the number of unhappy wives they received, but during the twentieth century they faced the issue more squarely. Statistics from the five-year period between 1923 and 1928 show seventy-eight such "domestic cases" admitted (in a period in which fifteen resident marriages were performed).[48]

A close look at these domestic cases reveals that Chinese immigrant women used the Mission Home to limit their vulnerability in the immigrant situation, in the process transforming the gender system of traditional China into a distinctive Chinese American form. They came to the Mission Home with a variety of complaints. The most frequent was wife abuse. When unhappy wives complained of mistreatment at the hands of their husbands, they were offered temporary shelter in the Mission Home while missionaries, predictably appalled by the complaints they heard, made it their business to shape unhappy marriages into the Victorian mode. Because they believed that "the fault usually lies with the husband," missionaries almost always tried to get husbands or their relatives to guarantee better treatment of wives before sending the women back to their homes.[49] They were not always successful in solving the problem. One young woman who twice sought help from the Mission Home and both times went back to her husband committed suicide in March of 1924.[50]

Other Chinese immigrant women approached the Home in order to gain leverage in polygamous marriages. One such woman, Mrs. Yung, requested help from the Mission Home after her husband took a concubine. Although concubinage was a recognized institution in China, Yung's own mother advised her to resist it. "I know," she wrote to her daughter in the Home, "how the second wife has brought all these accusations against you, causing your husband to maltreat you and act savagely. . . . You must make him send the concubine back to China. . . . It isn't right to acquire a concubine and especially this concubine." Mr. Yung, backed up by his father, apparently refused, but when Mrs. Yung complained to the Mission Home, Protestant women drew the boundary of morality to strengthen the position of the unhappy wife by excluding the threat to her authority: they arranged for the deportation of the concubine.[51]

Still other Chinese immigrant women came to the Mission Home to flee from parentally arranged marriages that were distasteful to them. As word got around that Mission Home workers were hostile to marriages arranged by parents, a number of young women found their way to the institution soon after their parents proposed unappealing matches. Bow Yoke, a young woman whose father had accepted $600 for agreeing to make her the second wife of a much older man, refused to go along with the plan. She fled to the Police Station, and then to the Mission Home, before it could be carried out.[52]

Still another group of married women sought help from missionaries when the death of their husbands left them dependent on the mercy of relatives. This was the case with one ex-prostitute who had been known to Mission Home officials for several years. The young woman had refused earlier invitations to come to the Mission Home because soon after becoming a prostitute she was ransomed by a man who paid $4,400 for her; she married her redeemer soon afterwards. She later explained to a Mission official that "he [her husband] was good to her and therefore she did not have to come to the Mission."[53] She did, however, come to the Mission Home when, after her husband's death, his nephew demanded that she return all the jewelry she had received as wedding presents from her husband.[54] Other widows, who feared that relatives would send them back to China or sell them or their children, also approached the Home.[55]

The possibility of Mission Home intervention offered Chinese immigrant women in any of these positions bargaining room to improve the terms of their marriages or their relations with relatives. In one quite typical case, a woman entered the Chinese Mission Home in 1925 and did not return to her husband until mission workers persuaded him to sign an agreement stipulating that: 1) he would not use opium; 2) he would treat her with "kindness and consideration" and "provide for them as comfortable a home as his income will permit"; 3) he would give her money to care for herself and her children; and 4) if she died he would give the children to the Mission Home or to their grandmother (rather than selling them).[56] To judge from these agreements, which rested solely on mission influence, immigrant wives found missionaries useful as go-betweens despite the risk of retribution from angry husbands.

Missionaries intervened not only in the marriages of strangers who approached them, but also in the marriages of women who had resided in and married from the Mission Home. Mission Home officials made it a point to visit "married daughters" in San Francisco as regularly as possible, and they called at the homes of those in other cities whenever they traveled. Visiting matrons urged ex-residents to follow home mission ideals; but ex-residents encountered quite different standards in Chinese immigrant communities. Conflicts between the two systems were most intense for women in the years just after their marriages, and frequently involved the two issues—Protestant church attendance and female reproduction—most directly related to the Victorian female values of piety and purity. Married Mission Home residents were caught in the middle, but they were not mere pawns of larger forces. They were an active part of the process of creating the gender system that came to characterize Chinese American communities.

We can outline the process they set in motion by examining a single case that reveals the connection between individual experience and wider shifts in the gender system of Chinese immigrant communities. Wong Ah So, the daughter of a poverty-stricken Hong Kong family, entered the United States in 1922, after a young immigrant man paid her mother $450, sweetened with promises that in America she could support her family by entertaining at Chinese banquets. The fancy entertaining she had been promised quickly turned into the harsh reality of prostitution in immigrant California. Her owner, in this case a Chinese woman, took most of her earnings, but Wong Ah So was able to send some money to her mother in Hong Kong.[57]

During this period, Wong Ah So's letters to her mother described her condition and expressed her clear understanding of her place in the traditional gender system in which she had been raised. "Daughter is not angry with you," she wrote in one letter later found and saved by missionary women, "It seems to be just my fate." She dutifully recited what she called "the three great obediences": "At home, a daughter should be obedient to her parents; after marriage, to her husband; after the death of her husband, to her son." She looked forward to gaining authority, not as a wife, but as a mother or mother-in-law. Trying to resign herself to her situation, she wrote, "Now I may be somebody's daughter, but some day I may be somebody's mother."[58]

Mission Home bride Ah Sue, her husband Ah Quin, and their twelve children. Ah Sue, who was brought to the Chinese Mission Home in 1879 by a suitor who died shortly afterwards, married Ah Quin in a Christian ceremony in the Mission Home in 1881. Ah Quin, who started in the United States as a cook, made a fortune as a railroad contractor and merchant in San Diego.

(*Courtesy of the San Diego Historical Society—Ticor Collection*)

But Wong Ah So's dreams fell on hard times. When the man who had helped smuggle her into the country belatedly demanded $1,000 for his services, Wong Ah So, who was afraid of him, borrowed the money to repay him. Shortly afterwards, she developed an illness, apparently venereal disease, that required daily treatment and interfered with her work as a prostitute. Impoverished, sick, and frightened, she did not protest when Donaldina Cameron located her and brought her to the Chinese Mission Home in San Francisco.

After a year in the Mission Home, Wong Ah So married a Chinese immigrant man who had established a foothold in Boise, Idaho. A few years later, she wrote a letter to Cameron at the

San Francisco Mission Home. "Thank you," she wrote, "for rescuing me and saving my soul and wishing peace for me and arranging for my marriage."[59] Wong Ah So had more than thank-you's on her mind, though: she had written to ask for help with her marriage. Her husband, she said, was treating her badly. Her complaints were three: first, her husband had joined the Hop Sing Tong; second, he refused to educate his daughters (by a previous wife); and third, he was so unhappy that Wong Ah So did not provide him with children that he had threatened to go to China to find a concubine to have a son for him.[60]

In this letter we can see how Wong Ah So's ideals had changed over the years since she had left China behind. As a former prostitute who had contracted a debilitating disease, she may have been unable to have the son whose birth would earn her female authority in traditional Chinese culture; in any case, what she wanted now was an education for her stepdaughters. She questioned the traditional ideals her husband still held. In response, her husband threatened to return to China to find a willing concubine, an act that would have reinforced Wong Ah So's vulnerability. To counter his threat, Wong Ah So invoked the aid of Mission Home women who, reading her carefully worded charges as an all-too-familiar indictment of "heathen" behavior, promptly sent a local Protestant woman to investigate.

Wong Ah So's case is especially revealing, but it was hardly unique. The clash between traditional and Victorian ideals in immigrant Chinatowns rendered certain tenets of the traditional Chinese gender system particularly vulnerable. For Chinese women who had decided to marry and for some who were already married, traditional Chinese family ideals clashed with the realities of immigrant life, such as the relative absence of in-laws and the difficulty young men had in finding wives. In such a situation, Chinese immigrant women used the Mission Home to help tip the balance between vulnerability and opportunity in immigrant Chinatowns—to facilitate forming marriages and to exert some control over relations within marriage itself. These marriages may or may not have fit the ideology of female moral authority home mission women put forth, but they did shape one set of possibilities for gender relations in Chinese American culture.

Domestic Service

Examining the marriages of rescue home residents is one way to chart the interaction between the ideology of female moral authority and forces outside the rescue homes, but marriages were not the only homes outside the rescue homes for ex-residents. Throughout the history of rescue home operations, most residents who did not marry as soon as they left the homes were funnelled into domestic service. Even ex-residents who attended college ordinarily worked as servants for Protestant families who provided their board while missionaries paid their school expenses. Domestic work, which reveals yet another pattern of the relationship between female moral authority and community values, provided the common-denominator employment experience for ex-residents from all the rescue homes.

In the 1870s, when Protestant women founded rescue homes, domestic service was the major source of paid employment for women of all ethnic groups. By the turn of the century, however, native-born white women had moved into industry, retail sales, office work, and the professions, leaving domestic service largely to immigrants and ethnic minority women. For Chinese immigrant women in California, domestic service, along with prostitution and seamstressing, provided major sources of employment well into the twentieth century.[61]

From the 1870s to the 1930s, rescue home matrons routinely placed ex-residents in domestic service.[62] Matrons' preference for domestic work had roots in the ideology of home mission women as well as the economic structure. For Protestant women, domestic service had intrinsic value as an occupation for rescue home residents. As they saw it, if a woman could not reign over her own home, the next best thing was to place her in someone else's. Home mission women thought that careful selection of employers could ensure ex-residents an extension of the caring, familial atmosphere home mission women tried to create in rescue homes. Furthermore, they expected that domestic service would prepare women for the ultimate goal of creating their own homes as married women. These expectations were conveyed in the language of matrons, who often reported that residents had found places in good Christian homes rather than that they worked as servants.

The placement of women in Christian homes reflected mission workers' continued attachment to the Victorian value of female piety; it also showed their devotion to the value of female purity. Matrons considered domestic service "honorable" work preferable to other, more lucrative employment that might tempt residents to depart from mission standards. While officials at the San Francisco Chinese Mission Home occasionally approved of residents' working as teachers, stenographers, or clerks, they drew the line at waitressing. "Positions in tea-rooms, restaurants and clubs allure many young girls from the Chinese community because of the higher pay," noted Donaldina Cameron, "but this type of work leads to many serious dangers for young and attractive Oriental girls."[63] At the Denver Cottage Home, too, matrons counseled residents to reject the "many temptations" surrounding them in favor of the "honest employment" offered by domestic work.[64] In insisting on domestic service, matrons' devotion to the values of the search for female moral authority overrode the economic interests of rescue home residents.[65]

Both rescue home pressure and the lack of alternatives led residents to accept work as servants. Few residents who did not marry had other homes outside the institutions. Many had no family resources to fall back on. Some had left their husbands to enter the rescue homes; others were orphans or daughters of poverty-stricken parents. Still others, especially unmarried mothers, were no longer welcomed by parents who considered them an embarrassment. At least one Cottage Home resident did not return to her family because she had been "ruined by her own father."[66] Some Chinese Mission Home residents had been taken from their parents by juvenile authorities. Most residents of the homes had few job alternatives. Because the industrial training schemes projected by the institutions had become, in practice, training in domestic skills, most residents had no other skills to offer employers.

Servants were in such demand in San Francisco, Salt Lake, and Denver that matrons quickly developed the networks of friends of friends they needed to place women in domestic work. Many ex-residents worked for wages; those with children often relied on informal day care services provided by rescue homes. Other ex-residents worked as servants while they attended vocational schools or colleges; these student-servants took jobs near their schools and received room and board in exchange for household work.

Matrons released optimistic reports on residents in domestic service. Chinese Mission Home workers, for example, described one resident as "working in a lovely American home, happy, independent, and well cared for."[67] Donaldina Cameron told national church officials that "in most instances," mission-trained women in domestic service were "giving satisfaction to their employers and finding comparative contentment in the work."[68]

Yet the use of ex-residents as domestic servants exposed a contradiction in the ideology of female moral authority. In the matter of domestic service, matrons' maternal feelings for their rescue home "daughters" clashed with their goal of buttressing the authority of middle-class wives and mothers in the home. Thus, when servants argued with their employers, matrons often took the side of the employers. The matron of the Salt Lake City Industrial Christian Home complained that no matter how many positions she found for servants, Home residents were unable to do the work. She did not question the extent of the drudgery expected, the rates paid, or the attitudes of employers toward their workers.[69] Most home mission women offered a kinder ear to complaints from servants, but, unless abuses were outrageous, they usually urged unhappy workers to rededicate themselves to their tasks.

The tensions between servants and their employers were somewhat different from those between residents and matrons within rescue home institutions.[70] Many departing residents were eager to begin work as domestic servants. Those who worked for wages needed the money; and most servants hoped employment would offer them freedom from the moral strictures of the rescue homes. In this last they were disappointed, for, in taking jobs as servants, ex-residents traded the moralistic routine of the rescue homes—which was generally mediated by the presence of a peer group as well as the self-consciously maternal attitudes of matrons—for hard work and loneliness bounded by employers' moral surveillance.

Candid servants' accounts indicate that the atmosphere of familial caring home mission women expected employers to provide was largely illusory. Such was the case with Jane Ying, a student-servant from the Chinese Mission Home, whose employer, Mrs. Webster, expected not only a great deal of work but also a cheerful attitude. Ying complained to Donaldina Cameron in 1923 that "things are just getting unbearable [even though] . . . they are nice people, dear people." She explained that "when I first came here I had just the sufficient three hours a day of work . . . but now . . . [I have to] cook two meals and wash dishes for three meals, for six people, and the[n] to clean this three story home. You'll have to admit that my room and board is not worth all that time."[71] After a few months of this treatment, Ying's resentment was obvious. When her employer asked her why she was "such a gloom cloud," Ying responded "that it was because I'm peculiar and for no other reason." She complained to Cameron that "[Mrs. Webster] felt quite shocked then and thot I was saucy, tho I was only stating a known fact."[72] For her part, Mrs. Webster grumbled to Cameron that Ying went out too often and stayed out too late.

Other servants resented the disdain with which employers treated them. In the case of ex-residents of the Chinese Mission Home, employers' attitudes were often rooted in racism. A case in point is that of Ng Shee, another student-servant from the Chinese Mission Home. Ng Shee had looked forward to her job in Los Angeles, expecting to prefer it to staying in the Mission Home. She was swiftly disillusioned. Within a few weeks of her move in 1918 she started voicing her complaints to Cameron, who she hoped would find her a new position. "Mrs. [Anderson]," she said of her employer, "is nice there is no doubt about that, but I am afraid everybody would not think so if they all lived with her and worked for her."[73]

Ng Shee's specific complaints reflected both the sexual tensions that confronted women who left the all-female Chinese Mission Home, and the racial tensions produced because most (but not all) were placed with white families. Accustomed to the company of Chinese girls and women, Ng Shee was lonely and disoriented in the Anderson's white Protestant household. Like many servants, she had to cope with her employers' assumptions of cultural and racial superiority. Ng Shee told Cameron that she was expected to scrub the floors every day, that she was told to eat in the kitchen, that she had not been offered a place to bathe, and that Mr. Anderson slept, with his door open, in the room next to hers. Ng Shee, who had expected to do light housework in exchange for her board while she attended school, found the workload—and the condescension—unbearable. She asked Cameron if she would have to quit school if she left her job. Apparently receiving an affirmative answer, she lamented, "when you suggested that it was best for me to be in a family I was indeed very glad . . . but [I] never expect[ed] to be treated like now and [am] greatly sorry that I have spoiled your dreams."[74] Not long afterwards, she left the Andersons to live with a Chinese woman who offered "sympathy and a refuge." Ng Shee refused Cameron's requests to return to the Chinese Mission Home.[75]

Ex-resident servants complained about heavy workloads, moral surveillance by employers, and the lack of dignity they felt as supervised employees rather than as accepted members of homes. These conditions, which they shared with domestic servants all across the country, led some residents to contrast their jobs unfavorably with their lives in rescue homes. One ex-resident of the Cottage Home who returned to Denver after a short stint as a cook "called up the Home because she felt that the Cottage Home had been a real home to her."[76] Disappointed servants soon began to search for alternatives. Some appealed directly to matrons to intervene for them; others relied on broader home mission networks for support. One Denver servant called a member of the Cottage Home board to report that "she was very ill and was ready to drop at her work."[77] The board member took her to her own home until she regained her health. In other cases, like that of Ng Shee, servants spent more and more time away from their jobs in an effort to find some of the independence they had sought in employment in the first place; prompting employers' complaints about bad attitudes and low moral standards.

Home mission women hoped that placing unmarried residents as servants would prepare them to become wives and mothers. But if recent historians are correct, domestic service was ultimately less effective in promoting marriage than it was in reinforcing servants' dependence on charitable institutions or in encouraging them to see prostitution as a better paid and less constricting alternative.[78] The trials of domestic servants make a mockery of success stories like those issued by Cottage Home officials, who once invited sponsors to savor the comments of an ex-resident who told them that her experience as a domestic servant convinced her that "God has forgiven me." "I am happier than I ever thought I could be," she went on. "I have a good home and I am trying to do my duty by the lady who is so kind to me."[79] It is clear, however, that for many unmarried mothers, domestic service was not evidence of God's forgiveness, but real-life punishment—expressed in the form of long hours, low wages, and loss of dignity—for their transgression of Victorian moral standards. For many Chinese Mission Home residents, the starkness of employer–employee relationships belied the mission image of a "good Christian home," and their distress was often deepened by their isolation in the midst of white families.

Residents' experiences in courtship, marriage, and domestic service highlight the ways Protestant women tried to form homes outside the rescue homes for departing residents. In all three areas, home mission women assumed that it would be possible to link female moral authority with the Christian home. Outside the institutions, however, this idealistic assumption ran counter to the diverse gender systems and patterns of race and class relations of turn-of-the-century America.

In establishing homes for ex-residents, matrons relied primarily on a strategy of seeking out prospective husbands who fit the Victorian model of the Christian gentleman. Yet for two reasons—because the communities from which rescue homes drew their clientèle gave little support to the "Christian gentleman" role, and because home mission women could not control the behavior of any men outside the homes—choosing a husband remained a risky gamble for residents. Because the connection home mission women assumed between Christian homes and women's emancipation locked women into marriage in a period when marriage involved significant legal and economic disabilities for women, it could be as much a problem as a solution for residents.

Yet, in the case of residents at the Chinese Mission Home, the support of Protestant women enabled some immigrant women caught in a conflict between gender systems to manipulate the gap between the two to meet their own ends. In part because of the actions of mission-educated immigrant women, the gender system that came to characterize Chinese American communities would be distinct from both the traditional Chinese system immigrants had brought to the United States and the Victorian system they encountered there.

Without a doubt, the weakest of the links home mission women tried to forge between the ideology of female moral authority and the ideal of the "Christian home" was domestic service. In the case of domestic service, Protestant women's conceptions of female moral authority folded in on themselves: their depictions of rescue home residents as their daughters clashed with their identification with employers whose household authority they wanted to uphold. The result for residents was minimal pay, sporadic assistance from home matrons, and, in the case of some women the Chinese Mission Home placed with white families, the sharp sting of racism.

Home mission women downplayed biological racism in the rescue homes, but they maintained a typically Victorian conception of a moral hierarchy of cultures. How else to interpret the hopes of home mission women that Ah Fah's marriage would demonstrate that "the first step upwards from heathenism to civilization is the organization of a home on Christian principles"?[80] Because they believed that their own influence came from their roles as Christian wives and mothers, Protestant women equated the emancipation of women with the adoption of middle-class Victorian family patterns, and presumed the superiority of Victorian culture.

So strongly did mission women believe in female piety and purity that they held to their ideology despite growing challenges to the Victorian culture that had spawned their ideas. By the turn of the century, domestic work seemed more intolerable than ever to rescue home residents, who saw other women employed in business, in retail work, and as professionals. Rescue home training in moral purity looked like mere prudishness to residents who knew that women outside the homes were dating young men and flirting with a sexual abandon that would have been anathema to "respectable" Victorians of previous generations. By the 1920s and 1930s, rumbles of discontent that had been audible in American society as early as the inception of rescue home programs had become a thunderous challenge to the Victorian equation of women with moral purity. When home mission women responded to this din with determination to reinforce moral standards, they widened the gap between matrons and residents and so contributed to the growing crisis in the Victorian women's campaign for female moral authority.

ANTICLIMAX

6

The Crisis of Victorian
Female Moral Authority,
1890–1939

In 1901, the Women's National Indian Association decided to drop
the word "Women's" from its title. The decision, proposed by
national officers at the group's annual convention, was a difficult
one to make. Officers and delegates knew that "great attachment
was felt for the old name of the Association, and [members felt]
pride in the fact that it was a women's society."[1] In the end,
however, the assembled delegates pushed aside their misgivings
and voted to become the National Indian Association.

According to the convention minutes, two arguments proved
persuasive. First, the newly installed United States Commissioner
of Indian Affairs seemed willing to adopt several reforms advocated by the women of the Association. Each hint of success at
influencing federal Indian policy led some members to wonder if
there were any further need for a women's society.[2] It is even
possible that one reason for the name change was to attract male
members in order to offset declining membership figures. If so,
members gained little from diffusing their female focus, for few
men joined the renamed National Indian Association.[3]

The second argument for the name change was put forth by national officer Patience Sparhawk, who told the convention delegates: "when men work together they make a camp; when women work together they make a nunnery; when men and women work together they make the home."[4] Such a statement, of course, contrasts sharply with Winifred Spaulding's belief that homes could be made by women alone. In accepting Sparhawk's statement, the members of the Association revealed that they had replaced their earlier emphasis on female morality with the conviction that it was "the natural and right way for men and women to work together in all great moral movements."[5]

In removing the word "women" from their title, the Women's National Indian Association became the first of the remaining three home mission groups to succumb to the forces that would, between 1890 and 1939, overwhelm the search for female moral authority. The Denver Cottage Home and the San Francisco Chinese Mission Home held on longer, perhaps because women's anger at male domination had such deep roots in western locations. In the end, though, all three groups would encounter two pivotal dynamics: the demands of institutional expansion and the transformation of Victorian culture.

The Perils of Institutional Stability

The significance of the Women's National Indian Association name change was not immediately apparent to home mission women. In the first decades of the twentieth century, women across the country enjoyed unprecedented success in persuading local, state, and national governments to devote resources to the protection of women and children. According to one historian, their victories contributed to the "domestication of politics" that distinguished many of the reforms of the Progressive era.[6] Home mission women lit some of the matches that ignited the brush fires of Progressivism; while the tenuous coalitions that masked the disparate aims of Progressive reformers lasted, missionaries' goals seemed near fulfillment. On at least a handful of issues, the search for female moral authority and Progressive reform were mutually reinforcing: images of female purity and piety lent strength to national campaigns for Prohibition, Indian reform, and the abolition of prostitution.

The reform impulse seemed to signal the beginning of the end of western distinctiveness. For the first time, home mission women in the West found it possible to believe that the cities that had seemed so threatening in the 1870s and 1880s might transform themselves into a social order more agreeable to Protestant women. In Salt Lake City, the Mormon Church, which had formally renounced the practice of polygamy in 1890, began to purge itself of recalcitrant polygamous leaders.[7] In San Francisco, an uproar over white slavery revitalized the campaign against Chinese prostitution.[8] By the turn of the century, women in Denver and San Francisco presided over an impressive number of charitable associations; women in Salt Lake City were not far behind.[9]

Rescue home sponsors measured their gains in terms of institutional stability; annual reports painted roseate pictures of financial improvements and building plans. In Denver, the Colorado Cottage Home opened a brand-new building in the suburbs. In San Francisco, the 1906 earthquake and fire leveled the Chinese Mission Home building but could not stop home mission momentum. In 1908, San Francisco women opened an imposing new Mission Home building, one large enough to be the headquarters for several Presbyterian mission boards in the San Francisco area; then quickly turned their attention to building yet another institution for Chinese American children. This institutional expansion of rescue homes was, as we will see, intertwined with three developments: the acquisition of stable funding sources, the strengthening of working relationships with law enforcement officials, and the rise of a social work bureaucracy.

The Acquisition of Stable Funding Sources

Rescue home expansion required a strong financial base. In Denver, the establishment of stable funding for the Colorado Cottage Home came only after a crisis at the institution. Ever since 1888, the Home had survived by collecting fees from those residents able to pay and balancing its books with monthly donations of two dollars from each of the local Colorado Woman's Christian Temperance Union auxiliaries.[10] Each auxiliary appointed a representative whose job it was to raise the monthly contribution and to keep local members apprised of events at the Home. This system was financially inefficient: it could not, for example, expand to meet unexpected outlays or increases in the Home population. Furthermore, auxiliaries were so often late with their donations that the Home treasurer spent much of her time reminding local representatives of their responsibilities. In July of 1903, matters got so bad that exasperated Union officials summarily closed the Home, telling the startled members that "no more girls will be cared for until a sufficient amount of money is raised to justify the re-opening."[11]

Almost immediately, a group of Union women determined to reopen the Colorado Cottage Home. They proposed to solve the financial mess by hiring a "solicitor" to travel around the state requesting donations for the Cottage Home. The solicitor they selected, Temperance Union member Dinnie Hayes, received a percentage commission for her trouble. With this financial incentive, Hayes proved to be a first-rate fund-raiser. By 1906, she had accumulated enough money to put a deposit on a new building; by 1911, its mortgage was paid off. In the meantime, she collected operating funds for the Home, easily keeping it solvent.[12]

The new system was a financial success, but its adoption had unforeseen consequences for the ideology of female moral authority that had sustained Cottage Home activities. The appointment of Solicitor Hayes made the local representatives expendable. Without the constant urgings of representatives, who had provided the useful service of keeping appeals for the Cottage Home on the Union agenda, some members lost the direct personal interest in the Home they had felt under the previous system. Hayes, who was understandably reluctant to depend on the tiny amounts of money available from middle-class married women, solicited largely from doctors, lawyers, and wealthy men.[13] Because the male community leaders Hayes approached were less likely than Temperance Union women to respond to rhetoric based on anger at male sexual license or the power of the sisterhood of women, the shift in the funding base of the Cottage Home reduced home mission reliance on calls to the Victorian female values of piety and purity. In the end, the new financial arrangements at the Colorado Cottage Home ensured financial stability at the cost of weakening the identification of women with the Victorian values that had paved women's way toward public influence; thus eroding home mission claims to female moral authority.

At the San Francisco Chinese Mission Home, too, the steps workers took to increase funding for the Mission Home ultimately sapped the concept of "woman's work for woman" that had long sustained home mission work. Unlike the Colorado Cottage Home Board, the Woman's Occidental Board, which sponsored the Chinese Mission Home, had never enjoyed complete control over its own finances; within the Presbyterian hierarchy, synod and mission officials retained the power to allocate funds for all mission programs. In practice, however, Presbyterian churchmen left the Mission Home to its own devices as long as the women raised enough money to pay for its operations. For many years, the women managed to do so, collecting some boarding fees from residents but depending mostly on small donations from local auxiliaries, on public fund-raising meetings, and on "scholarships" from "American mamas" who agreed to support individual Home residents.[14] This personalized system had the advantage of constantly renewing the interest of members and donors in the day-to-day work of the Home; its advocates raised funds by telling middle-class women supporters the individual life-stories of "Chinese slave girls" kept at the mercy of lascivious men.

As the Chinese Mission Home grew, however, several attempts to consolidate Presbyterian mission programs whittled away at its *de facto* independence. San Francisco churchmen took the first step towards consolidation in the 1890s, when they ordered the Woman's Occidental Board to cut back on Chinese Mission Home expenses in light of the nationwide depression. Despite obvious annoyance at this unusual intervention in their financial affairs, the women did so.[15] San Francisco women themselves took the next step when they designed their new Mission Home, which opened in 1908, to be the headquarters for all Presbyterian mission work, male and female, on the Pacific Coast. By 1920, the Chinese Mission Home program had expanded to a point that surpassed its members' personalized fund-raising program.[16] When Chinese Mission Home women sought and received financial assistance from national Presbyterian mission boards, the boards found the leverage they needed to exert control over the Home operation.

In 1922, the Chinese Mission Home came under the jurisdiction of the national Presbyterian Woman's Board of Home Missions, which itself came under the aegis of the Board of National Missions a year later.[17]

The attitude the national board would take toward the Chinese Mission Home was determined by Katharine Bennett, a national officer who represented a newer, more social scientific approach to missionary work. To Bennett, the personalized program of the Chinese Mission Home was an awkward local exception to a smoothly functioning and carefully specialized national bureaucracy of mission work. She recommended selling the Mission Home building at 920 Sacramento Street and dividing its residents among a separate mission building in Oakland, a local YWCA, and a much smaller rescue work operation.[18]

The national officials who arranged for the acquisition of the Chinese Mission Home adopted most of Bennett's recommendations, but they added some provisions designed to reassure Home matron Donaldina Cameron, who objected strenuously to the entire plan.[19] These provisions included a promise that when the board sold the Mission Home building, Cameron could move the rescue work to a "better adapted" facility, and the assurance that a local committee would share supervisory power with the national board. These concessions allowed San Francisco women to believe that the national board would not only provide adequate funding for their program but might also underwrite the construction of new mission buildings. Their hopes were dashed, however, as the national board resisted Cameron's subsequent proposals for expansion.

During the process of consolidation, officials dismantled the methods by which San Francisco home mission women had sustained their personal identification with residents of the Chinese Mission Home. Mission Home workers, fearing that their plan of allowing donors to act as "American mamas" led to favoritism, stopped soliciting individual scholarships. The national board insisted that San Francisco women discontinue the popular public meetings of the local board, which featured entertainment by Chinese Mission Home residents chosen to represent the transformation from "slavery" to mission freedom. Their demands

broke another bond between San Francisco women and their special work for Chinese women, for Home supporters had considered
the carefully orchestrated meetings a highlight of their work.[20]

Thus, in San Francisco, as in Denver, financial security for rescue
home operations concealed costs of a different kind: it chipped
away at the relationships between rescue home supporters and
rescue home residents, relationships that had been justified in
terms of the Victorian female values of purity and piety. Home
mission women who sought funding from national boards learned
to emphasize their rescue homes' contributions to the national
mission bureaucracy rather than their significance as symbols of
female moral authority in western cities.

The Development of Working Relationships
with Government and Law Enforcement Personnel

The shift in the financial bases of rescue homes thus offered a form
of institutional stability that loosened the ties between local women
and rescue home projects. Rescue home workers sought another
kind of institutional stability by developing firm working relationships with government and law enforcement personnel. Because
home mission women had worked long and hard to convince government officials of the legitimacy of their programs, they saw each
sign of government acceptance as a measure of success. Yet in the
end, Protestant women's ties to officialdom proved to be as par-
adoxical for the search for female moral authority as the acquisition
of stable funding bases.

The strengthening of ties to government officials happened most
smoothly where tension between women and men was least pronounced: in the case of the Women's National Indian Association.
Although the Indian Association had begun its life as a reform
group angry about government mistreatment of the Indians, it did
not hesitate to invoke the aid of legislators. When Congress passed
the Dawes Act of 1887, the major Indian reform bill of the nineteenth century, Association members rushed to take credit for its
passage.[21] Once reform legislation was in place, Association members prodded reluctant government officials to extend allotment
and temperance to all the tribes; to improve the quality of the

Indian Service personnel by "separating" the Indian question from
partisan politics; and to spend more money for schooling, health
care, and the employment of women field matrons.[22]

By the turn of the century, government officials had become so
responsive to their pleas that the Women's National Indian Association substituted congratulatory comments on federal progress
for its earlier criticism of government officials. Along with this shift
came a corresponding decline in their anger at men for failing to
value women's moral priorities; as we have seen, by 1901, the
members of the Association had begun to argue that it was "the
natural and right way for men and women to work together," thus
emphasizing the similarities rather than the differences between
male and female reformers.[23]

In western cities, where the tension between the two groups of
reformers had always been more pronounced than in the Women's
National Indian Association, Protestant women had a more difficult time influencing government officials. In the early years of
home mission work, rescue workers in western cities cast themselves as daring female reformers who advocated unpopular causes
in the face of men's determined resistance. The obstacles they
faced had been illustrated at the Industrial Christian Home in Salt
Lake City, where women secured government support for their
home for polygamous wives only to find the Home given over to
the control of local men who doubted its value. Together with poor
response from Mormon women, the battles between missionary
women and community men crippled the institution, which closed
in 1893, after only seven years of operation.

In Denver and San Francisco, by contrast, home mission women
established rescue homes free from such overt male control. Within
these rescue homes, they turned their search for female moral
authority inward, deflecting their anger away from Christian men
and community authorities and concentrating their efforts on the
women in the institutions. As their institutions prospered, their
sense of themselves as isolated female voices overwhelmed by a
male-dominated social order slowly subsided. By the turn of the
century, they had forgotten the lesson of the Salt Lake City Industrial Christian Home, and they were hard at work cementing
working relationships with law enforcement authorities. Government support provided rescue home workers with a source of of-

ficial power previously unavailable to them; it also, however, diluted their appeals to Victorian female values.

Antoinette Hawley, turn-of-the-century president of the Colorado Woman's Christian Temperance Union, observed firsthand the transition from embattled Protestant women to righteous civic leaders. In 1918, Hawley took the time to reflect on her many years of association with the Temperance Union. In the "early days," she noted, "it was hard to get an audience [but] it is different now. Some of the most prominent women are joining our organization." Hawley noticed with evident nostalgia that "there is a decided difference in the reformers of today, who . . . do not seem to care to be conspicuous merely because they are working for a cause."[24]

As women temperance reformers in Denver became less "conspicuous" and more "prominent," they became eager to cooperate with the law enforcement authorities they had once seen as intractable opponents. In 1896, for example, Temperance Union women created a Department of Christian Citizenship and Enforcement of Law. The chairperson of this department called on home mission women to demand that reluctant officials enforce moral legislation. In 1896, for example, women took out public advertisements asking Denver police to enforce Sunday closing laws. Over the next decade, Colorado Union women set themselves up as watchdogs over violations of curfew ordinances and other such minor offenses, until they could, after the state enacted Prohibition in 1914, comment that "no subject so engrosses us at this time as does that of law enforcement." In 1920, they pledged "every assistance to the officials who endeavor to apprehend and convict law breakers," a threat they carried out by personally investigating local pool halls, dance halls, and drug stores and reporting culprits to the police. By 1928, Union president Adrianna Hungerford described the Law Enforcement Department as "a clearing house for reports of the violation of prohibition."[25]

Not all local law enforcement officials welcomed this assistance, but there is no doubt that home mission women, who had always been eager to persuade state and local governments to support their aims, were enjoying unprecedented success in doing so. Yet here lay a trap for the search for female moral authority, for, once having shifted responsibility for moral guidance to the state, middle-class women could no longer define morality as they wished or insist that its boundaries be drawn according to their relatively inclusive ideals. Furthermore, because government sponsorship diminished the chances that morality would be identified solely as a female responsibility, cooperation with government weakened the link between morality and women that was a central component of Victorian culture.

The development of ties to law enforcement officials affected rescue homes as well as the organizations that sponsored them. In San Francisco, Chinese Mission Home workers who had long despaired about police corruption and government hostility came to rely on local, state, and national authorities to provide a steady stream of residents for their institution. Their first important liaison was with the court system. As early as the 1880s, they took advantage of the quasi-legal powers of the Society for the Prevention of Cruelty to Children to assign Chinese children who had been taken from their parents to Mission Home care.[26] As the California juvenile justice system, an innovation of the Progressive period, developed, the Mission Home relied on its judges to grant matrons custody over delinquent children. By the 1920s, these ties to the justice system had become indispensable to the Chinese Mission Home; by the 1930s, girls sent to the Home as "juvenile delinquents" were the largest single group of Home residents.[27]

San Francisco women strengthened their ties to local police officers, too. Matrons took the first steps in this direction in the 1890s when they enlisted a few sympathetic police officers to help rescue parties take prostitutes from particularly dangerous brothels. At the end of the decade, they went even further, allowing law enforcement officials to use the Chinese Mission Home as a holding tank for women jailed in raids on prostitution. This technique was quickly abandoned, but relations between the police and the Chinese Mission Home tightened as San Francisco police decided to rid Chinatown of organized crime during the "tong wars" of the early 1900s. San Francisco police inspector John Manion revealed the tenor of the twentieth-century police relationship with mission women when he called matron Donaldina Cameron his "very good friend"; Cameron, in turn, considered him "absolutely trustworthy."[28] On the basis of this friendship, Manion once acted as godfather for a Home resident.

The Chinese Mission Home also worked closely with immigration officials. Cooperation began when home mission women, shocked at the inadequacy of the Pacific Mail Dock facilities for women, took immigrant women detainees into the Mission Home (by all accounts a preferable accommodation) during their period of detention by United States officials. Mission women interviewed detainees in the Home and advised immigration officials on the disposition of specific cases. When new detention facilities at Angel Island were opened in 1910, Home officials lost their bid to continue to house detainees, but maintained, and in fact, strengthened, their ties to immigration officials.[29]

By 1921, a visitor to the Mission Home could say with some assurance, "with the Chinese, with the courts, with the police, Miss Cameron is the commanding factor along the coast."[30] Over the years, Chinese Mission Home workers had shed the initial distrust they felt for police and government officials and established firm working relationships with law enforcement authorities. These relationships served home mission women by providing the Chinese Mission Home with residents. They offered some benefits to rescue home residents, too, because Mission Home officials acted as informal legal advocates for Chinese women and girls faced with bewildering immigration requirements. Notwithstanding the frequent cultural misunderstandings between matrons and Home residents, mission women were inclined to be more responsive to residents' needs than either law enforcement or immigration officials.[31]

Yet, as these relationships solidified, Chinese Mission Home officials like Donaldina Cameron found themselves spending less time appealing to middle-class women supporters in the name of women's work for women and more time pleading cases before male law enforcement officials. Since these men could be expected to be more responsive to pleas for individual leniency than to rhetoric that stressed the sisterhood of women and anger at men, the development of working relationships with law enforcement officials, like the shift in the financial bases of rescue home operations, eroded the ideology of female moral authority, even as it gave home mission women a new arena in which to exert influence.

The Rise of a Social Work Bureaucracy

Rescue home workers were proud of their newfound financial stability and of their ties to government officials. They were, however, much less enthusiastic about the third development that would affect their institutions, the rise of a social work bureaucracy. Rescue homes were not the only welfare institutions thriving in the late nineteenth century; in fact, charitable institutions of all kinds prospered during the period. The rise of professional social work was in many respects a response to this very success—it promised system and method for overburdened institutions, and it created a new type of institutional worker, the professional social worker dedicated to the ideals of scientific charity.[32]

Scientific charity gained its first foothold in the late nineteenth century when benevolent leaders consolidated charitable institutions into citywide umbrella organizations. In Denver, local charities combined into a Charity Organization Society in 1889.[33] In San Francisco, a parallel organization, the Associated Charities of San Francisco, was established at about the same time.[34] Both the Denver and San Francisco charity organization programs reflected the techniques of "scientific philanthropy": advocates favored moral exhortation over financial aid, hoped to end duplication of services by sharing information about aid recipients, and tried to avoid promoting the "pauperization" they felt resulted from letting recipients depend on charitable aid. Scientific philanthropy held wide appeal for aspiring professionals who wanted to bring rigorous business efficiency to charitable work. In both cities, charity organization movements proved popular among the middle- and upper-class donors who supported benevolent work.

Women's home mission groups, however, were not enthusiastic about either the local charity organization societies or the tenets of scientific philanthropy. Neither the Chinese Mission Home nor the Colorado Cottage Home participated in efforts to organize local networks: neither was among the members of the new or-a

ganizations. Some clues to the reasons they resisted the consolidation movement can be gleaned from a survey of charitable work in San Francisco undertaken by Millicent Shinn in 1889. Shinn, a college-educated supporter of the charities organization movement, singled out Protestant churches for their unwillingness to participate in consolidation activities. Their reluctance, she informed her readers, "shows that they have no very potent sense of the dangers of alms, or the need of cooperation to avert them." She noted that "they are ... a little suspicious of system and method [and] afraid that Christian spontaneity may be diminished." Furthermore, they were "probably the less disposed to value organization because the charities of a church are rarely in the hands of its business men, but of the clergy and women, who, while energetic and competent enough, have not the bent toward organized combination acquired in the constant handling of large affairs."[35]

Shinn's observations fit both the Colorado Cottage Home and the San Francisco Chinese Mission Home. Matrons at both institutions were so anxious to protect the reputation of their residents that they were reluctant to share their names with other institutions. They had faith, in Shinn's terms, in the power of "Christian spontaneity"; furthermore, they believed that effective charity depended on the concern of women for other women. Judged by the standards of charity organization advocates, they were too sympathetic to be businesslike. As a result, they resisted the trend toward local charity organization that proved so attractive to other groups.

The reservations of rescue home workers had no discernible effect on the growth of charity organization societies, which soon came under state control. In 1891, Denver charity organizations were put under the jurisdiction of a State Board of Charities, which held investigative power. Charitable work for children came under the control of a different state department, the Bureau of Child and Animal Protection, in 1901; by 1911, the Bureau had gained the power to inspect and license all maternity homes and to supervise and set procedures for adoptions.[36] In San Francisco, too, local charity organizations came under state control. In 1903, charities were placed under the aegis of the State Board of Charities and Corrections. By 1911, this Board had acquired the power to investigate private institutions; soon afterwards, it gained control over licensing. Its supervisory functions were shared with a State Board of Control formed in 1911 to bring business efficiency to California charities.[37]

Although the Colorado Cottage Home and the Chinese Mission Home avoided affiliating with local charity organization societies, they were unable to sidestep the state agencies that evolved from them. For the San Francisco Chinese Mission Home, there was a financial inducement to become involved with the state bureaucracy: Home officials discovered that their institution would be eligible for state compensation payments if there were twenty children in the Home who could be considered "orphans, half-orphans, or abandoned children."[38] But the same state officials who promised financial aid also held investigative power. On the whole, state investigators were impressed with the Chinese Mission Home, labeling it a fine operation.[39] Still, state and local governments imposed requirements that home mission women found difficult to meet. In the 1920s, the state condemned the mission building to which some young Chinese girls had been moved as "unsanitary and unsafe," although it deferred taking action until a new building had been completed.[40] In 1932, a more serious problem resulted from the passage of legislation limiting the amount of state aid available to migrants to California. This law restricted Donaldina Cameron's ability to welcome residents who came to the Home from outside state borders.[41]

In Denver, too, government supervision of charitable institutions resulted in requirements that were difficult for Cottage Home officials to meet. By 1924, Home officials were complaining "of recent stringent rulings of the Board of Health on institutions which will affect Cottage Home."[42] By 1929, attempts to comply with building codes for institutions had resulted in a debt of $1,360.[43] In practice, then, state officers who established minimum standards for typical charitable institutions subjected rescue homes to an obstacle course of governmental regulations. To the extent that scientific attitudes and state-enforced requirements overshadowed Protestant women's personal concern for rescue home residents, they, too, helped weaken the ideological groundwork of rescue work for women.

One conclusion to be drawn from the story of the institutional development of rescue homes is that home mission women had an ambiguous relationship to Progressive reform. Because they were eager to use the government to protect women and children, they had welcomed the spirit of Progressivism that enlivened western cities after the turn of the century, contributing to it a rhetoric of female moral authority derived from Victorian culture. Yet perhaps they are better seen as foremothers of Progressivism than as its stalwarts; certainly they were only halfhearted converts to its distinctive blend of religiously inspired morality, bureaucratic consolidation, and social scientific expertise.[44] The story of their institutional development suggests that they found losses as well as gains in state control, and they resisted adopting social scientific attitudes. Their reluctance was unusual; women's welfare institutions that survived into the mid–twentieth century did so because they adapted to the social scientific mainstream. Significantly, however, such adaptation often came at the cost of losing their identity as women's institutions.[45]

Rescue home workers in Denver and San Francisco avoided taking this path; they tried to maintain their institutions without losing their focus on women. Yet each step they took to strengthen their institutions—the attempts to find stable financial bases, to strengthen relations with law enforcement and government personnel, and to respond, however reluctantly, to the dictates of state officials—undermined the foundations of rescue home work. As rescue homes shifted away from their original base of support— Protestant women supportive of calls to Victorian female values— home mission workers who held on to the concept of women's work for women argued for it in less gender-specific terms. Like many Progressive reformers, they won the battle to add women's concerns to government, but lost the ability to choose—and to argue for—those concerns as expressions of women's values.[46] Although they eschewed other alternatives and continued to carry out work by women for women, they were less and less likely to defend their work in these terms. In this respect, the name change of the Women's National Indian Association is revealing: the consequence was an erosion of the ideology of female moral authority that had served as women's primary route to authority within Victorian culture.

Victorian Values in a Modern Age

While the ideological structures home mission women built on Victorian female values eroded, the very ground beneath their feet began to shift. During the nineteenth century, Victorian culture, with its gender system and racial hierarchy, maintained a substantial degree of hegemony in American society. In the years after 1890, however, Victorian culture was supplanted by a form of culture historians are beginning to label "modernism."[47] The most radical modernists questioned all the verities of Victorianism, from the exaggerated divisions between men and women, to the evolutionary ladder from savagery to civilization. Seeking to move in a new direction, they ridiculed rather than respected the pious Protestantism of their predecessors. The triumph of modernism was neither immediate nor complete, but each step in its direction loosened the laces with which Victorians tied women to piety and purity—the ties that had sustained rescue home activities, influenced matrons' relationships with residents, and supported the Victorian search for female moral authority. The road to modernism is only beginning to be mapped by historians, but three aspects of the complex cultural changes involved can be outlined here: the transformation of the Victorian gender system, the decline in the cultural authority of Protestant evangelicalism, and the rise of a concept of cultural relativism that challenged Victorian racial hierarchies.

The Transformation of the Victorian Gender System

For rescue home operations, the most significant of these changes was the shift from a Victorian gender system that idolized female purity, to a modern one that acknowledged female passion. Of course, the hegemony of Victorian gender ideals had never been absolute. From their inception, rescue homes struggled with the challenges posed by alternative gender systems in which female purity was either devalued or conceived of in different ways. In the eyes of some residents, Victorian morality had always suffered by comparison with the less restrictive sexual practices of working-class and ethnic minority communities. In the years after 1890, new assaults on the ideal of female purity and sexual self-control added to the power of this comparison.[48]

The challenges to Victorian morality originated well outside rescue homes. They began among the "free lovers" of the late nineteenth century who argued that sexual relationships should reflect love rather than marital obligation.[49] By the turn of the century, they were visible among urban working-class women, whose economic contributions bought them enough freedom from family surveillance to build a peer culture that flaunted sexuality.[50] The challenges swept along among Greenwich Village radicals whose readings of Freud convinced them that female passion was modern and healthy, while self-control was old-fashioned and repressive.[51] By the 1920s, they were making inroads among the urban middle classes.[52]

Doubts about the Victorian cultural prescriptions that equated womanhood with sexual passionlessness multiplied; soon, the Victorian gender system came under siege from within as well as without. In urban areas, a more casual system of "dating" replaced the formal constraints on courtship that had previously characterized Victorian middle-class culture.[53] Furthermore, the meaning of marriage itself changed. As one historian has explained, the most modern of middle-class couples eschewed Victorian marriages based on ideals of self-control and self-sacrifice; they favored modern marriages in which sexual pleasure was a cardinal index of marital contentment. Over the course of the twentieth century, "true women" and "Christian gentlemen" would be replaced with "partners in pleasure" with high expectations for heterosexual emotional intimacy.[54]

Taken together, these changes added up to a modern gender system; one that threatened to render obsolete the images of female purity, true women, and Christian gentlemen so dear to the hearts of home mission women. The transformation posed significant problems for rescue home matrons, whose efficacy depended on a consensus of support for Victorian values. Consider, for example, an incident from the Colorado Cottage Home in 1909. President Harriet Dunklee interviewed a woman who entered the Cottage Home. In standard home mission terminology, she noted that "on talking [with her] I found her a pure minded young girl who still loved her betrayer and believed in him." This young woman, however, had no intention of fitting into Dunklee's Victorian categories. Even at the end of their talk, "she showed his picture and asked if he was not fine looking." Dunklee, registering amazement, blamed the young woman's parents. They had, she thought, endorsed immorality by approving their daughter's engagement and then allowing her to "go out evenings" with her fiancé.[55]

What was happening was a twofold process. Each harbinger of the new gender system pushed pious Protestant women further from the mainstream of American society. At the same time, the increasing frequency of modern gender arrangements outside rescue homes reinforced residents' resistance to matrons' moralism. Home mission women, of course, sensed that the bond between women and moral purity was endangered, but they were unable to imagine a search for female moral authority resting on any basis other than female purity. Having side-stepped social science alternatives, they dug in their heels in defense of Victorianism. In the process, they aligned themselves against modern courtship patterns as well as against their older enemies—seduction, betrayal, and prostitution. Thus, another mother who came "heart-broken" to tell her story to Cottage Home president Dunklee found little sympathy. Dunklee reported, "I was obliged to tell her that I thought she was wholly to blame as this man was allowed too much freedom when he visited their home."[56]

Many rescue home residents were less resistant than matrons to modern concepts of sexuality, courtship, and marriage, and the gap between residents and matrons widened as modern ideals spread. The distance between the two can be seen in the comments of Soo Ah Young, a resident of the San Francisco Chinese Mission Home. Young left a record of her thoughts on meeting a suitor, Mr. Ping, chosen for her by matron Donaldina Cameron. "I hardly can tell you if I like Mr. [Ping]," she wrote to Cameron, "because we both hardly talk together you know I never walk with the boys in my life, and he never walk with the girls in his life, so I think its offly hard for me to walk with him, it offly hard for him too."[57]

Soo Ah Young, like many second-generation Chinese American women, had in mind an image of dating that neither Ping nor Donaldina Cameron shared. She was disappointed that on their date "he [Ping] take me out to S.P. Station and set there nothing to do, and he makes me walk from East 20th Street to the S.P. station, and then after we set there, then he took me out to dinner, then we came back." He was, she reported worriedly, "so China man . . . so old fashion typ[e], he doesn't know to walk with the girl."[58] There is an interesting, if ultimately unresolvable, ambiguity about the use of the phrase "walk with the girl" here. On the one hand, it reflects missionaries' complaints that Chinese men expected Chinese women literally to walk behind them rather than beside them on city streets. On the other, the phrase refers to a practice of young couples' walking out in public that had long been a feature of urban working-class life, associated with a casual sexuality that deeply offended middle-class Victorians.[59]

Home mission women were haunted by the breakdown of the Victorian assumption that women were naturally sexually pure. At the Denver Cottage Home, workers who had long argued that "purity is the characteristic of woman above all the other virtues" began to worry that "with the emancipation of womanhood from many slavish traditions has come a breaking down of ideals that represent in its noblest form the feminine conception of life." They lamented that "drunkenness is increasing . . . rapidly among . . . women," a phenomenon that suggested to them that "young women do not realize their power for good."[60]

Seeing slippage all around them, home mission women prescribed the enforcement of a female morality they once thought was inherent in women. Amy Wong, a married former resident of the Chinese Mission Home, felt the effects. When she came to the Mission Home asking for help in a marital dispute, Protestant women decided that she, not her husband, was in the wrong. They suggested that she sign an agreement that echoed those they ordinarily presented to husbands. According to its terms, her husband would take her back if she gave up smoking, drinking, gambling, and attending the Chinese theater, and if she agreed "not to be out later than ten o-clock at night without my husband's knowledge and consent, or in his company." Additionally, she was to attend church and part-time school regularly, and to spend the rest of her time working to earn money for further education.[61] The Wong agreement is the only one of its kind among Mission Home sources, but the enforcement of female purity and piety it sought was indicative of the reactions of rescue home matrons whose central assumptions had lost substantial support in American society.

Such an attitude boded ill for the tenuous lines of communication that had been established between rescue home residents and matrons. In response, rescue home residents spent more energy than ever before in evading the moral judgments of rescue home matrons. Ordinarily this involved deception rather than outright rebellion. For example, in 1907, a Denver Cottage Home resident accepted the offer of Home officials to care for her child while she worked outside the institution; then she quietly moved into a rooming house with a man to whom she was not married. When a visiting Mission official discovered that she had taken "the downward plunge into sin," the former resident tried to convince her visitor that she had legally married her roommate. Her pretense failed and the mission official retired from the field "with a heavy heart."[62]

A more dramatic incident occurred at the San Francisco Chinese Mission Home in 1924. Rose Seen, an unhappy fourteen-year-old resident, longed to be reunited with her lover, Bill, a Chinese man who had been charged with contributing to her delinquency. To avoid mission scrutiny, Seen communicated with her boyfriend by suspending notes on sticks from her window at the front of the Mission Home. In one such missive, addressed "to my dearest beloved husband," she pleaded with Bill "to find some easy job and go to work so just to make them think you are not lazy and go to church on Sunday so pretend that you were a Christian cause Miss Cameron does not allow the girls to marry a boy that doesn't go to work."[63] Mission Home officials confiscated this note and reported Bill to his probation officer, while Seen remained in the Home. During the next year, she and another resident convinced Mission Home officials of their sincerity and were entrusted with the funds of a student group. In December 1925, however, both young women ran away from the Home, taking the money and some jewelry, hoping to reunite with Bill and his friends.[64] Seen's contemporaries might have found her actions entirely understandable, but mission workers, still guided by Victorian assumptions of female purity, were astonished by the incident and at a loss to explain it.

The Contraction of Protestant Evangelicalism

As modernism gained strength and Victorianism faded, female purity lost its position as a central symbol within American society. Female piety, too, lost its salience. Middle-class Americans continued to identify women with piety, but they paid far less heed to Protestant piety in general, whether displayed by women or men. Turn-of-the-century American Protestantism had been a significant social force, strong enough to support worldwide missionary programs as well as to fuel such Progressive reforms as Prohibition and campaigns against white slavery. Some historians believe that in this period Protestantism was so powerful as to be virtually indistinguishable from Americanism. By 1925, however, it had fallen into the midst of a religious "depression."[65]

One cause of the decline was the spread of skepticism, a modern attitude that pulled liberal evangelicals away from their more conservative counterparts. Protestants divided themselves into two opposing camps, the liberals and the fundamentalists. Fundamentalists claimed for their own the evangelical heritage that had once been touted by Protestants of every variety. Yet, in the years after 1920, fundamentalists withdrew from political action, and as the social range of evangelicalism contracted, social reform was left to the liberals. The South provided a particularly congenial stronghold for both fundamentalists and liberals, whose dedication to social gospel ideals underlay mid–twentieth-century campaigns for world peace and racial egalitarianism. Outside the South and the rural Midwest, the forces of secularism were stronger, and neither fundamentalists nor social gospel thinkers retained much more than a shadow of the cultural authority wielded by turn-of-the-century Protestantism.[66]

By the 1920s, even missionary work, the need for which had been one of the few things that both camps agreed on, was falling victim to the rivalry. It also suffered from a long-term attrition of acceptable missionary candidates. Throughout the last half of the nineteenth century, national missionary boards worried about the shortage of young men willing to become missionaries. For women, the lure of missionary careers lingered longer. In Victorian America, a missionary career was one of the few professional jobs open to women; furthermore, it combined the appeal of exoticism with the social authority of speaking for Protestant America. By the turn of the century, however, the kind of ambitious young women who might earlier have become missionaries were increasingly attracted to business, government, social work, or academia.[67]

By the 1920s, Protestantism had become a target for ridicule rather than a focus for the aspirations of self-consciously modern young people. In the literature of the modern period, writers used pious women as stock characters, but they presented them as caricatures of self-denial, repression, or religious fanaticism, rather than as heroines. Regarded in this light, rescue home matrons served as a warning rather than a model for rescue home residents. Even the most devout residents, those who once might have become native helpers, had difficulty keeping pity out of their voices. As one wrote to Ethel Higgins of the Chinese Mission Home, "you [and Donaldina Cameron] have sacrificed pleasure for the sake of humanity."[68] It was not a choice this young woman or her peers would be willing to make.

Although the transformation from Victorianism to modernism was a complex one, the direction of the change is clear. In the transition, the Victorian female values of piety and purity were discredited; without them, the search for female moral authority could not survive.

The Development of Cultural Relativism

One last consequence of the emergence of modernism is important for our story, and that is the dismantling of the Victorian hierarchy of race relations. As we have seen, Victorians understood differences between ethnic groups as a function of "racial" difference arranged along an evolutionary ladder. Although missionary women had come to distinguish between culture and biological race, they had maintained the notion of a hierarchy of cultures. In the early twentieth century, however, pioneering intellectuals moved well beyond the ideas of the missionary women, putting forth a notion of cultural relativism—the belief that no culture is inherently more valuable, or more moral, than any other—that has been enormously influential in modern thinking.[69]

Advocates of cultural relativism faced fierce opponents. In the first decades of the twentieth century, both racialism and biological racism were at high tide, and visible in such reforms as the wide-spread immigration quotas enacted in the 1920s. But if the concept of cultural relativism did not immediately translate into a society-wide repudiation of racism, it did set in motion the forces that would topple critical academic and political support for racial hier-archies over the course of the twentieth century.

The accompanying shift in attitudes could be seen in the modern literary notion of the allure of native cultures. In the 1920s, white Americans "in the know" were fascinated spectators of the Harlem Renaissance and avid readers of sensational tales of "yellow slav-ery" that played as much on sexual titillation as on moral outrage. Like their Victorian predecessors, they saw native cultures as sen-sual; but they reversed the value judgments that Victorians had made. Newly hostile to the forces that repressed sexual expression, they rejected the notion of innate female purity and looked to other cultures for inspiration.[70] In such a context, missionaries' attempts to fit women of native cultures into a Protestant mold were regarded as, at best, meddling; at worst, moral extremism.

As native cultures appeared more enticing and less "immoral," matrons were pressured to minimize the distance between rescue home residents and their communities of origin; a new, more social scientific generation of mission personnel saw the gap between the two as a problem to be remedied rather than as an index of the successful adoption of Victorian female moral authority. In San Francisco, a small group of mission workers tried to bridge the gap between the Chinese Mission Home and Chinatown. As one commented, "it is our observation that the girls at Ming Quong Home [the children's home associated with the Mission] are stead-ily growing further away from their own people and race."[71] De-ciding that "everything should be done to cement the relationship between the Home and the Chinese community," they began to make plans to move the institution for Chinese girls closer to Chinatown.[72] Complaining that the Oakland location of the chil-dren's home limited the girls' social contacts with Chinese Amer-icans without securing their acceptance by white society, officials recommended change. "Our present family," they explained, "[is] divided into two camps. Those who do not wish to move to the Chinese community are the girls who have no connections outside the Home, and who have been with us since they were little children. Those who grasped at once the meaning of the plan and look forward to its accomplishment are the girls who remember their own family life and have not been here as long."[73]

The dilemma at the Chinese Mission Home suggests another consequence of the rise of cultural relativism and the accompanying challenge to Victorian racial hierarchies. As Victorian structures crumbled, the unique complex of factors that had encouraged some ethnic minority women to become native helpers disappeared. The native helpers who remained did not become, as mission women had hoped they would, heroines to young women in ethnic minority communities. In fact, native helpers, who were devoted to mission ideals that distanced them from their own communities but were unable to command authority in white society outside the missions (or equal authority within them), became increasingly isolated.

Victimized by their countrymen and attracted by the unique opportunities for education offered by rescue homes, Ah Tsun Wing and Tien Fu Wu worked at the Chinese Mission Home for much of their lives. Both were devoted missionary advocates, but neither they nor the matrons of the Home were able to inspire young residents to follow in their footsteps. The close personal relations with matrons that had drawn Wu into mission work were increasingly strained for younger residents; furthermore, the educations that Wing and Wu had found in the Home were now available to Chinese American women outside the institution, for San Franciscans had belatedly created public school accommodations for Asian Americans. In this changed context, Wing and Wu were leaders without followers; truly, exceptional women.

Native helper Susan LaFlesche Picotte of the Omaha tribe proved to be equally exceptional. When reformer Alice Fletcher visited the Omaha Indians in the 1880s, tribal "progressives" like Susan LaFlesche Picotte seemed to her to be its brightest future.[74] Educated at well-known eastern schools, dedicated to religion and family on the white middle-class model, and devoted to their tribe, they seemed to Fletcher to provide the leadership necessary for its future development. Anthropologist and noted cultural relativist Margaret Mead, who visited the tribe in the 1930s, drew very different conclusions. She believed that the group of Omaha who had "gone white," as she put it, were so deviant from the rest of the tribe as to merit little consideration in her study of changing tribal culture. She dismissed the impact of white-educated Indians with the comment that because they were mostly "orphans, children of the poor, or children of aberrant and unpopular people who welcomed the coming of a new way of life"; they held little influence among the tribe.[75] To Mead, women like Susan La-Flesche Picotte were unique rather than representative, and therefore of little consequence.

Picotte was also unique in the annals of the Connecticut Indian Association, which never again put an Indian woman through medical school. When no young women as promising as Picotte seemed to be at hand, the Association agreed to finance the medical education of a young Indian man named Lewis Johnson. On learning that Johnson's "conduct has been far from what we approved of, or could allow," they cut off his funds, and thereafter concentrated on training young Indian women to be nurses rather than doctors.[76]

Neither Indian nurses nor their mission-educated Chinese American counterparts captured the imagination of white contemporaries the way Wu, Wing, and Picotte had a generation earlier. In a society in which avant-garde modernists questioned the very categories of the transformation from "savagery to civilization" that native helpers had signified to Victorian Protestant women, there was little soil for home mission seeds.

The Demise of Rescue Work for Women

Over the first decades of the twentieth century, the transformation of Victorian culture seen in the rise of a modern gender system, the contraction of Protestant evangelicalism, and the development of cultural relativism put home mission women in the awkward position of defending Victorian values to a modern age. Home mission women were increasingly unable to find an audience, much less cultural authority, in American society; home mission programs were weakened by the erosion of the ideology of female moral authority. Still devoted to their assumptions that piety and purity were the central values of womanhood, Victorian mission women were stranded in a modern world. When they tried to enforce their view of female morality in the one arena where they had enough authority to do so—their relationships with rescue home residents—they only increased the distance between themselves and the women they hoped to serve in their institutions. By the end of the 1920s, rescue homes had come to be regarded as repressive institutions out of step with modern American culture. One by one, home mission organizations dwindled, and the rescue homes they sponsored closed down.

The home mission organization whose commitment to women as women had always been the weakest—the Connecticut branch of the Women's National Indian Association—was the first of the remaining three to go under. Over the years, Connecticut women had provided loans for building homes on reservations, educated Indian women to be doctors and nurses, and funded women missionaries in Fort Hall, Idaho. By 1900, however, all of these projects were defunct. The group stumbled on with little purpose until 1906, when member Annie Beecher Scoville tried to interest members in an ambitious plan for revitalization.

Scoville proposed, in effect, that the Connecticut Association return to the tactics that had generated enthusiasm among members in earlier years. She argued that Indian reformers' willingness to rely on government had been a mistake, because the government could not work with "heart" and would therefore necessarily fail.[77] She suggested that the Association set up a medical mission, consisting of a house staffed by a Protestant woman trained in medicine and with enough extra rooms to allow her to take Indian children in as students. Scoville was particularly anxious to put the proposed mission on either the Omaha or the Winnebago reservation, since recent government investigations had shown how desperate was the condition of these tribes, who were once the darlings of Indian reformers.[78]

The possibility of establishing a medical mission among the Omaha appealed to Connecticut members because they might, in so doing, reestablish their relationship with Omaha doctor Susan LaFlesche Picotte. Although Picotte's communication with the group had fallen off, she still dreamed of presiding over a hospital on her reservation. Recently widowed and the mother of two school-age children, she had moved to the new reservation town of Walthill, Nebraska. In Walthill, she devoted her time to medical practice, church activities, and civic affairs; she was eager to acquire financial support for a hospital.

Discussion of the Omaha project created more excitement than the Connecticut group had generated in years. Membership in the Hartford branch actually rose; the new plan temporarily silenced members' queries about the need for the Association.[79] The Commissioner of Indian Affairs looked favorably on the mission project; Presbyterian officials offered to donate a piece of land on the Omaha reservation; and Alice Fletcher made a special appearance to urge the Association to adopt the project. Fletcher "paid a glowing tribute to Dr. Susan LaFlesche, as a woman and as a doctor, and said that too much could not be said in praise of her work among her people."[80]

In the end, though, the hopes of Connecticut Association leaders that they might "return to our first love" came too late.[81] Investigation of the hospital site revealed "malarious conditions"; reports of factionalism on the reservation worried the women. But the determining factor in their decision was financial: they simply did not have and could no longer raise the several thousand dollars it would cost to put their plans in operation. Hoping to retain the interest the Omaha project had aroused among members, Connecticut leaders opened a hospital on the Oneida reservation, where a suitable building was already available.[82] When a tornado blew down the tiny mission hospital a few years after its dedication, it took with it much of the active energy of the Connecticut Indian Association. Only the determination of Sara Kinney, the group's first and only president, held the Association together. When Kinney died soon after conducting the 1922 annual meeting, the Connecticut Indian Association voted to disband.[83]

The demise of the Connecticut Indian Association resulted from several factors, among them a general decline in Indian reform activity, but it also illustrated the consequences of the erosion of female moral authority for home mission work.[84] Having set aside their conviction that their work was especially appropriate for women, intended to benefit women, or based on ties between women, members' personal identification with home mission work flagged. By the time that leaders tried to resurrect their personal focus on women, it was too late to save the organization.

Home mission organizations that reinforced their commitment to Victorian female values held on a little longer. In Denver, the Colorado Woman's Christian Temperance Union overcame its financial problems well enough to keep the Colorado Cottage Home functioning until 1930, when a group of members who represented a significant minority of a new generation of temperance union members raised a chorus of criticism. Their objections to the Home show the rising influence of professional standards of social work. The critics charged that "the home has been used as a tool in practicing blackmail on unmarried mothers, funds of the organization collected for a supposedly charitable purpose have fallen into other channels, children are 'farmed' out of the home without going through the legal process of adoption, and that babies in the home are neglected and given improper sanitary care."[85]

None of the critics' charges were ever proved. Perhaps they never could have been, for there is reason to believe that the critics tried to discredit the Home largely as a way to wrest Union leadership away from Adrianna Hungerford. Hungerford, who had been president of the Union for more than twenty-five years, had managed to fend off all previous challenges to her power. Ironically, she shared her critics' belief that the Cottage Home had outlived its usefulness, but she stoutly defended the institution because she believed that the bulk of the membership favored its continuation. As she put it, the "Cottage Home . . . is rooted deep in the hearts of women in the state; it has a sentimental interest and when they lose faith in its efficacy they and they alone will order it closed."[86]

When the critics were unable to convince Hungerford of the validity of their concerns, they took their case to newspaper reporters. In response to this public embarrassment, Hungerford expelled the "insurgent" members and ordered an audit of the Cottage Home books to disprove their charges.[87] The angry insurgents vowed to oust Hungerford from the presidency at the fall convention. They put forth as an opposition candidate Mrs. F. I. Smith, a long-time Cottage Home official, a choice that confirms that the real issue in the battle was control of the organization. The convention election was bitterly contested, but Hungerford retained her hold on the presidency by a vote of 283 to 109.[88] With her leadership vindicated, Hungerford tried to smooth the ruffled feathers of her detractors; she agreed to close the Colorado Cottage Home.[89]

Despite the critics' charges, the Cottage Home did not lack

residents; in fact, the institution received more women in the 1920s than ever before. In 1928, Home official Anna Keenan had confidently told members, "Cottage Home is doing the same type of work that it has done all the years of its existence."[90] What had declined was not the need for services for pregnant women, but the connection middle-class Protestant women had made between institutions for unmarried mothers and their own search for female moral authority. The critics' suggestion that the Home had been used by blackmailers indicates how much times had changed since the establishment of the institution in the 1880s, when its founders saw it as the best way to protect the reputations of victimized pregnant women. By 1930, the Cottage Home, once the jewel in the crown of the Colorado Woman's Christian Temperance Union, had become a mere pawn in its organizational struggles. The institution closed its doors in 1931.

The last of the mission home projects, the San Francisco Chinese Mission Home, clung to life until 1939. Indeed, Donaldina Cameron was so adept at keeping her sensational rescues of Chinese prostitutes before the public eye that she was able to offset objections from mission officials who pointed out that the number of Chinese prostitutes was steadily decreasing. For a few years during the mid–1920s, it looked as if Cameron might overcome the national officials who wanted to scale down her work for Chinese immigrant women. In 1925, she proudly opened Ming Quong Home, a lavish institution for Chinese girls located in Oakland. Mindful of the national board's promise to get her a "better adapted" building for rescue work, she made plans to construct a mission complex in San Mateo that would include a main building, an industrial building, and a baby cottage. Cameron had enormous powers of persuasion, and she was able to infect a few mission officials with her enthusiasm for the San Mateo project. In the meantime, she resisted all attempts to sell the old Mission Home building at 920 Sacramento Street, hoping that it could be used as a receiving home for rescue cases, a day nursery, and a boarding home for working girls.[91]

Cameron's plans, however, came to an abrupt halt when one national leader, H. N. Morse, recommended that the project be scrapped. His reasons provided a catalogue of the forces that were making Cameron's work vulnerable: he cited the decline in the

Chinese immigrant population in the wake of immigration restriction, the inevitable decline in rescue work, the availability of other state-supported institutions for delinquents, and the relatively large amount of national mission money already spent on Chinese work.[92] Following Morse's lead, national home mission officials steeled themselves to hold the line against expansion and pointedly reminded Cameron of their plan to sell the building at "920." In the early 1930s, national board officials announced in their publication *Women and Missions* that the Chinese Mission Home was "no longer vitally necessary," and started to speak publicly of proposed changes.[93] They realized that the outcome of their campaign to close the Home hinged on how effectively they could deal with the major obstacle to their plans: the polite but determined opposition of Cameron, who held almost charismatic sway over a small group of San Francisco mission home women. Hoping to relieve Cameron of administrative responsibility for the San Francisco homes—and of day-to-day contact with San Francisco workers—they assigned her to carry on nationwide rescue work and to lead a campaign for legislation against the prostitute/slave trade. Cameron, who had lived as well as worked in the Chinese Mission Home for more than thirty years, was due to retire in 1934. She was delighted to accept the new assignment and to delay her retirement, but she put off handing over control of "920" on the grounds that she needed to find someone to carry on her San Francisco work.[94]

Soon, however, even Cameron could no longer hold back the changes. In 1936, her beloved Ming Quong Home was sold to Mills College at the behest of national officials and the Ming Quong superintendent, Ethel Higgins; who, along with some of the younger San Francisco women, felt that the building was too showy and too far away from Oakland's Chinese community.[95] In the same year, the national board decided to turn "920" into a Chinese language school.[96] Reminding officials of their promise to find quarters that would house the rescue work "PERMANENTLY AND ADEQUATELY," Cameron tried to delay the transfer, but the patience of the national officials had run out.[97] In 1937 they asked San Francisco doctor Frederick Payne to "secretly investigate" the Mission Home so that "we may be able to make out a case for the Board giving up this work."[98] Payne surveyed local public welfare, Board of Health, and juvenile court officials and found that only the juvenile court protested the plan to end the rescue work; the others, he reported, thought "we have just provided a soft basket where the Juvenile Court could dump its rubbish, at a minimum expense to the county."[99]

Armed with this information, national officials moved to close the programs for Chinese women and girls at the Chinese Mission Home. In early 1939, Cameron's successor Lorna Logan moved the mission to rented quarters on Wetmore Street with room for no more than six residents. Soon after, national board official Edna Voss congratulated Logan on "turning the tide from backward-thinking to a forward-looking attitude."[100] What Voss meant by "forward-looking" was that Logan would preside over "a program of broad community service" rather than rescue work focused on Chinese women and girls.[101] Like the Connecticut Indian Association and the Colorado Cottage Home, the Chinese Mission Home had succumbed to the forces of institutional and cultural change that rendered rescue work for women anomalous in the early decades of the twentieth century.

Epilogue

A Legacy to Ponder: Female Moral Authority and Contemporary Women's Culture

With the removal of the Chinese Mission Home from its rescue home headquarters in 1939, this story of the search for female moral authority in the American West comes to an end. Its most significant elements—the designation of purity and piety as female values and the identification of women with morality—withered in the harsh climate of modern culture. For most of the modern period, the search for female moral authority remained dormant, budding only occasionally, most notably in the interwar women's peace movement.

Today the particular constellation of symbols—piety, purity, morality, the Christian home—once advanced by Victorian Protestant women is most strongly identified with the religious New Right, an aggressively political reformulation of fundamentalism. But, although the New Right would like to recapture the momentum enjoyed by turn-of-the-century Protestantism, it retains more of the shape than the substance of the original. Contemporary fundamentalists have aligned themselves firmly against the emancipation of women; furthermore, they put forth a concept of the Christian home based on a reinforcement of patriarchal authority. Both positions would have angered home mission women in the West.

This book has stressed three elements of the Victorian search for female moral authority: its origins in a "women's culture" rooted most firmly among white middle-class women, its use of the female values of that culture to strengthen the social authority of women, and its assumption that those values applied (or should apply) to women of ethnic minority groups as well as to white women. Assumptions very much like these are visible today, not in the New Right, but among those feminists who advocate the development of a women's culture based on a peculiarly twentieth-century version of female values: one that depicts women as peace-makers, cooperators, and experts in empathy. In recent years, the development of cultural feminism has allowed some women to overcome the modern distaste for the term *morality* and to call for a moral society informed by women's voices.

As cultural feminists have discovered, such a strategy has enormous political potential. Because "women's values" resonate with many women's experiences, cultural feminist appeals hold considerable power to inspire women to political action. Cultural feminism has been a major force in contemporary antipornography and antinuclear campaigns and in the ecology movement. Because contemporary women's culture (much like its Victorian equivalent) is adapted from familiar gender roles, it allows maximum communication between feminists and women who adhere to conventional standards of female behavior. Cultural feminists and women of the so-called Moral Majority agree on the need to legislate against pornography; both feminist lobbyists and conservative legislators work to provide shelters for battered women.[1]

The concept of women's culture has been at least as important to the academic field of women's studies as it has been to political organizing. In the past two decades, feminist scholars in a variety of disciplines have defined their task as one of understanding the contemporary world of women, learning to value women's insights and to strengthen bonds between them. Like their activist counterparts, these scholars have brought to the surface a long-submerged reserve of female experience (in psychologist Carol

Gilligan's terms, "a different voice") that seems to offer hope for a more humane future.

But their studies also demonstrate some of the limitations of using women's culture as a point of departure for research or for politics. Chief among these is the assumption of the universality of female values. The attempt to base feminism on any particular set of female values puts its advocates in the same problematic relationship to women labeled "deviant" that Victorian missionary women found themselves. Cultural feminism may increase communication between feminists and conservative women, but because it encourages the reinforcement of gendered identities, it short-circuits communication between cultural feminists and women who challenge the gender role definitions of contemporary society. To take only the most obvious instance, what is a feminism based on nonviolence as a "women's value" to make of women who enter the armed forces?[2]

As this example suggests, gender definitions that are established enough to allow feminists to use them as an effective wedge for political authority may already be in danger of being overthrown. Victorian missionary women suffered an anticlimactic end to their own search for female moral authority. By the 1890s, when they had just barely managed to institutionalize the Victorian values of female purity and piety in rescue homes, the forces that would transform Victorian culture were already in motion. To avoid their predicament, we have to be alert to the forces outside feminism that are changing gender definitions in our own time.

Because of their focus on change over time, feminist historians have avoided some of these traps. Among the first to see the significance of women's culture, they have explored at great length its nineteenth- and early–twentieth-century forms, repeatedly contrasting them with modern equivalents and exposing the ahistorical bias of modern assumptions. Along the way, they have used their focus on the bonds between women to rescue Victorian domesticity from the stigma of insufferable sentimentality, to point out the historical interdependence between women's institutions and feminism, and to highlight the uses of separatism for achieving women's emancipation.[3]

But whether the women's culture in question is modern or historical, focusing on the "female values" at its center draws attention away from the power relations at its boundaries. Consequently, I have tried to concentrate on the points at which Victorian women searching for female moral authority challenged male public authority, and the way they structured relations with women outside the white middle classes.

To the extent that focusing on women makes men peripheral to the analysis, it hampers the creation of effective strategies for dislodging the male-dominated power structures that affect most women's lives. This was a problem that Protestant missionary women were unable to solve. Concentrating their efforts on establishing homes for women alone allowed them much-needed and otherwise unavailable space to care for the victims of male abuse. It also allowed them to lose sight of how widespread those abuses were. Unable to exert much control over men outside the rescue homes and increasingly dependent on them for financial and legal help, they exempted "Christian men" from their critiques of male dominance. In the end, home mission matrons watched their charges return to a world outside the homes where male dominance was so ubiquitous that the concept of female moral authority was more an illusion than a reality.

As it turned out, missionaries had expressed more female moral authority over the women in rescue homes than over the men outside them. This dynamic, too, was related to the conception of women's culture, because the same emphasis on "female values" that allowed Victorian women to point out the oppressions women shared across cultural boundaries predisposed them to underestimate the differences among groups of women. In our own day, as in Victorian times, the symbols of women's culture have been derived, in the main, from the experience of white, middle-class women who have assumed that those values fit all others. While this universalizing tendency of cultural feminism has invited cooperation across cultural boundaries, it has also encouraged the kind of cultural misunderstandings home mission women experienced in rescue homes. It is sadly significant that while contemporary cultural feminists have discussed at great length the power of "women's values" for building support for feminist goals, they have been much less forthcoming about the complexities of relations among women across racial and cultural boundaries.

The all-too-recent recognition of the significance of supportive relationships among women is a central insight of cultural feminism. As historian Gerda Lerner has noted, "whenever [women] are confined by patriarchal restraint or segregation into separateness (which always has subordination as its purpose), they transform this restraint into complementarity and redefine it."[4] Because we live in a time when the future of feminism depends on establishing viable intercultural relations among women, it is important to be especially alert to the constraints any particular formation of "women's values" places on the transforming potential of these relationships. Cultural feminists who call for a new morality need to remember that the stereotyped images of Chinese prostitutes, Indian wives, polygamous Mormon women, and unmarried mothers spread by home mission women expressed, not only missionaries' indignation at the mistreatment of women, but also their misunderstanding—if not cavalier rejection—of alternative systems of morality. When pushed, they were willing to stigmatize women who disagreed with them as basically "immoral."

The weaknesses of the women's culture model stem, at least in part, from a lack of clear definition. Despite its obvious appeal as an analytic category, close examination reveals just how slippery a concept "culture" really is. This is by no means a problem limited to feminists or even to feminist historians. Over the past two decades, social historians of all kinds have been busy exploring the variety of cultures (from working-class culture to black culture) that make up American society. Like feminist historians, they have focused primarily on the values and symbols that make each cultural group distinctive. It is time now to explore the relations between these various groups. If we can learn one thing from the story of Protestant women in the West, it is that, for the moment at least, we need to pay less attention to the values at the center of women's culture and more attention to the relationships at its boundaries.

Abbreviations

A quick reminder of organizational titles might be helpful in locating specific records in the notes and the bibliography that follow. Susan LaFlesche Picotte was sponsored by the Connecticut Indian Association, a branch of the larger Women's National Indian Association. The Colorado Cottage Home was sponsored by the Colorado Woman's Christian Temperance Union, a state branch of the national Woman's Christian Temperance Union. The Chinese Mission Home was sponsored by San Francisco Presbyterian women, and was subject to a number of organizational permutations over its history. The founders of the Home initially associated with the Presbyterian Woman's Foreign Missionary Society of Philadelphia. From 1874 to 1876 they were known as the "California Branch" of the Society, from 1877 to 1881 as its "Occidental Branch," and from 1882 to 1888 as its "Occidental Board." In 1889, San Francisco women diverged from the parent Society to become the independent Woman's Occidental Board of Foreign Missions. In 1920, the Board was subsumed under the various national mission boards of the Presbyterian Church. The Industrial Christian Home in Salt Lake City was sponsored by the Industrial Christian Home Association and funded by the federal government; its records are listed in the "Government Documents" section of the bibliography.

ORGANIZATIONS

CIA	Connecticut Indian Association
WNIA	Women's National Indian Association
CWCTU	Colorado Woman's Christian Temperance Union
WFMS-CB	Woman's Foreign Missionary Society, California Branch
WFMS-OBo	Woman's Foreign Missionary Society, Occidental Board
WFMS-OBr	Woman's Foreign Missionary Society, Occidental Branch
WOBFM	Woman's Occidental Board of Foreign Missions

REPOSITORIES

CH	Cameron House, San Francisco, California
CSA	Connecticut State Archives, Hartford, Connecticut
CSL	California State Library, Sacramento, California
DPL	Denver Public Library, Western History Department, Denver, Colorado
HFL	Huntington Free Library and Reading Room, The Bronx, New York
HI	Hoover Institution, Stanford University, Stanford, California
HIA	Hampton Institute Archives, Hampton, Virginia
LDS	Church of Jesus Christ of Latter-day Saints, Historical Department, Salt Lake City, Utah
MCAH	United Methodist Church, Commission on Archives and History, Madison, New Jersey
MCP	Medical College of Pennsylvania, Archives and Special Collections on Women in Medicine, Philadelphia, Pennsylvania
NA	National Archives, Washington, D.C.
NAA	National Anthropological Archives, Washington, D.C.
NSHS	Nebraska State Historical Society, Lincoln, Nebraska
NWU	Nebraska Wesleyan University, United Methodist Church Archives, Lincoln, Nebraska
POH	Presbyterian Office of History, Philadelphia, Pennsylvania

SFTS	San Francisco Theological Seminary, San Anselmo, California
SLCPL	Salt Lake City Public Library, Special Collections, Salt Lake City, Utah
UC	University of Colorado Library, Western History Department, Boulder, Colorado
USHS	Utah State Historical Society, Library, Salt Lake City, Utah

Notes

Introduction: The Search for Female Moral Authority

1. The term *cultural feminism* was first used by Brooke in "The Retreat to Cultural Feminism," in Redstockings, *Feminist Revolution* (New Paltz, N.Y., 1975), pp. 65–68. Its subsequent development can be traced in Cheris Kramarae and Paula Treichler, eds., *A Feminist Dictionary* (Boston, Mass., 1985); and Lisa Tuttle, ed., *Encyclopedia of Feminism* (New York, 1986). Among contemporary feminist thinkers, those most frequently identified as cultural feminists include Mary Daly, Sally Miller Gearhart, Susan Griffin, Janice Raymond, and Adrienne Rich.

2. Hester Eisenstein, *Contemporary Feminist Thought* (Boston, Mass., 1983), p. xviii. See also Josephine Donovan, *Feminist Theory: The Intellectual Traditions of American Feminism* (New York, 1985), chaps. 2 and 7; and Alison Jaggar, *Feminist Politics and Human Nature* (Totowa, N.J., 1983), pp. 84, 93–98, 104. This development has, in turn, led to renewed scholarly interest in the relationship between women and morality. See, for example, Barbara Andolsen et al., eds., *Women's Consciousness, Women's Conscience: A Reader in Feminist Ethics* (Minneapolis, Minn., 1985); Marilyn Pearsall, ed., *Women and Values: Readings in Recent Feminist Philosophy* (Belmont, Calif., 1986); Eva Feder Kittay and Diana Meyers, eds., *Women and Moral Theory* (Totowa, N.J., 1987); Beverly Wildung Harrison, *Making the Connections: Essays in Feminist Social Ethics,* ed. Carol Robb (Boston, Mass., 1985); and Linda Nicholson, "Women, Morality, and History," *Social Research* 50 (Autumn 1983): 504–36.

3. Carol Gilligan, *In a Different Voice: Psychological Theory and Women's Development* (Cambridge, Mass., 1982); Annie Cheatham and Mary Clare Powell, *This Way Daybreak Comes: Women's Values and the Future* (Philadelphia, Pa., 1986). See also Joyce Trebilcot, ed., *Mothering: Essays*

in Feminist Theory (Totowa, N.J., 1984); Marilyn French, *Beyond Power: On Women, Men, and Morals* (New York, 1985); Mary Field Belenky et al., *Women's Ways of Knowing: The Development of Self, Voice, and Mind* (New York, 1986); Catherine Keller, *From a Broken Web: Separation, Sexism, and Self* (Boston, Mass., 1986); and Sara Ruddick, "Maternal Thinking," *Feminist Studies* 6 (Summer 1980): 343–67.

4. Marilyn Chapin Massey, *Feminine Soul: The Fate of an Ideal* (Boston, Mass., 1985); Nel Noddings, *Caring: A Feminine Approach to Ethics and Moral Education* (Berkeley, Calif., 1984).

5. Brooke, "The Retreat to Cultural Feminism"; Alice Echols, "The Taming of the Id: Feminist Sexual Politics, 1968–1983," in Carole Vance, ed., *Pleasure and Danger: Exploring Female Sexuality* (Boston, Mass., 1984), pp. 53–54; Nancy Hewitt, "Beyond the Search for Sisterhood: American Women's History in the 1980s," *Social History* 10 (October 1985): 299–321.

6. Echols, "The Taming of the Id"; idem, "The New Feminism of Yin and Yang," in Ann Snitow et al., eds., *Powers of Desire: The Politics of Sexuality* (New York, 1983), pp. 440–59; Ellen Willis, "Radical Feminism and Feminist Radicalism," in Jean Friedman et al., eds., *Our American Sisters: Women in American Life and Thought*, 4th ed. (Lexington, Ky., 1987), pp. 531–35; Gayle Rubin, "Thinking Sex: Notes for a Radical Theory of the Politics of Sexuality," in Vance, *Pleasure and Danger*, pp. 167–319.

7. See especially Linda Alcoff, "Cultural Feminism *vs.* Post-Structuralism: The Identity Crisis in Feminist Theory," *Signs* 13 (Spring 1988): 405–36; and Alice Jardine, *Gynesis: Configurations of Woman and Modernity* (Ithaca, N.Y., 1985). As Jardine points out, French feminists are often misread on this point; the first Americans to welcome them did so because they thought they reflected rather than challenged cultural feminist assumptions.

8. Carol Gilligan's moral challenge to patriarchy met with such immediate popular acclaim that *Ms.* named her "Woman of the Year" for 1984. For a sampling of critical responses, see *Social Research* 50 (Autumn 1983): entire issue; *Psychology of Women Quarterly* 9 (December 1985): 549–50; Linda Kerber et al., "On *In a Different Voice:* An Interdisciplinary Forum," *Signs* 11 (Winter 1987): 304–33; and Joan Scott, "Gender: A Useful Category of Historical Analysis," *American Historical Review* 91 (December 1986): 1053–75.

9. Adrienne Rich, introduction to "Women and Honor: Some Notes on Lying," in M. Pearsall, ed., *Women and Values*, p. 352.

10. The Victorian assumption of female sexual purity has been all but reversed in our own time. For overviews of this development, see Linda

Gordon and Ellen DuBois, "Seeking Ecstasy on the Battlefield: Danger and Pleasure in Nineteenth-Century Feminist Sexual Thought," *Feminist Studies* 9 (Spring 1983): 7–26; and Barbara Epstein, "Family, Sexual Morality, and Popular Movements in Turn-of-the-Century America," in Snitow et al., *Powers of Desire,* pp. 117–30.

11. The phrase "woman's work for woman" was used to describe a variety of domestic and foreign mission projects; between 1870 and 1895, it also served as the title of one of the Presbyterian women's mission society magazines. See Anne Firor Scott, "As Easily as They Breathe . . . ," in Scott, *Making the Invisible Woman Visible* (Urbana, Ill., 1984), pp. 270–71.

12. Estelle Freedman, *Their Sisters' Keepers: Women's Prison Reform in America, 1830–1930* (Ann Arbor, Mich., 1981); Barbara Epstein, *The Politics of Domesticity: Women, Evangelism, and Temperance in Nineteenth-Century America* (Middletown, Conn., 1981); Ruth Rosen, *The Lost Sisterhood: Prostitution in America, 1900–1918* (Baltimore, Md., 1982). Missing from this list—and badly needed—is a feminist examination of women's participation in the American social purity movement. For an older interpretation, see David Pivar, *Purity Crusade: Sexual Morality and Social Control, 1868–1900* (Westport, Conn., 1973). On the roughly parallel British movement, see Judith Walkowitz, "Male Vice and Female Virtue: Feminism and the Politics of Prostitution in Nineteenth-Century Britain," in Snitow et al., *Powers of Desire,* pp. 409–38.

13. For critiques of this image and for the research agendas of historians of women in the West, see Elizabeth Jameson, "Toward a Multicultural History of Women in the Western United States," *Signs* 13 (Summer 1988): 761–91; Lillian Schlissel et al., eds., *Western Women: Their Land, Their Lives* (Albuquerque, N.M., 1988), pp. 1–9; Susan Armitage and Elizabeth Jameson, eds., *The Women's West* (Norman, Okla., 1987), pp. 9–18, 145–64; and Joan Jensen and Darlis Miller, "The Gentle Tamers Revisited: New Approaches to the History of Women in the American West," *Pacific Historical Review* 49 (May 1980): 173–214.

14. Susan Armitage, "Through Women's Eyes: A New View of the West," in Armitage and Jameson, *Women's West,* p. 13.

15. Richard White, "Race Relations in the American West," *American Quarterly* 38 (Bibliography 1986): 396–416; Patty Limerick, *The Legacy of Conquest: The Unbroken Past of the American West* (New York, 1987), pp. 26–29.

16. Patricia Hill, *The World Their Household: The American Woman's Foreign Mission Movement and Cultural Transformation, 1870–1920* (Ann Arbor, Mich., 1985), pp. 54–55.

17. Gerda Lerner, "Women's Rights and American Feminism," in Ler-

ner, *The Majority Finds Its Past: Placing Women in History* (New York, 1979), p. 48; idem, *The Creation of Patriarchy* (New York, 1986), appendix, pp. 236–37. For a somewhat different formulation, see Nancy Cott, *The Grounding of Modern Feminism* (New Haven, Conn., 1987), p. 16.

18. Donovan, *Feminist Theory*, chap. 2.

19. The pattern-setting works here were Clifford Griffen, *Their Brothers' Keepers: Moral Stewardship in the United States, 1800–1865* (New Brunswick, N.J., 1960); Michael Katz, *The Irony of Early School Reform: Educational Innovation in Mid-Nineteenth-Century Massachusetts* (Boston, Mass., 1968); and David Rothman, *The Discovery of the Asylum: Social Order and Disorder in the New Republic* (Boston, Mass., 1971).

20. Fred Matthews, " 'Hobbesian Populism': Interpretive Paradigms and Moral Vision in American Historiography," *Journal of American History* 72 (June 1985): 92–115; Thomas Haskell, "Capitalism and the Origins of the Humanitarian Sensibility, Part 1," *American Historical Review* 90 (April 1985): 339–61.

21. Although they would admit that race and class domination overlap, most historians who study the history of racial ideology have taken care to distinguish between the two. See, for example, Thomas Gossett, *Race: The History of an Idea in America* (Dallas, Tex., 1963); George Stocking, *Race, Culture and Evolution: Essays in the History of Anthropology* (Chicago, Ill., 1968); Robert Berkhofer, *The White Man's Indian: Images of the American Indian from Columbus to the Present* (New York, 1978); Reginald Horsman, *Race and Manifest Destiny: The Origins of American Racial Anglo-Saxonism* (Cambridge, Mass., 1981); and White, "Race Relations in the American West." As a group, historians have been particularly resistant to the recent tendency of social scientists to explain racial and ethnic inequality primarily as a product of economic inequality— exemplified in Steven Steinberg, *The Ethnic Myth: Race, Ethnicity and Class in America* (Boston, Mass., 1981).

22. Linda Gordon, *Heroes of Their Own Lives: The Politics and History of Family Violence, Boston 1880–1960* (New York, 1988), pp. 293–99; Elizabeth Pleck, *Domestic Tyranny: The Making of Social Policy Against Family Violence from Colonial Times to the Present* (New York, 1987), pp. 12–13; Susan Porter Benson, "Business Heads and Sympathizing Hearts: The Women of the Providence Employment Society," *Journal of Social History* 12 (Winter 1978): 302–12; John Cumbler, "The Politics of Charity: Gender and Class in Late Nineteenth-Century Charity Policy," *Journal of Social History* 14 (Fall 1980): 99–112; Mary Odem, "Working-Class Parents, Delinquent Daughters, and the Juvenile Court," paper

presented to the American Historical Association, Pacific Coast Branch, San Francisco, August 1988.

23. My understanding of the gender system is adapted from a landmark article by Gayle Rubin, "The Traffic in Women: Notes on the 'Political Economy' of Sex," in Rayna Reiter, ed., *Toward an Anthropology of Women,* (New York, 1975), pp. 157–210.

24. See, for example, Hill, *The World Their Household.*

25. Pioneering attempts to explore these themes are Joan Jacobs Brumberg, "Zenanas and Girlless Villages: The Ethnology of American Evangelical Women, 1870–1910," *Journal of American History* 69 (September 1982): 347–71; and Sarah Deutsch, "Women and Intercultural Relations: The Case of Hispanic New Mexico and Colorado," *Signs* 12 (Summer 1987): 719–39.

Chapter 1: Institutional Origins

1. Mary Ryan, *Cradle of the Middle Class: The Family in Oneida County, New York, 1790–1865* (Cambridge, Mass., 1981); Paul Johnson, *A Shopkeeper's Millennium: Society and Revivals in Rochester, New York, 1815–1837* (New York, 1978); William McLoughlin, *Revivals, Awakenings, and Reform: An Essay on Religion and Social Change in America, 1607–1977* (Chicago, Ill., 1978).

2. Ryan, *Cradle of the Middle Class,* chap. 2; Barbara Welter, "The Feminization of American Religion," in Mary Hartman and Lois Banner, eds., *Clio's Consciousness Raised: New Perspectives on the History of Women* (New York, 1974), pp. 137–57; Richard Shiels, "The Feminization of American Congregationalism, 1730–1835," *American Quarterly* 33 (Spring 1981): 46–62.

3. Barbara Welter, "The Cult of True Womanhood: 1820–1860," *American Quarterly* 18 (Summer 1966): 151–74; Nancy Cott, *The Bonds of Womanhood: 'Woman's Sphere' in New England, 1780–1835* (New Haven, Conn., 1977); Kathryn Kish Sklar, *Catharine Beecher: A Study in American Domesticity* (New Haven, Conn., 1973); Carroll Smith-Rosenberg, "The Female World of Love and Ritual: Relationships between Women in Nineteenth-Century America," *Signs* 1 (Autumn 1975): 1–30; Ellen DuBois et al., "Politics and Culture in Women's History: A Symposium," *Feminist Studies* 6 (Spring 1980): 65–75.

4. For an overview, see John D'Emilio and Estelle Freedman, *Intimate Matters: A History of Sexuality in America* (New York, 1988), especially p. 57. Agreement on this point is widespread, despite the notable challenge

222   NOTES FOR PAGES 4–6

by Peter Gay in *The Bourgeois Experience: Victoria to Freud,* vol. 1, *Education of the Senses* (New York, 1984).

5. Lois Boyd and R. Douglas Brackenridge, *Presbyterian Women in America: Two Centuries of a Quest for Status* (Westport, Conn., 1983), pp. 3–14; Keith Melder, *Beginnings of Sisterhood: The American Woman's Rights Movement, 1800–1850* (New York, 1977), chap. 3.

6. Anne Boylan, "Timid Girls, Venerable Widows, and Dignified Matrons: Life Cycle Patterns among Organized Women in New York and Boston, 1797–1840," *American Quarterly* 38 (Winter 1986): 779–97; idem, "Women in Groups: An Analysis of Women's Benevolent Organizations in New York and Boston, 1797–1840," *Journal of American History* 71 (December 1984): 497–523; Nancy Hewitt, *Women's Activism and Social Change: Rochester, New York, 1822–1871* (Ithaca, N.Y., 1984).

7. Carroll Smith-Rosenberg, "Beauty, the Beast, and the Militant Woman: A Case Study in Sex Roles and Social Stress in Jacksonian America," *American Quarterly* 23 (October 1971): 562–84; Mary Ryan, "The Power of Women's Networks: A Case Study of Female Moral Reform in Antebellum America," *Feminist Studies* 5 (Spring 1979): 66–87; Barbara Berg, *The Remembered Gate: Origins of American Feminism— The Woman and the City, 1800–1860* (New York, 1978).

8. Paula Baker, "The Domestication of Politics: Women and American Political Society, 1780–1920," *American Historical Review* 89 (June 1984): 633. On similar antiseduction efforts, see Barbara Meil Hobson, *Uneasy Virtue: The Politics of Prostitution and the American Reform Tradition* (New York, 1987), pp. 66–70; and Michael Grossberg, *Governing the Hearth: Law and the Family in Nineteenth-Century America* (Chapel Hill, N.C., 1985), pp. 45–49.

9. Carroll Smith-Rosenberg, *Religion and the Rise of the American City: The New York City Mission Movement, 1812–1870* (Ithaca, N.Y., 1971), pp. 100–101, 110–12; Hobson, *Uneasy Virtue,* pp. 118–24.

10. Ryan, *Cradle of the Middle Class,* chap. 4; Hewitt, *Women's Activism,* chap. 4; Carroll Smith-Rosenberg, "The Cross and the Pedestal: Women, Anti-Ritualism, and the Emergence of the American Bourgeoisie," in *Disorderly Conduct: Visions of Gender in Victorian America* (New York, 1985), pp. 129–64.

11. Kathleen McCarthy, *Noblesse Oblige: Charity and Cultural Philanthropy in Chicago, 1849–1929* (Chicago, Ill., 1982), pp. 3–26; Joanne Meyerowitz, *Women Adrift: Independent Wage Earners in Chicago, 1880–1930* (Chicago, Ill., 1988), pp. 45–47; Scott, "As Easily as They Breathe . . . ."

12. M. Katherine Bennett, comp., "How It Grew: The Story of Woman's Organization in the Presbyterian Church in the United States of

America," narrative and drama presented at Quadrennial Meeting, Atlantic City, N. J., May 15, 1942, p. 29; and idem, "The Past a Promise for the Future," *Home Mission Monthly* 38 (March 1924): 106, quoted in Boyd and Brackenridge, *Presbyterian Women,* p. 15.

13. R. Pierce Beaver, *All Loves Excelling: American Protestant Women in World Mission* (Grand Rapids, Mich., 1968); Hill, *The World Their Household;* Jane Hunter, *The Gospel of Gentility: American Women Missionaries in Turn-of-the-Century China* (New Haven, Conn., 1984); Brumberg, "Zenanas and Girlless Villages."

14. The only book-length study of home mission women is John McDowell, *The Social Gospel in the South: The Woman's Home Mission Movement in the Methodist Episcopal Church, South, 1886–1939* (Baton Rouge, La., 1982).

15. WFMS-CB, *Annual Report,* 1874, p. 13; Woman's Home Missionary Society, *Annual Report,* 1882, p. 39.

16. The only study of the WNIA is Helen Wanken, " 'Woman's Sphere' and Indian Reform: The Women's National Indian Association, 1879–1901," (Ph.D. diss., Marquette Univ., 1981). Mary Bonney and Amelia Quinton initially called the group "The Indian Treaty-Keeping and Protective Association." The name "Women's National Indian Association" was adopted in 1883.

17. Francis Prucha, *American Indian Policy in Crisis: Christian Reformers and the Indian, 1865–1900* (Norman, Okla., 1976), chap. 4; Robert Mardock, *The Reformers and the American Indian* (Columbia, Mo., 1971), chaps. 9–11. Susette LaFlesche's life is recounted in Dorothy Wilson, *Bright Eyes: The Story of Susette LaFlesche, an Omaha Indian* (New York, 1974); and Margaret Crary, *Susette LaFlesche: Voice of the Omaha Indians* (New York, 1973).

18. Wanken, " 'Woman's Sphere' and Indian Reform," pp. 59–61. The Connecticut branch, displaying typical independence, was reluctant to give credit for the group's organization to Quinton. Instead, its members traced its roots to an 1880 meeting at which Kinney and four other Hartford women, assembled for a different purpose, proposed beginning work for Indian reform. See Ellen Johnson, *Historical Sketch of the Connecticut Indian Association from 1881 to 1888* (Hartford, Conn., 1888), box 6, Thomson-Kinney Papers, CSA.

19. Daughters of the American Revolution of Connecticut, *In Memoriam: Sara Thomson Kinney* (Windsor, Connecticut, 1923).

20. L. M. Hensel, *Report of Our Omaha Mission* (Philadelphia, Pa., 1888); WNIA, *Report on Missionary Work* (Philadelphia, Pa., 1888), pp. 5–6; WNIA, *Report of Missionary Work* (Philadelphia, Pa., 1889), pp. 3–4.

21. U.S. Congress, Senate, *Record of Indian Students Returned from Hampton Institute*, S. Ex. Doc. 31, 52nd Cong., 1st sess., February 9, 1892; WNIA, *Our Work: What? How? Why?* (Philadelphia, Pa., 1893), pp. 18–23; Wanken, " 'Woman's Sphere' and Indian Reform," pp. 153–81.

22. WNIA, *Annual Meeting and Report*, 1892, p. 10.

23. WNIA, *Annual Meeting and Report*, 1888, p. 9.

24. WNIA, *Annual Meeting and Report*, 1883, pp. 15–16; WNIA, *Missionary Work of the WNIA* (Philadelphia, Pa., 1884), p. 1; Wanken, " 'Woman's Sphere' and Indian Reform," pp. 137–39.

25. John Mack Faragher, *Women and Men on the Overland Trail* (New Haven, Conn., 1979); John Mack Faragher and Christine Stansell, "Women and Their Families on the Overland Trail, 1842–1867," *Feminist Studies* 2 (1975): 150–60; Julie Roy Jeffrey, *Frontier Women: The Trans-Mississippi West, 1840–1880* (New York, 1979); Carolyn Stefanco, "Pathways to Power: Women and Voluntary Associations in Denver, Colorado, 1876–1893" (Ph.D. diss., Duke Univ., 1987), pp. 96–97, 108, 113, 133, 231; Gayle Gullett, "City Mothers, City Daughters, and the Dance Hall Girls: The Limits of Female Political Power in San Francisco, 1913," in Barbara Harris and JoAnn McNamara, eds., *Women and the Structure of Society* (Durham, N.C., 1984), pp. 149–59.

26. Ralph Mann, "Frontier Opportunity and the New Social History," *Pacific Historical Review* 53 (November 1984): 463–91; Gunther Barth, *Instant Cities: Urbanization and the Rise of San Francisco and Denver* (New York, 1975); Peter Decker, *Fortunes and Failures: White Collar Mobility in Nineteenth-Century San Francisco* (Cambridge, Mass., 1978); Robert Tank, "Mobility and Occupational Structure on the Late Nineteenth-Century Urban Frontier: The Case of Denver, Colorado," *Pacific Historical Review* 47 (May 1978): 189–216.

27. Carol Roland, "The California Kindergarten Movement: A Study in Class and Social Feminism" (Ph.D. diss., Univ. of California, Riverside, 1980), p. 13. On the development of charities in San Francisco, see M. W. Shinn: "Poverty and Charity in San Francisco, I and II," *Overland Monthly*, November 1889, pp. 535–47, and December 1889, pp. 586–92; and idem, "Charities for Children in San Francisco," *Overland Monthly*, January 1890, pp. 78–100.

28. Mrs. E. V. Robbins, "The Occidental Board, 1873–1911," handwritten reminiscence, 1912, POH, pp. 5–7.

29. Ibid., p. 35.

30. Don Doyle, *The Social Order of a Frontier Community: Jacksonville, Illinois, 1825–1870* (Urbana, Ill., 1978); Gregory Singleton, *Religion in the City of the Angels: American Protestant Culture and Urbanization, Los*

Angeles, 1850–1930 (Ann Arbor, Mich., 1979); Gayle Gullett, "Feminism, Politics, and Voluntary Groups: Organized Womanhood in California, 1886–1896," (Ph.D. diss., Univ. of California, Riverside, 1983).

31. Robbins, "The Occidental Board, 1873–1911," pp. 12–14.

32. As Susan Johnson concluded after a study of the diaries of men in the California gold rush, men, too, wondered "whether or not men had either reason or ability to exercise restraint when apart from their collective better half." Susan Johnson, " 'Into this vortex': Men and the Meaning of Morality in Gold Rush California," (unpublished paper, Yale Univ., October 5, 1987), pp. 4–5.

33. For analyses of the extent to which western entrepreneurs and community builders profited from prostitution and liquor, see Jacqueline Baker Barnhart, *The Fair but Frail: Prostitution in San Francisco, 1840–1900* (Reno, Nev., 1986), pp. 72–81; Thomas Noel, *The City and the Saloon: Denver, 1858–1916* (Lincoln, Nebr., 1982), chap. 5; and Elliott West, *The Saloon on the Rocky Mountain Frontier* (Lincoln, Nebr., 1979), chap. 5. On vice operators' resistance to moral reform, see Neil Shumsky, "Vice Responds to Reform: San Francisco, 1910–1914," *Journal of Urban History* 7 (November 1980): 31–47.

34. Barth, *Instant Cities,* passim. For overviews of political patterns and resistance to moral reform in Denver and San Francisco, see Lyle Dorsett, *The Queen City: A History of Denver* (Boulder, Colo., 1977); and Robert Cherny and William Issel, *San Francisco: Presidio, Port, and Pacific Metropolis* (San Francisco, Calif., 1981).

35. To date, historians have paid more attention to Donaldina Cameron, the most famous matron of the Chinese Mission Home, than to the operation of the institution itself. See Mildred Crowl Martin, *Chinatown's Angry Angel: The Story of Donaldina Cameron* (Palo Alto, Calif., 1977); Laurene Wu McClain, "Donaldina Cameron: A Reappraisal," *Pacific Historian* 27 (Fall 1983): 25–35; and Carol Green Wilson, *Chinatown Quest: The Life Adventures of Donaldina Cameron* (Stanford, Calif., 1931).

36. WFMS-CB, *Annual Report,* 1874, pp. 5–9; Mrs. I. M. Condit, "The Occidental Board: An Historical Sketch," *Occidental Leaves* (San Francisco, Calif., 1893), pp. 8–9; Mrs. H. B. Pinney et al., "The Story of the Decades: A Historical Sketch of the Woman's Occidental Board of Foreign Missions," in WOBFM, *Annual Report,* 1920, p. 9.

37. WFMS-CB, *Annual Report,* 1875.

38. Ibid., pp. 7–8; Condit, "Occidental Board," pp. 8–9; Pinney et al., "Story of the Decades," p. 10.

39. Lucie Cheng Hirata, "Free, Endentured, Enslaved: Chinese Pros-

titutes in Nineteenth-Century America," *Signs* 5 (1979): 3–29; Sucheng Chan, "Chinese Women in California, 1860–1910: A Demographic Overview," in Chan, ed., *Living Under Exclusion: The Chinese in the United States, 1882–1943* (forthcoming); Barnhart, *Fair but Frail,* pp. 25–39, 45–50.

40. Accounts of the growth of anti-Chinese sentiment include Alexander Saxton, *The Indispensable Enemy: Labor and the Anti-Chinese Movement in California* (Berkeley, Calif., 1971); Ronald Takaki, *Iron Cages: Race and Culture in Nineteenth-Century America* (New York, 1979); Jack Chen, *The Chinese of America* (San Francisco, Calif., 1980); and Elmer Sandmeyer, *The Anti-Chinese Movement in California* (Urbana, Ill., 1939).

41. Mrs. W. H. Hamilton, "Historical Sketch of the Occidental Board For First Seven Years," typed MS, n.d., SFTS, pp. 10–11.

42. Ibid.

43. *Occident,* September 27, 1876; Hamilton, "Historical Sketch," pp. 10–11. On the relationship between blacks and Chinese immigrants, see Leigh Johnsen, "Equal Rights and the 'Heathen Chinee': Black Activism in San Francisco, 1865–75," *Western Historical Quarterly* 11 (January 1980): 57–68; David Hellwig, "Black Reactions to Chinese Immigration and the Anti-Chinese Movement: 1850–1910," *Amerasia* 6 (Fall 1979): 25–44; and Arnold Shankman, "Black on Yellow: Afro-Americans View Chinese Americans, 1850–1935," *Phylon* 39 (Spring 1978): 1–17.

44. Hamilton, "Historical Sketch," pp. 10–11; *Occidental Board Bulletin,* January 1, 1901, pp. 1–2.

45. Mrs. E. V. Robbins, *History of the Woman's Occidental Board of Foreign Missions* (n.p, 1905), p. 7; Lorna Logan, *Ventures in Mission: The Cameron House Story* (Wilson Creek, Wash., 1976), p. 13.

46. Mrs. I. M. Condit, *A Quarter of a Century* (San Francisco, Calif., 1898), pp. 8–9; Hamilton, "Historical Sketch," p. 9.

47. Condit, *Quarter of a Century,* pp. 8–9; WFMS-CB, *Annual Report,* 1876, pp. 4–5; Pinney et al., "Story of the Decades," p. 11.

48. Condit, "Occidental Board," p. 9.

49. *Occident,* August 14, 1878.

50. For a sense of the variety of contexts in which women's historians have found the WCTU to be important, see Epstein, *Politics of Domesticity;* Gordon and DuBois, "Seeking Ecstasy on the Battlefield"; Ellen DuBois, "The Radicalism of the Woman Suffrage Movement: Notes Toward the Reconstruction of Nineteenth-Century Feminism," *Feminist Studies* 3 (Fall 1975): 63–71; Mari Jo Buhle, *Women and American Socialism, 1870–1920* (Urbana, Ill., 1981); and Baker, "Domestication of Politics."

51. Woman's Christian Temperance Union, *Annual Report*, 1884, p. 26.

52. Stefanco, "Pathways to Power," pp. 95–134; Sherilyn Brandenstein, "The Colorado Cottage Home," *Colorado Magazine* 53 (Summer 1976): 229–42.

53. Daniel Scott Smith, "The Long Cycle in American Illegitimacy and Prenuptial Pregnancy," in Peter Laslett et al., eds., *Bastardy and Its Comparative History* (Cambridge, Mass., 1980), pp. 370–71; Daniel Scott Smith, "The Dating of the American Sexual Revolution: Evidence and Interpretation," in Michael Gordon, ed., *The American Family in Social-Historical Perspective*, 2nd ed. (New York, 1978), p. 435; Daniel Scott Smith and Michael Hindus, "Premarital Pregnancy in America, 1640–1971: An Overview and Interpretation," *Journal of Interdisciplinary History* 5 (Spring 1975): 537–70.

54. David Brundage, "The Producing Classes and the Saloon: Denver in the 1880s," *Labor History* 26 (Winter 1985): 31, 33.

55. Catherine Beach, "Beginnings of Cottage Home Work," *WCTU Messenger,* November 1906; "Promoted," *WCTU Messenger,* March 1912; *Union Signal* clipping, hand-dated January 31, 1889, folder 15, box 7, CWCTU Collection, UC.

56. Beach, "Beginnings of Cottage Home Work"; "Inception of the Cottage Home," *WCTU Messenger,* November 1904.

57. The membership figure is from 1888. For a sense of the enthusiasm Union members felt for the venture, see CWCTU, *Annual Report,* 1889, p. 34, and 1895, pp. 58–59.

58. CWCTU, *Annual Report,* 1888, p. 22; "Cottage Home Closed," *Denver Times,* April 16, 1903.

59. CWCTU, *Annual Report,* 1889, p. 21.

60. For similar examples, see Katherine Harris, "Feminism and Temperance Reform in the Boulder WCTU," *Frontiers* 4 (Summer 1979): 20; and idem, "A Study of Feminine and Class Identity in the WCTU, 1920–1979," *Historicus* 1 (Fall–Winter 1981): 57.

61. Stefanco, "Pathways to Power," p. 108.

62. "History of the State Union," folder 3, box 5, CWCTU Collection, UC; CWCTU, *Annual Report,* 1893, pp. 48–49, and 1894, p. 42.

63. The only account of the Industrial Christian Home is Gustive Larson, "An Industrial Home for Polygamous Wives," *Utah Historical Quarterly* 38 (Summer 1970): 263–75.

64. Frances Willard, introduction to *The Women of Mormonism; or, The Story of Polygamy as Told by the Victims Themselves,* ed. Jennie Froiseth (Detroit, Mich., 1882), p. xviii.

65. Nineteenth-century political alignments in Salt Lake City can be followed in Thomas Alexander and James Allen, *Mormons and Gentiles: A History of Salt Lake City* (Boulder, Colo., 1984); Leonard Arrington and Davis Bitton, *A History of the Latter-day Saints* (New York, 1979), chap. 9; and Richard Poll, ed., *Utah's History* (Provo, Utah, 1978), chaps. 13–14.

66. Cornelia Paddock, "An Industrial Home for Mormon Women," *Christian Register,* January 7, 1886. Paddock noted that the Mormon, Episcopal, and Catholic hospitals were exceptions to her generalization, but, like most evangelical Protestant women, she considered these organizations insufficient. "We have," she said, "no orphan asylums, no reformatories, no homes for the aged, no asylums for the blind, no schools for the feeble-minded, no infirmaries,—nothing, in fact, which, elsewhere, comes under the head of charities and reforms." Paddock was well known in home mission circles for her sensational anti-Mormon novel, *The Fate of Madame LaTour: A Tale of Great Salt Lake* (New York, 1881).

67. There is an enormous literature on the institution of Mormon polygamy. The best recent study is Lawrence Foster, *Religion and Sexuality: Three American Communal Experiments of the Nineteenth Century* (New York, 1981); but see also Louis Kern, *An Ordered Love: Sex Roles and Sexuality in Victorian Utopias—The Shakers, the Mormons, and the Oneida Community* (Chapel Hill, N.C., 1981); and Jessie Embry, *Mormon Polygamous Families: Life in the Principle* (Salt Lake City, Utah, 1987).

68. Although the earliest demographic studies of polygamy found that only 10%–20% of Mormon men practiced polygamy, recent work based on more complete source materials has netted considerably higher figures. The shift can be followed in: Davis Bitton, "Mormon Polygamy: A Review Article," *Journal of Mormon History* 4 (1977): 101–18; Phillip Kunz, "One Wife or Several? A Comparative Study of Late Nineteenth-Century Marriage in Utah," in Thomas Alexander, ed., *The Mormon People: Their Character and Traditions* (Provo, Utah, 1980), pp. 53–74; Larry Logue, "A Time of Marriage: Monogamy and Polygamy in a Utah Town," *Journal of Mormon History* 11 (1984): 3–26; and Lowell "Ben" Bennion, "The Incidence of Mormon Polygamy in 1880: 'Dixie' versus Davis Stake," *Journal of Mormon History* 11 (1984): 27–42.

69. The tension Mormon women felt is evident in their diaries and personal accounts. Perhaps the most evocative of these is Annie Clark Tanner, *A Mormon Mother: An Autobiography* (Salt Lake City, Utah, 1969).

70. Helen Mar Whitney, *Why We Practice Plural Marriage, by a Mormon Wife and Mother* (Salt Lake City, Utah, 1884); *Mormon Women's Protest: An Appeal for Freedom, Justice and Equal Rights* (Salt Lake City,

Utah, 1886); Richard Burton, *City of the Saints,* ed. Fawn Brodie (New York, 1963), pp. 484–93. For interpretations, see Jeffrey, *Frontier Women,* pp. 147–78; Julie Dunfey, " 'Living the Principle' of Plural Marriage: Mormon Women, Utopia, and Female Sexuality in the Nineteenth Century," *Feminist Studies* 10 (Fall 1984): 523–36; Kathleen Marquis, " 'Diamond Cut Diamond': Mormon Women and the Cult of Domesticity in the Nineteenth Century," *University of Michigan Papers in Women's Studies* 2 (1974): 105–23; and Joan Iverson, "Feminist Implications of Mormon Polygamy," *Feminist Studies* 10 (Fall 1984): 505–22.

71. *Salt Lake Evening Chronicle,* November 7, 1882, p. 2, quoted in Thomas Lyon, "Evangelical Protestant Missionary Activities in Mormon Dominated Areas: 1865–1900," (Ph.D. diss., Univ. of Utah, 1962), p. 241. The best analysis of the ideology of non-Mormon women is Dunfey, " 'Living the Principle.' "

72. Grossberg, *Governing the Hearth,* pp. 120–26; Gustive Larson, "Government, Politics and Conflict" and "The Crusade and the Manifesto," in Poll, ed., *Utah's History,* chaps. 13 and 14; Gustive Larson, *The "Americanization" of Utah for Statehood* (San Marino, Calif., 1971); Howard Lamar, *The Far Southwest: A Territorial History* (New Haven, Conn., 1966); Robert Dwyer, *The Gentile Comes to Utah: A Study in Religious and Social Conflict, 1862–1890* (Washington, D.C., 1941).

73. This conclusion is based on my examination of two dozen such novels written by women. Typical examples include Jeannette Walworth, *The Bar-Sinister: A Mormon Study* (Rathway, N.J., 1885); and Jennie Bartlett, *Elder Northfield's Home; or, Sacrificed on the Mormon Altar* (New York, 1882).

74. The most significant of the apostate accounts are Ann Eliza Young, *Wife No. 19, or The Story of a Life in Bondage* (Hartford, Conn., 1875); and Fanny Stenhouse, *Tell It All: The Story of a Life's Experience in Mormonism* (Hartford, Conn., 1874).

75. The only existing study of the Ladies' Anti-Polygamy Society is Barbara Hayward, "Utah's Anti-Polygamy Society, 1878–1884" (M.A. thesis, Brigham Young Univ., 1980). The Society's call to action, written by famed antislavery novelist Harriet Beecher Stowe, was taken from Stowe's introduction to Stenhouse, *Tell It All.*

76. Edward James, ed., *Notable American Women, 1607–1950: A Biographical Dictionary* (Cambridge, Mass., 1971), 2:620–22; Frances Willard and Mary Livermore, eds., *A Woman of the Century* (Buffalo, N.Y., 1813), p. 534; Albert Watkins, ed., *History of Nebraska* (Lincoln, Nebr., 1913), 3:742–43; Ernest Cherrington, ed., *Standard Encyclopedia of the Alcohol Problem* (Westerville, Ohio, 1928), 14:1914–15.

77. Angie Newman, quoted in James, ed., *Notable American Women,* 2:621.

78. Woman's Home Missionary Society, *Annual Report,* 1882–83, pp. 15–17.

79. Woman's Home Missionary Society, *Annual Report,* 1883–84, pp. 49, 66–68, and 1884–85, p. 58; "The Industrial Home," *Salt Lake Tribune,* March 16, 1886.

80. "The Industrial Home," *Salt Lake Tribune,* March 16, 1886; "A Philanthropic Enterprise," *Salt Lake Tribune,* March 19, 1886.

81. U.S. Congress, Senate, S. Rept. 1279, 49th Cong., 1st sess., June 5, 1886.

82. "The Proposed Industrial Home," *Deseret News,* October 20, 1886, p. 639; "Something More About the Industrial Home," *Deseret News,* October 27, 1886, p. 647.

83. These letters are reprinted in U.S. Congress, Senate, S. Rept. 1279, 49th Cong., 1st sess., June 5, 1886.

84. "Utah Again Before Congress," Journal History of the Church of Jesus Christ of Latter-day Saints, October 3, 1888, LDS.

85. Angie Newman to Grover Cleveland, November 18, 1886, U.S. Interior Department, Territorial Papers, Utah, 1850–1902, Letters Received Relating to Polygamy, January 27, 1879–December 17, 1897, NA.

86. U.S. Congress, S. Ex. Doc. 57, 50th Cong., 1st sess., January 14, 1888; Jeannette Ferry, *The Industrial Christian Home Association of Utah,* (Salt Lake City, Utah, 1893), pp. 19–20, 63. For a typical Mormon reaction, see "The Law Is the Lion in the Way," *Deseret Evening News,* Journal History of the Church of Jesus Christ of Latter-day Saints, October 16, 1886, LDS.

87. "Mrs. Newman's Remarks," *Salt Lake Tribune,* October 12, 1887.

88. U.S. Congress, House of Representatives, H. Mis. Doc. 6, 52nd Cong., 2nd sess., December 5, 1892, p. 4.

89. "Industrial Christian Home," *Salt Lake Tribune,* October 18[?], 1887; Ferry, *Industrial Christian Home,* p. 62.

90. U.S. Congress, Senate, S. Ex. Doc. 57, 50th Cong., 1st sess., January 14, 1888; "The National Capital," *Salt Lake Tribune,* December 30, 1887.

91. "Mrs. Newman's Petition Criticized," *Woman's Exponent,* July 15, 1886, p. 28; "Pursuing Its Old Vile Methods," *Deseret News,* March 27, 1890, in Dyer scrapbooks, USHS.

92. Industrial Christian Home Association flier, reprinted in U.S. Congress, Senate, S. Mis. Doc. 31, 51st Cong., 1st sess., December 19, 1889.

93. U.S. Congress, Senate, S. Mis. Doc. 34, 51st Cong., 1st sess., December 19, 1889; "Utah Industrial Home," *Salt Lake Tribune,* October

3, 1888; "Utah Industrial Home," *Salt Lake Tribune,* October 9, 1888; "The Industrial Home," *Salt Lake Tribune,* December 5, 1888.

94. U.S. Congress, Senate, S. Mis. Doc. 15, 51st Cong., 2nd sess., December 9, 1891, p. 4.

95. "The Public Buildings for Salt Lake City, Utah. A Plan for Limiting Its Cost to a Sum Not Exceeding $75,000.00," carbon of original MS, LDS.

96. The motivations of the syndicate members were discussed in local newspaper coverage, including "The Industrial Home Threatened," *Salt Lake Tribune,* February 10, 1890; "For the East Side," *Salt Lake Herald,* March 14, 1890; "The Public Building Job," *Salt Lake Tribune,* March 15, 1890; untitled clipping, *Salt Lake Herald,* March 15, 1890; "Gaze on the Noble Army," *Salt Lake Tribune,* March 22, 1890; and "The Federal Building," *Salt Lake Herald,* March 28, 1890; all in Dyer scrapbooks, USHS. Salt Lake City directories for 1890 confirm the East Side addresses of the syndicate members.

97. See, for example, "The East Side Will Relent," *Salt Lake Tribune,* March 28, 1890; and "The Government Building," *Deseret News,* March 15, 1890, both in Dyer scrapbooks, USHS.

98. U.S. Congress, Senate, S. Mis. Doc. 15, 51st Cong., 2nd sess., December 9, 1891, p. 4.

Chapter 2: The Ideology of Female Moral Authority, 1874–1900

1. Winifred Spaulding, "YWCTU Work," *WCTU Bulletin,* January 1892.

2. Glenna Matthews, *"Just a Housewife": The Rise and Fall of Domesticity in America* (New York, 1987), p. 19; Colleen McDannell, *The Christian Home in Victorian America, 1840–1900* (Bloomington, Ind., 1986); Maxine Van de Wetering, "The Popular Concept of 'Home' in Nineteenth-Century America," *Journal of American Studies* 18 (April 1984): 5–28. It is important to emphasize that this domestic ideology bore no necessary resemblance to household reality. The gap between the two is explored in Mary Ryan, "The Explosion of Family History," *Reviews in American History* 10 (December 1982): 180–95.

3. Herbert Ross Brown, *The Sentimental Novel in America* (Durham, N.C., 1942); F. L. Pattee, *The Feminine Fifties* (New York, 1942); Helen Waite Papashvily, *All the Happy Endings* (New York, 1956).

4. The best-known of these is Christopher Lasch, *Haven in a Heartless World: The Family Besieged* (New York, 1977).

5. The best-known of these is Barbara Welter, "The Cult of True Womanhood."

6. Although I have chosen to refer to it as "Victorian," there is little scholarly agreement about how to designate the form of marriage that emerged in the early nineteenth century. Two terms—*democratic,* favored by Steven Mintz and Susan Kellogg, and *republican,* favored by Robert Griswold and Michael Grossberg—imply a degree of individual egalitarianism that better fits Victorian men than women. Carl Degler's term, *modern,* minimizes the changes that occurred in the early twentieth century. Although several historians, including Degler, Griswold, and Ellen Rothman, have emphasized the "companionate" aspects of Victorian marriages, others, including Christina Simmons, Elaine Tyler May, John D'Emilio, Estelle Freedman, Nancy Cott, and Margaret Marsh, note that the term *companionate* and the set of expectations for husband–wife intimacy it implies were products of the early twentieth century. See Steven Mintz and Susan Kellogg, *Domestic Revolutions: A Social History of American Family Life* (New York, 1988), pp. xvi, 43–65, 107–31; Robert Griswold, *Family and Divorce in California, 1850–1890: Victorian Illusions and Everyday Realities* (Albany, N.Y., 1982); pp. 1–17; Grossberg, *Governing the Hearth,* pp. 4–9; Carl Degler, *At Odds: Women and the Family in America from the Revolution to the Present* (New York, 1980), pp. 3–25; Ellen Rothman, *Hands and Hearts: A History of Courtship in America* (New York, 1984); Christina Simmons, "Companionate Marriage and the Lesbian Threat," *Frontiers* 4 (1979): 54–59; idem, " 'Marriage in the Modern Manner': Sexual Radicalism and Reform in America, 1914–1941," (Ph.D. diss., Brown Univ., 1982), especially pp. vi, vii, xii; Elaine Tyler May, *Great Expectations: Marriage and Divorce in Post-Victorian America* (Chicago, 1980); D'Emilio and Freedman, *Intimate Matters,* pp. 265–70; Cott, *Grounding of Modern Feminism,* pp. 156–58; and Margaret Marsh, "Suburban Men and Masculine Domesticity, 1870–1915," *American Quarterly* 49 (June 1988): 165–86.

7. Freedman, *Their Sisters' Keepers;* Epstein, *Politics of Domesticity;* Smith-Rosenberg, "Beauty, the Beast, and the Militant Woman"; Ryan, "Power of Women's Networks"; Rosen, *Lost Sisterhood.*

8. On this point, see Linda Gordon, who has referred to the transition from traditional to Victorian marriages as the "reconstruction of patriarchy" in "Child Abuse, Gender, and the Myth of Family Independence: A Historical Critique," *Child Welfare* 64 (May–June 1985): 213–15. See also Lebsock, *Free Women of Petersburg,* pp. 15–53; Faragher, *Women and Men on the Overland Trail;* and Gordon, *Heroes of Their Own Lives,*

pp. 57–58. It is instructive to compare dynamics within the Victorian family to those of the black slave family, where men were prevented from exercising the Victorian privileges of white middle-class husbands. See Willie Lee Rose, "The Domestication of Domestic Slavery," in Rose, *Slavery and Freedom* (New York, 1982); Angela Davis, *Women, Race, and Class* (New York, 1981), pp. 1–29; Deborah Gray White, *Ar'n't I a Woman?: Female Slaves in the Plantation South* (New York, 1985), chap. 5; and Jacqueline Jones, *Labor of Love, Labor of Sorrow: Black Women, Work, and the Family from Slavery to the Present* (New York, 1985), pp. 30–43. On the extent to which marriage remained a "labor contract" in the 1920s and 1930s, see Cott, *Grounding of Modern Feminism*, pp. 185–95.

9. Grossberg, *Governing the Hearth*, pp. 246–47, 251–53; Norma Basch, *In the Eyes of the Law: Women, Marriage, and Property in Nineteenth-Century New York* (Ithaca, N.Y., 1982).

10. Charles Rosenberg, "Sexuality, Class, and Role in Nineteenth-Century America," *American Quarterly* 25 (May 1973): 131–53; Daniel Scott Smith, "Family Limitation, Sexual Control, and Domestic Feminism in Victorian America," *Feminist Studies* 1 (Winter–Spring 1973): 40–58.

11. Rosen, *Lost Sisterhood*, p. 52; Ronald Howard, *A History of American Family Sociology, 1865–1900* (Westport, Conn., 1981), p. 19.

12. This reluctance was widespread among Victorian women reformers, as shown in Linda Gordon, *Woman's Body, Woman's Right: Birth Control in America* (New York, 1977), p. 110; Epstein, *Politics of Domesticity*, chap. 5; DuBois, "Radicalism of the Woman Suffrage Movement"; Gordon and DuBois, "Seeking Ecstasy on the Battlefield"; Brumberg, "Zenanas and Girlless Villages"; and Elizabeth Pleck, "Feminist Responses to 'Crimes against Women,' 1868–1896," *Signs* 8 (Spring 1983): 451–70.

13. Many of the same points were made by temperance workers and foreign missionary women. See Pleck, *Domestic Tyranny*, pp. 49–66; and Joan Jacobs Brumberg, "The Ethnological Mirror: American Evangelical Women and Their Heathen Sisters, 1870–1910," in Harris and McNamara, *Women and the Structure of Society*, pp. 108–28.

14. See, for example, CWCTU, *Annual Report*, 1893, p. 34, and 1894, p. 41.

15. Spaulding, "YWCTU Work."

16. Elizabeth Pleck found a similar dynamic in the Chicago Protective Agency for Women and Children. See Pleck, *Domestic Tyranny*, pp. 95–98; and Pleck, "Feminist Responses to 'Crimes against Women,' " pp. 465–67. Home mission policy differed from that of social welfare agencies of the 1940s and 1950s, which, according to Linda Gordon, "shared a

hostility to separation and divorce, and a policy of urging preservation of marriage at almost all costs." Gordon, *Heroes of Their Own Lives,* p. 160.

17. Minutes, June 22, 1887, Minute Book 1, CIA, Thomson-Kinney Papers, CSA.

18. *Bulletin,* December 1894.

19. Sarah Deutsch, *No Separate Refuge: Culture, Class, and Gender on an Anglo-Hispanic Frontier in the American Southwest, 1880–1940* (New York, 1987), pp. 63–86; Hunter, *Gospel of Gentility,* pp. 52–89.

20. Spaulding, "YWCTU Work."

21. "Social Purity," *WCTU Bulletin,* December 1891.

22. This deflection has received a great deal of emphasis in Brumberg, "Zenanas and Girlless Villages"; Gordon and DuBois, "Seeking Ecstasy on the Battlefield"; and Barbara Welter, "'She Hath Done What She Could': Protestant Women's Missionary Careers in Nineteenth-Century America," *American Quarterly* 30 (Winter 1978): 624–38.

23. *Anti-Polygamy Standard,* July 1881, p. 28.

24. Irving Wallace, *The Twenty-Seventh Wife* (New York, 1961), pp. 395–415; James, *Notable American Women,* 3:697.

25. Linda Kerber, *Women of the Republic: Intellect and Ideology in Revolutionary America* (Chapel Hill, N.C., 1980); Mary Beth Norton, *Liberty's Daughters: The Revolutionary Experience of American Women, 1750–1800* (Boston, Mass., 1980), pp. 256–94.

26. WFMS-OBo, *Annual Report,* 1883.

27. D'Emilio and Freedman, *Intimate Matters,* pp. xviii, 150–56; Nancy Cott, "Passionlessness: An Interpretation of Victorian Sexual Ideology, 1790–1850," *Signs* 4 (Winter 1978): 219–36; Degler, *At Odds,* pp. 279–97; Gordon, *Woman's Body, Woman's Right,* pp. 95–115; Smith-Rosenberg, "Beauty, the Beast, and the Militant Woman."

28. CWCTU, *Annual Report,* 1895, pp. 48–49.

29. WFMS-OBo, *Annual Report,* 1882, p. 38, and 1884, pp. 59–63; Woman's Home Missionary Society, *Annual Report,* 1883–84, pp. 61–64; CWCTU, *Annual Report,* 1895, pp. 48–49; CWCTU, *Annual Report,* 1889, pp. 60–61, and 1893, p. 41; WOBFM, *Annual Report,* 1894, p. 14, and 1897, p. 16; *Occident,* May 6, 1897, p. 3.

30. *WCTU Bulletin,* October 16, 1892; CWCTU, *Annual Report,* 1896, p. 11; Alice Hatfield, "An Appeal," *Occident,* May 17, 1899, p. 18.

31. James Buckley, *Constitutional and Parliamentary History of the Methodist Episcopal Church* (New York, 1912), pp. 290–307; Rosemary Skinner Keller, "Creating a Sphere for Women in the Church: How Consequential an Accommodation?" *Methodist History* 18 (January 1980):

83–94. The other women elected were Mary Nind, Amanda Rippey, Lizzie Van Kirk, and temperance leader Frances Willard.

32. Angie Newman, "New Century Church Club," *Union Signal*, July 24, 1890, p. 3; *Christian Advocate*, October 2, 1890, p. 643.

33. *Christian Advocate*, October 2, 1890, p. 643.

34. *Daily Nebraska State Journal*, May 7, 1892, p. 2.

35. *Christian Advocate*, June 2, 1892, p. 360.

36. Saranne O'Donnell, "Distress from the Press: Antifeminism in the Editorials of James Monroe Buckley, 1880–1912," in Hilah Thomas et al., eds., *Women in New Worlds* (Nashville, Tenn., 1982), 2:76–93.

37. Hobson, *Uneasy Virtue*, pp. 66–70; Baker, "Domestication of Politics"; Jack Blocker, "Separate Paths: Suffragists and the Women's Temperance Crusade," *Signs* 10 (Spring 1985): 460–76.

38. Carolyn Stefanco, "Networking on the Frontier: The Colorado Women's Suffrage Movement, 1876–1893," in Armitage and Jameson, *Women's West*, pp. 265–76; Harris, "Feminism and Temperance Reform."

39. "Our Leaders," folder 3, box 5, CWCTU Collection, UC; Stefanco, "Pathways to Power," p. 103.

40. Stefanco, "Pathways to Power," p. 129.

41. CWCTU, *Annual Report*, 1895, pp. 52–53.

42. *WCTU Messenger*, November 1900.

43. Stefanco, "Pathways to Power," p. 187.

44. WNIA, *Annual Meeting and Report*, 1888; Sara Kinney to Mrs. Bull, "Letters, 1888–89," box 4, Thomson-Kinney Papers, CSA; Minutes of executive committee meeting, January 8, 1889, Minute Book 2, CIA, Thomson-Kinney Papers, CSA.

45. WNIA, *Annual Meeting and Report*, 1888, pp. 25–26.

46. Sara Kinney to Mrs. Bull, "Letters, 1888–89," box 4, Thomson-Kinney Papers, CSA.

47. Beverly Beeton, *Women Vote in the West: The Woman Suffrage Movement, 1869–1896* (New York, 1986), pp. 23, 37, 52.

48. Editorials, *Anti-Polygamy Standard*, March 1883.

49. *Woman's Home Missions*, April 1886, p. 53; U.S. Congress, Senate, S. Rept. 1279, 49th Cong., 1st sess., June 5, 1886; Angie Newman, *Woman's Suffrage in Utah*, U.S. Congress, Senate, S. Mis. Doc. 122, 49th Cong., 1st sess., June 8, 1886, p. 9. The issue of suffrage in Utah was troubling even to the most devoted suffrage partisans. National Woman Suffrage Association Vice-President Jennie Froiseth refused the request of well-known Mormon women that she call a meeting to organize Utah suffragists after woman suffrage had been revoked by antipolygamy leg-

islation in 1887. See "The Sister Suffragists," *Salt Lake Tribune,* January 8, 1889; and "The Gulf Between Them," *Salt Lake Tribune,* January 11, 1889.

50. WFMS-OBo, *Annual Report,* 1884, p. 20.

51. WOBFM, *Annual Report,* 1889, p. 44.

52. Ibid.; WFMS-OBo, *Annual Report,* 1887, p. 52; and Mary Browne, "San Francisco Chinese Home and Work," *Woman's Work,* July 1895, pp. 184–85.

53. WOBFM, *Annual Report,* 1890, pp. 39–40.

54. WFMS-OBo, *Annual Report,* 1884, pp. 39–45.

55. M. G. C. Edholm, "A Stain on the Flag," *The Californian* 1 (1914): 159–70.

56. WOBFM, *Annual Report,* 1896, p. 23.

57. WOBFM, *Annual Report,* 1890, pp. 39–40.

58. WFMS-OBo, *Annual Report,* 1880, p. 36.

59. WFMS-OBo, *Annual Report,* 1879, p. 11.

60. Robbins, *Woman's Occidental Board of Foreign Missions,* p. 7; Logan, *Ventures in Mission,* p. 13. In the twentieth century, when San Francisco mission women supported legislation providing for the deportation of tong members who engaged in the traffic in women, they added a significant demand that "the testimony of any slave girl, be they white, black, or yellow, [be] sufficient, standing alone and of itself, to convict any owner, part-owner, or part-keeper, or any person, knowing of the Chinese system of slavery, who shall visit for immoral purpose any such girl." "Resolution," file #220, CH.

61. For the first, see McClain, "Donaldina Cameron: A Reappraisal"; for the second, Betty Lee Sung, *Mountain of Gold: The Story of the Chinese in America* (New York, 1967); and Thomas Chinn, ed., *A History of the Chinese in California: A Syllabus* (San Francisco, Calif., 1969), who reacted to the earlier, sensationalized accounts such as Alexander MacLeod, *Pigtails and Gold Dust: A Panorama of Chinese Life in Early California* (Caldwell, Idaho, 1948); and Richard Dillon, *The Hatchet Men: The Story of the Tong Wars in San Francisco's Chinatown* (New York, 1962).

62. Hirata, "Free, Endentured, Enslaved"; Judy Yung, *Chinese Women of America: A Pictorial History* (Seattle, Wash., 1986); Sucheng Chan, "The Exclusion of Chinese Women, 1874–1943"; and idem, "Chinese Women in California."

63. WFMS-OBo, *Annual Report,* 1885, pp. 44–52.

64. James Axtell, ed., *The Indian Peoples of Eastern America: A Documentary History of the Sexes* (New York, 1981), pp. 103–40; Berkhofer, *White Man's Indian,* p. 6; Roy Pearce, *The Savages of America: A Study*

of the Indian and the Idea of Civilization, rev. ed. (Baltimore, Md., 1976), p. 93.

65. Rayna Green, "The Pocahontas Perplex: The Image of Indian Women in American Culture," *Massachusetts Review* 16 (1975): 698–714; Katherine Weist, "Beasts of Burden and Menial Slaves: Nineteenth Century Observations of Northern Plains Indian Women," in Patricia Albers and Beatrice Medicine, eds., *The Hidden Half: Studies of Plains Indian Women* (Washington, D.C., 1983), pp. 29–52; Glenda Riley, "Some European (Mis)Perceptions of American Indian Women," *New Mexico Historical Review* 59 (July 1984): 237–66.

66. "Indian Mothers and Indian Girls," *Indian's Friend,* June 1890, p. 1; "Mrs. Dorchester's Plea for Indian Girls and Women," *Bulletin,* November 1890, Scrapbook 1, CIA, Thomson-Kinney Papers, CSA.

67. Mrs. Egerton Young, "The Transformed Indian Woman," *Indian's Friend,* March 1898, pp. 9–10.

68. "The Navaho Women," *Indian's Friend,* June 1891, p. 4; "The Navaho Women," *Indian's Friend,* August 1894, pp. 8–9.

69. Sara Kinney, "Helping Indians to Help Themselves," *Indian's Friend,* February 1890, pp. 1, 3; Young, "Transformed Indian Woman"; "Woman's Work in Indian Homes," *Indian's Friend,* August 1894, pp. 9–10.

70. Scholars debate the extent to which Indian women enjoyed freedoms denied to their white counterparts, but they agree that nineteenth-century observers generally underestimated their status in native society. See Valerie Sherer Mathes, "A New Look at the Role of Women in Indian Society," *American Indian Quarterly* 2 (1975): 131–39; Clara Sue Kidwell, "The Power of Women in Three American Indian Societies," *Journal of Ethnic Studies* 6 (Fall 1978): 113–22; Priscilla Buffalohead, "Farmers, Warriors, Traders: A Fresh Look at Ojibway Women," *Minnesota History* 48 (Summer 1983): 236–44; Katherine Weist, "Plains Indian Women: An Assessment," in W. Raymond Wood and Margot Liberty, eds., *Anthropology on the Great Plains* (Lincoln, Nebr., 1980), pp. 255–71.

71. Bea Medicine, "American Indian Family: Cultural Change and Adaptive Strategies," *Journal of Ethnic Studies* 8 (Winter 1981): 13–24; John Price, "North American Indian Families," in Charles Mindel and Robert Habenstein, eds., *Ethnic Families in America: Patterns and Variations,* 2nd ed. (New York, 1981), pp. 245–68.

72. *Southern Workman,* February 1885, p. 22.

73. Alice Fletcher, "The Allotted Indian's Difficulties," *Outlook,* April 11, 1896, "Alice Fletcher," box 6, Thomson-Kinney Papers, CSA; Alice Fletcher, "Indian Woman and Her Problems," *Indian's Friend,* October 1899, p. 3.

74. Several scholars have begun to investigate the contradictory effects the inculcation of Christianity had on the status of women in native societies. See especially Carol Devens, "Separate Confrontations: Gender as a Factor in Indian Adaptation to European Colonization in New France," *American Quarterly* 38 (Bibliography 1986): 461–80; Mary Young, "Women, Civilization, and the Indian Question," in Mabel Deutrich and Virginia Purdy, eds., *Clio Was a Woman: Studies in the History of American Women* (Washington, D.C., 1980), pp. 98–112; and Diane Rothenberg, "The Mothers of the Nation: Seneca Resistance to Quaker Intervention," in Mona Etienne and Eleanor Leacock, eds., *Women and Colonization: Anthropological Perspectives* (New York, 1980), pp. 63–87.

75. Hobson, *Uneasy Virtue,* pp. 56–59, 70–72; Meyerowitz, *Women Adrift,* pp. 48–55; Regina Kunzel, "From Seduced Victim to Sex Delinquents: Evangelicals, Social Workers, and Unmarried Mothers, 1890–1945," paper presented to the American Historical Association, Pacific Coast Branch, San Francisco State University, August 1988.

76. Studies of refuges for unmarried mothers suggest that those that housed largely white populations attracted more interest from reformers—and were less coercive institutions. See Steven Ruggles, "Fallen Women: The Inmates of the Magdalen Society Asylum in Philadelphia, 1836–1908," *Journal of Social History* 16 (Summer 1983): 65–82; Marian Morton, "Seduced and Abandoned in an American City: Cleveland and Its Fallen Women, 1869–1936," *Journal of Urban History* 11 (August 1985): 443–69; and Kunzel, "From Seduced Victims to Sex Delinquents."

77. CWCTU, *Annual Report,* 1895, pp. 48–49. On the meaning of the "betrayal" image, see Joan Jacobs Brumberg, " 'Ruined' Girls: Changing Community Responses to Illegitimacy in Upstate New York, 1890–1920," *Journal of Social History* 18 (Winter 1984): 247–72.

78. "The Colorado Cottage Home," pamphlet, 1897, folder 7, box 7, CWCTU Collection, UC; CWCTU, *Annual Report,* 1899, pp. 68–69.

79. "Mother's Meetings," *WCTU Bulletin,* April 17, 1893.

80. Brumberg, " 'Ruined' Girls"; Mintz and Kellogg, *Domestic Revolutions,* pp. 56–60; Deborah Gorham, "The 'Maiden Tribute of Modern Babylon' Reexamined: Child Prostitution and the Idea of Childhood in Late-Victorian England," *Victorian Studies* 21 (Spring 1978): 353–79.

81. CWCTU, *Annual Report,* 1892, pp. 37–38, 1899, p. 30, 1889, pp. 68–69; Brumberg, " 'Ruined' Girls," pp. 250–52; "In Need of Funds," *Rocky Mountain News,* October 19, 1896.

82. Davis Bitton and Gary Bunker, *The Mormon Graphic Image, 1834–1914: Cartoons, Caricatures, and Illustrations* (Salt Lake City, Utah, 1983); Gail Casterline Farr, "In the Toils or Onward for Zion: Images of the Mormon Woman, 1852–1890" (M.A. thesis, Utah State Univ., 1974).

83. Charles Cannon, "The Awesome Power of Sex: The Polemical Campaign Against Mormon Polygamy," *Pacific Historical Review* 43 (February 1974): 61–82.

84. *Anti-Polygamy Standard,* May 1880, p. 10.

85. Stenhouse, *Tell It All;* Ronald Walker, "The Stenhouses and the Making of a Mormon Image," *Journal of Mormon History* 1 (1974): 51–72.

86. U.S. Congress, Senate, S. Rept. 1279, 49th Cong., 1st sess., June 5, 1886, pp. 16–17.

87. Adelaide Smith, *Womanhood and Polygamy* (New York, n.d.).

88. Young, *Wife No. 19.* The only biography of Young is Wallace, *Twenty-Seventh Wife.*

89. *Anti-Polygamy Standard,* July 1881, p. 28; Froiseth, *Women of Mormonism;* and Paddock, "Industrial Home for Mormon Women."

90. *Anti-Polygamy Standard,* May 1880, p. 10.

91. U.S. Congress, Senate, S. Rept. 1279, 49th Cong., 1st sess., June 5, 1886, p. 14. Angie Newman noted one exception, a law against rape that she commented sarcastically "was evidently framed for the Gentiles."

92. Jennie Froiseth, "The Home and Mormonism," *Home Science* 1 (October 1884): 226–32.

93. Foster, *Religion and Sexuality,* pp. 216–20; Embry, *Mormon Polygamous Families,* pp. 178–79.

94. Froiseth, "Home and Mormonism," p. 227.

95. Whitney, *Why We Practice Plural Marriage; Mormon Women's Protest;* and Burton, *City of the Saints;* U.S. Congress, Senate, S. Rept. 1279, 49th Cong., 1st sess., June 4, 1886, p. 44, letter of Mormon women to Senate Committee on Education and Labor.

96. Dunfey, " 'Living the Principle.' "

97. Angie Newman, "Protest of a Loyal Woman," *Salt Lake Tribune,* March 9, 1886.

98. Mary Tanner, "Reasoning on Mrs. Newman's Statements," *Woman's Exponent,* August 15, 1886, pp. 41–42.

Chapter 3: Some Women's Culture and Other Women's Needs: Motivations, Maternalism, and the Language of Gratitude

1. Information about Chin Leen* is in file #14, CH.

2. "China Girl Kidnapped from Mate," *San Francisco Bulletin,* November 26, 1927; "Chinese Girl Bride Stolen from Groom," *San Francisco Examiner,* November 26, 1927, file #14, CH.

*Pseudonym.

3. Ethel Higgins, typescript, file #14, CH.

4. Frank Wong* to Donaldina Cameron, December 1, 1927, file #14, CH.

5. Donaldina Cameron to Rev. W. M. Case, December 31, 1927, file #14, CH.

6. Donaldina Cameron to Frank Wong*, December 8, 1927, file #14, CH.

7. "Chinese Girl Bride to Be Sent Home," *San Francisco Examiner,* November 27, 1927, file #14, CH.

8. For an introduction to this divided literature, see Walter Trattner, "Introduction: The State of the Field—And the Scope of the Work," in *Social Welfare in America: An Annotated Bibliography* (Westport, Conn., 1983), pp. xvii–xxx.

9. Margaret Culbertson biographical file, POH; "The Industrial Home," *Salt Lake Tribune,* September 3, 1889; WFMS-CB, *Annual Report,* 1876, p. 18; "The Industrial Home," *Salt Lake Tribune,* October 14, 1886; *WCTU Messenger,* February 1907.

10. Martin, *Chinatown's Angry Angel,* especially pp. 25–59; Barbara Sicherman and Carol Hurd Green, eds., *Notable American Women: The Modern Period* (Cambridge, Mass., 1980), pp. 130–32.

11. WFMS-OBr, *Annual Report,* 1881, pp. 42–43.

12. "As Seen by a Visitor," *WCTU Messenger,* May 1907; "Year of the Cottage Home," *WCTU Messenger,* June 1905; "Cottage Home," pamphlet, circa 1925, folder 7, box 7, CWCTU Collection, UC.

13. *Woman's Work,* July 1892, p. 179; WOBFM, *Annual Report,* 1896, p. 66; WFMS-OBr, *Annual Report,* 1878, p. 7.

14. "Indignantly Denied," *Rocky Mountain News,* June 23, 1891, p. 4; WOBFM, *Annual Report,* 1903, pp. 54–55.

15. "Charges Not Sustained," *Salt Lake Tribune,* April 10, 1887.

16. WOBFM, *Annual Report,* 1895, p. 57; CWCTU, *Annual Report,* 1906, pp. 70–72; Ethel Higgins to Mrs. C. S. Brattan, February 19, 1921, file #109, CH; Ethel Higgins to C. W. Mathews, August 28, 1922, file #108, CH.

17. See, for example, Catharine Beecher and Harriet Beecher Stowe, *The American Woman's Home* (New York, 1869), pp. 13–19.

18. Many historians have assumed that a sharp split exists between women's "private" and men's "public" activities; but of late, historians of women have been urged to move "beyond the public-private dichotomy," to borrow the title from the Seventh Berkshire Conference on the

*Pseudonym.

History of Women, held at Wellesley College in June 1987. Historians who question the dichotomy emphasize, as I have in Chapter 2 of this book, the ways women participated in public activities in spite of their assignment to a "private" sphere. Despite its analytic drawbacks, the dichotomy was a widespread convention of Victorian family and gender discourse.

19. CWCTU, *Annual Report*, 1893, p. 109.

20. *Occident*, February 18, 1880, p. 6.

21. Grace King, "Presbyterian Chinese Mission Home," MS report for California State Board of Charities and Corrections, November–December 1919, p. 9, Cadwallader Papers, SFTS.

22. "Executive Meeting," *WCTU Bulletin*, April 3, 1893; CWCTU, *Annual Report*, 1893, p. 13; *Occident*, April 13, 1881, p. 7.

23. "Easter at the Cottage Home," *WCTU Messenger*, May 1906; "Christmas at Cottage Home," *WCTU Messenger*, January 1922.

24. *Occidental Board Bulletin*, November 1, 1901, p. 15.

25. WFMS-CB, *Annual Report*, 1876, pp. 20–21; WOBFM, *Annual Report*, 1895, pp. 58–59; *Occidental Board Bulletin*, November 1, 1901, p. 15; King, "Presbyterian Chinese Mission Home," p. 9.

26. U.S. Congress, House of Representatives, H. Mis. Doc. 6, 52nd Cong., 2nd sess., December 5, 1892, p. 3; Ferry, *Industrial Christian Home*, p. 18.

27. "Life in the Home," *WCTU Messenger*, February 1907, "Mrs. F. I. Smith," *WCTU Messenger*, June 1914.

28. Woman's Home Missionary Society, *Annual Report*, 1883–84, pp. 61–64; U.S. Congress, Senate, S. Rept. 1279, 49th Cong., 1st sess., June 5, 1886, p. 34.

29. "Charges Not Sustained," *Salt Lake Tribune*, April 10, 1887; U.S. Congress, House of Representatives, H. Mis. Doc. 104, 52nd Cong., 1st sess., February 24, 1892, pp. 4–5.

30. A. B. Williams to Secretary of the Treasury, U.S. Interior Department, Territorial Papers, Utah, 1850–1902, Letters Received Related to Polygamy, January 27, 1879–December 17, 1897, NA.

31. "Charges Not Sustained," *Salt Lake Tribune*, April 10, 1887; U.S. Congress, Senate, S. Mis. Doc. 15, 51st Cong., 2nd sess., December 9, 1890, pp. 2–3.

32. Mrs. L. A. Kelley, "The New Headquarters and Mission Home," *Occidental Leaves* (San Francisco, Calif., 1893), 26–27; WOBFM, *Annual Report*, 1919, pp. 42–51, and 1920, pp. 25–26.

33. "Chinese Mission Home, Industrial Department," 1934 correspondence file, CH.

34. *Far West,* November 1919, p. 18; King, "Presbyterian Chinese Mission Home," pp. 10–11; "The Campers Return," *"920" Newsletter,* August 1936.

35. For figures on the number of Chinese women professionals in this period, see Lucie Cheng Hirata, "Chinese Immigrant Women in Nineteenth-Century California," in Carol Berkin and Mary Beth Norton, eds., *Women of America: A History,* pp. 223–41; and Chan, "Chinese Women in California." On the importance of mission-supported education for Chinese American women, see Yung, *Chinese Women of America,* p. 50.

36. See, for example, Rothman, *Discovery of the Asylum;* Anthony Platt, *The Child-Savers: The Invention of Juvenile Delinquency,* 2nd ed. (Chicago, Ill., 1977); and David Rothman, *Conscience and Convenience: The Asylum and Its Alternatives in Progressive America* (Boston, Mass., 1980).

37. Even in the case of coercive institutions, recent research by historians of women has revealed that a surprisingly high percentage of institutional commitments originated in requests from neighbors or relatives rather than from reformers. See Gordon, *Heroes of Their Own Lives,* pp. 38, 83; Pleck, *Domestic Tyranny,* p. 84; Barbara Brenzel, *Daughters of the State: A Social Portrait of the First Reform School for Girls in North America, 1836–1905* (Cambridge, Mass., 1983), pp. 7–8, 88, 119, 122; and Odem, "Working-Class Parents, Delinquent Daughters," p. 1.

38. From the beginning, Mormon women leaders sought to avoid conflict with Mormon men. Eliza Snow, the most prominent Mormon woman of the nineteenth century, the leader of the Female Relief Society, and a celebrated poet, spent a good deal of her time trying to convince Mormon women that they had no interests that should not be subsumed under those of Mormon men. "I have apologies to offer here / For ladies who demand a wider sphere," she once wrote. "They seek with noble, yet with fruitless aim / Corruptions and abuses to reclaim / With all their efforts to remove the curse / Matters are daily growing worse." Eliza Snow, *Poems, Religious, Historical, and Political* 2 (Salt Lake City, Utah, 1877): 173–78. Nonetheless, Mormon women shared a sense of sisterhood sustained by their own female rituals, some of which are examined in Maureen Ursenbach Beecher and Lavina Fielding Anderson, eds., *Sisters in Spirit: Mormon Women in Historical and Cultural Perspective* (Urbana, Ill., November 1987) and in Maureen Ursenbach Beecher, "The 'Leading Sisters': A Female Hierarchy in Nineteenth Century Mormon Society," *Journal of Mormon History* 9 (1982): 25–39.

39. Dunfey, " 'Living the Principle,' " pp. 530–34.

40. "The Industrial Home," *Woman's Exponent,* December 1, 1886, pp. 99–100.

41. "The Industrial Home," *Deseret News,* Journal History of the Church of Jesus Christ of Latter-day Saints, November 8, 1886; Ferry, *Industrial Christian Home,* pp. 18–19.

42. Letter to Senate Committee on Education and Labor, May 12, 1886, in U.S. Congress, Senate, S. Rept. 1279, 49th Cong., 1st sess., June 5, 1886, p. 44.

43. Ferry, *Industrial Christian Home,* pp. 17–18, 26–27; U.S. Congress, Senate, S. Ex. Doc. 57, 50th Cong., 1st sess., January 24, 1888, p. 3.

44. "Priestcraft's Victims," *Salt Lake Tribune,* August 21, 1887.

45. "Charges Not Sustained," *Salt Lake Tribune,* April 10, 1887.

46. Descriptions of some of the cases rejected by the Board of Control were published in Ferry, *Industrial Christian Home,* pp. 19–20.

47. "The First Year's Work," *Salt Lake Tribune,* October 6, 1887.

48. "At the Industrial Home," *Salt Lake Tribune,* October 25, 1887.

49. U.S. Congress, Senate, S. Mis. Doc. 7, 53rd Cong., 2nd sess., December 5, 1893, p. 8.

50. "The Industrial Home," *Salt Lake Tribune,* October 13, 1887.

51. CWCTU, *Annual Report,* 1915, p. 96.

52. The concept of working-class culture was first elaborated for American social historians by Herbert Gutman. See his *Work, Culture, and Society in Industrializing America: Essays in Working-Class and Social History* (New York, 1976).

53. Christine Stansell, *City of Women: Sex and Class in New York, 1789–1860* (New York, 1986), chap. 9; Kathy Peiss, "Charity Girls and City Pleasures: Historical Notes on Working-Class Sexuality, 1880–1920," in Snitow et al., *Powers of Desire,* pp. 74–87; Kathy Peiss, *Cheap Amusements: Working Women and Leisure in Turn-of-the-Century New York* (Philadelphia, Pa., 1986), pp. 109–11; Meyerowitz, *Women Adrift,* pp. 16–17, 104–7.

54. "From the President of the Cottage Home Board," *WCTU Messenger,* August 1909.

55. Hobson, *Uneasy Virtue,* pp. 18–19, 60, 101, 118–24. Many homes for unmarried mothers developed from charitable efforts for prostitutes. See Ruggles, "Fallen Women"; Morton, "Seduced and Abandoned"; and Katherine Aiken, "The National Florence Crittenton Mission, 1883–1925: A Case Study in Progressive Reform" (Ph.D. diss., Washington State Univ., 1980), chap. 1.

56. CWCTU, *Annual Report,* 1889, pp. 68–69.

57. According to Betsy Jameson's analysis, labor leaders in Colorado absorbed a great deal of the middle-class ideal of the genteel family. See

Elizabeth Jameson, "High-Grade and Fissures: A Working-Class History of the Cripple Creek, Colorado, Gold Mining District, 1890–1905," (Ph.D. diss., Univ. of Michigan, 1987), pp. 254–95.

58. Brumberg, " 'Ruined' Girls," p. 250.

59. "Jottings by the Way," *WCTU Messenger*, May 1911.

60. "Cottage Home," *WCTU Messenger*, March 1905.

61. Brundage, "Producing Classes and the Saloon," p. 38.

62. "Cottage Home Report," *WCTU Messenger*, October 1906; "From the President of the Cottage Home Board," *WCTU Messenger*, August 1909; "Colorado Cottage Home," *WCTU Messenger*, November 1905.

63. "From the President of the Cottage Home Board," *WCTU Messenger*, August 1912.

64. Stefanco, "Pathways to Power," p. 107.

65. CWCTU, *Annual Report*, pp. 95–96.

66. "Cottage Home Questions and Answers," *WCTU Messenger*, November 1903.

67. For information on the traditional Chinese gender system, see Margery Wolf and Roxane Witke, eds., *Women in Chinese Society* (Stanford, Calif., 1975). Scholarship on the Chinese family has been flourishing of late, and is too extensive to be reviewed here. For a sense of the issues at stake, see Maurice Freedman, "The Family in China, Past and Present," *Pacific Affairs* 34 (Winter 1961–62): 323–36; Charlotte Ikels, "The Family Past: Contemporary Studies and the Traditional Chinese Family," *Journal of Family History* 6 (Fall 1981): 334–40; and James Watson, "Chinese Kinship Reconsidered: Anthropological Perspectives on Historical Research," *China Quarterly* 92 (December 1982): 589–622.

68. Sue Gronewald, "Beautiful Merchandise: Prostitution in China, 1860–1936," *Women and History*, no. 1 (Spring 1982).

69. Olga Lang, *Chinese Family and Society* (New Haven, Conn., 1946), chap. 4.

70. Margery Wolf, "Women and Suicide in China," in Wolf and Witke, *Women in Chinese Society*, pp. 111–42.

71. Ibid.; Lang, *Chinese Family and Society*, chap. 5.

72. Lang, *Chinese Family and Society*, pp. 53, 108–9; Marjorie Topley, "Marriage Resistance in Rural Kwangtung," in Wolf and Witke, *Women in Chinese Society*, pp. 67–88; Janice Stockard, "Marriage and Marriage Resistance in the Canton Delta, 1860–1930," (Ph.D. diss., Stanford Univ., 1985), pp. 62–70.

73. Chan, "Exclusion of Chinese Women"; George Peffer, "Forbidden Families: Emigration Experiences of Chinese Women Under the Page Law, 1875–1882," *Journal of American Ethnic History* 6 (Fall 1986): 28–46; Vincente Tang, "Chinese Women Immigrants and the Two-Edged

Sword of Habeas Corpus," in Genny Lim, ed., *The Chinese American Experience* (San Francisco, Calif., 1984), pp. 48–56; Stanford Lyman, "Marriage and the Family Among Chinese Immigrants to America, 1850–1960," *Phylon* 29 (Winter 1968): 321–30, 323–24.

74. Hirata, "Chinese Immigrant Women," p. 241; Chan, "Chinese Women in California."

75. Hirata, "Chinese Immigrant Women," p. 237.

76. Hirata, "Free, Endentured, Enslaved," pp. 19–20.

77. See, for example, WOBFM, *Annual Report*, 1894, pp. 33–34; WFMS-OBo, *Annual Report*, 1886, pp. 50–51.

78. WOBFM, *Annual Report*, 1894, pp. 33–34. The earliest reference I have found to this kind of rescue work is in WFMS-OBo, *Annual Report*, 1885, p. 27.

79. *Occident*, July 23, 1884, p. 6; WFMS-OBo, *Annual Report*, 1885, pp. 26–27.

80. Nellie Tong* to Donaldina Cameron, June 25, 1922, file #237, CH.

81. WOBFM, *Annual Report*, 1897, p. 61.

82. WOBFM, *Annual Report*, 1900, p. 73; *Occident*, February 28, 1900, p. 18.

83. *Occident*, May 25, 1881, p. 7.

84. Chan, "Exclusion of Chinese Women."

85. See, for example, *Occident*, November 12, 1890, p. 16; WOBFM, *Annual Report*, 1900, p. 72. Several such cases are included in file #227, CH.

86. WFMS-OBo, *Annual Report*, 1882, p. 33.

87. Typed biographical sketch and letter to Donaldina Cameron, February 22, 1917, file #99, CH; Major Document 56, Box 24, Survey of Race Relations, HI.

88. These numbers have been collected from yearly tabulations in the Home's annual reports.

89. "A Model Refuge," *Salt Lake Herald*, Journal History of the Church of Jesus Christ of Latter-day Saints, April 6, 1887; "The Proposed Refuge," *Salt Lake Herald*, Journal History, November 20, 1886; "The Woman's Home," *Salt Lake Herald*, Journal History, November 24, 1886.

90. "Home Investigation," *Salt Lake Tribune*, April 9, 1887; "Charges Not Sustained," *Salt Lake Tribune*, April 10, 1887.

91. "Home Investigation," *Salt Lake Tribune*, April 9, 1887.

92. "Charges Not Sustained," *Salt Lake Tribune*, April 10, 1887.

93. "Echoes of the Investigation," *Salt Lake Tribune*, April 11, 1887.

---

*Pseudonym.

94. *Occidental Board Bulletin,* February 1, 1901, pp. 1–2.

95. Ibid.

96. WFMS-OBr, *Annual Report,* 1881, p. 45.

97. WOBFM, *Annual Report,* 1889, p. 46, and 1904, pp. 55–56; Frances Cahn and Valeska Bary, *Welfare Activities of Federal, State, and Local Governments in California, 1850–1934* (Berkeley, Calif., 1936); James Leiby, "State Welfare Administration in California, 1879–1929," *Pacific Historical Review* 41 (May 1972): 169–88.

98. These figures range from five (of 88 residents) in 1923 to one (of 30 residents) in 1931. It is, of course, impossible to know whether conflict with Home officials, or more mundane reasons, such as reconciliation with family members, might have motivated such women.

99. See WOBFM, *Annual Report,* 1897, pp. 60–61, and 1899, pp. 74–81.

100. WOBFM, *Annual Report,* 1903.

101. Resident to her friend outside the Mission Home, September 10, 1927, file #158, CH. This letter had been confiscated by mission officials.

102. WOBFM, *Annual Report,* 1898, p. 18. In this case, the comment referred to Margaret Culbertson of the Chinese Mission Home. Such maternalism was widespread among nineteenth-century women reformers in a variety of institutions. On matrons of homes for working girls, for example, see Meyerowitz, *Women Adrift,* pp. 52–53; and Peiss, *Cheap Amusements,* p. 166.

103. The Chinese ideographs for Lo Mo mean "old mother," but "mother" is a colloquial, spoken usage. I am grateful to Judy Yung for assistance interpreting the term. See also Martin, *Chinatown's Angry Angel,* p. 61.

104. McClain, "Donaldina Cameron," p. 30.

105. "From the President of Cottage Home Board," *WCTU Messenger,* February 1908.

106. CWCTU, *Annual Report,* pp. 43–45.

107. "From the President of Cottage Home Board," *WCTU Messenger,* August 1906.

108. Gronewald, "Beautiful Merchandise," p. 9; Medical ledger, CH; "Statement," file #69, CH; "Statement," file #27, CH; California State Senate, Special Committee on Chinese Immigration, *Chinese Immigration: Its Social, Moral, and Political Effect* (Sacramento, Calif., 1878), p. 124. For a suggestive comparison between prison matrons and brothel madams, see Hobson, *Uneasy Virtue,* p. 128.

109. "From the President of Cottage Home Board," *WCTU Messenger,* August 1908.

110. Resident to Donaldina Cameron, February 16, 1925, file #129, CH.

111. Resident to Donaldina Cameron, n.d., 1931 correspondence file, CH.

112. "Corrections on Tentative Report of the Presbyterian Chinese Mission Home, San Francisco, California," May 7, 1935, 1939 correspondence file, CH. Cameron was referring to church attendance, but her remark is generally applicable to the relationship between matrons and residents.

113. "From the President of Cottage Home Board," *WCTU Messenger,* March 1913.

114. Ibid.

115. "Devotional Department," *WCTU Messenger,* September 1914.

116. "Mrs. F. I. Smith, President," *WCTU Messenger,* September 1918.

117. "From the President of Cottage Home Board," *WCTU Messenger,* March 1913.

118. For example, 8 out of 50 in 1905, 3 out of 33 in 1915, and 12 out of 58 in 1925 made this decision.

119. "Cottage Home Nursery," *WCTU Messenger,* August 1910.

120. *Occidental Board Bulletin,* January 1, 1903.

121. See, for example, "Mrs. F. I. Smith, President," *WCTU Messenger,* September 1918; "A Grateful Patient," *WCTU Messenger,* May 1912; "What We Have to Be Thankful For," WFMS-OBo, *Annual Report,* 1886, pp. 57–58; "Letter from Ah Tsun," WFMS-OBr, *Annual Report,* 1881, p. 47.

122. "Cottage Home Report," *WCTU Bulletin,* June 1892.

123. "Mrs. F. I. Smith, President," *WCTU Messenger,* September 1918.

124. See, for example, "From the President of the Cottage Home Board," *WCTU Messenger,* May 1907.

125. "Home Investigation," *Salt Lake Tribune,* April 9, 1887.

126. See, for example, ex-resident to Donaldina Cameron, January 29, 1916, October 21, 1916, and December 4, 1916, file #71, CH.

127. Resident's brother to Donaldina Cameron, April 2, 1912, file #224, CH.

128. "From the President of Cottage Home Board," *WCTU Messenger,* June 1913.

129. "Devotional Report," *WCTU Messenger,* June 1914.

130. Scattered statistics compiled from annual reports suggest that relatively few residents desired baptism, the first step toward conversion. For example, in 1886, 7 out of 50 residents were baptized, apparently the highest figure in a decade. In 1898, 9 out of 67 residents were baptized.

131. Resident to her friend outside the Home, quoted in Ethel Higgins to Mrs. C. S. Brattan, February 19, 1921, file #108, CH.

132. Ethel Abercrombie to Ethel Higgins, August 28, 1928, file #160, CH.

Chapter 4: Home Mission Women, Race, and Culture: The Case of "Native Helpers"

1. Tien Fu Wu to Donaldina Cameron, June 13, 1915, about Ah Ho*, file #269, CH.

2. Maddie* to Donaldina Cameron, June 10, 1915, file #269, CH.

3. Tien Fu Wu to Donaldina Cameron, June 13, 1915, file #269, CH.

4. For several decades, the social science concept of assimilation has set the terms of debate about relations between white and ethnic minority Americans. For the pattern-setting discussion of the issues, see Milton Gordon, *Assimilation in American Life: The Role of Race, Religion, and National Origins* (New York, 1964).

5. Micaela di Leonardo, *The Varieties of Ethnic Experience: Kinship, Class, and Gender among California Italian-Americans* (Ithaca, N.Y., 1984), p. 221.

6. For particularly intelligent discussions of modern concepts, see Barbara Fields, "Ideology and Race in American History," in J. Morgan Kousser and James McPherson, eds., *Region, Race, and Reconstruction: Essays in Honor of C. Vann Woodward* (New York, 1982), pp. 143–78; and Karen Blu, *The Lumbee Problem: The Making of an American Indian People* (London, 1980), p. 7.

7. Berkhofer, *White Man's Indian,* pp. 55–61. On scientific racism, see Horsman, *Race and Manifest Destiny;* John Haller, *Outcasts from Evolution: Scientific Attitudes of Racial Inferiority, 1859–1900* (Urbana, Ill., 1971); William Stanton, *The Leopard's Spots: Scientific Attitudes Toward Race in America, 1815–1859* (Chicago, Ill., 1960); Reginald Horsman, "Scientific Racism and the American Indian in the Mid–nineteenth Century," *American Quarterly* 27 (May 1975): 152–68; Francis Prucha, "Scientific Racism and Indian Policy," in Prucha, *Indian Policy in the United States* (Lincoln, Nebr., 1981), pp. 180–97.

8. "News From Dr. Picotte," *Bulletin,* February 1897.

9. Gossett, *Race,* chap. 7; Stocking, *Race, Culture, and Evolution,* chap. 6.

10. Daniel Joseph Singal, *The War Within: From Victorian to Modernist Thought in the South, 1919–1945* (Chapel Hill, N.C., 1982), p. 5; Henry

---

*Pseudonym.

May, *The End of American Innocence: A Study of the First Years of Our Own Time, 1912–1917* (New York, 1959).

11. For the first, see Prucha, "Scientific Racism and Indian Policy"; and Robert Seager II, "Some Denominational Reactions to Chinese Immigration to California, 1856–1892," *Pacific Historical Review* 28 (February 1959): 59–66; for the second, see Stuart Creighton Miller, *The Unwelcome Immigrant: The American Image of the Chinese, 1785–1882* (Berkeley, Calif., 1969), especially chap. 4. These two extremes do not, of course, exhaust all the possibilities. Some scholars contend that racism and ethnocentrism are sharply distinct phenomena and argue that missionaries could be ethnocentric and anti-racist at the same time. See Michael Coleman, *Presbyterian Missionary Attitudes toward American Indians, 1837–1893* (Jackson, Miss., 1985); and idem, "Presbyterian Missionary Attitudes toward China and the Chinese, 1837–1900," *Journal of Presbyterian History* 56 (Fall 1978): 185–200.

12. *Occidental Board Bulletin,* May 1, 1902, pp. 3–4; *Occident,* April 27, 1887, p. 11.

13. *Far West,* March 1908, p. 6.

14. Ruth Etnier, "Training Indian Girls," *Indian's Friend,* February 1901, p. 2.

15. "Good Cheer" speech, circa 1895, box 5, Thomson-Kinney Papers, CSA.

16. Chinese Mission Home workers also unsuccessfully challenged the San Francisco public school system, which had provided no education at all for Chinese children between 1871 and 1885 and maintained a segregated "Oriental School" from 1885 through the 1920s. See Victor Low, *The Unimpressible Race: A Century of Educational Struggle by the Chinese in San Francisco* (San Francisco, Calif., 1982), p. 96; and Charles Wollenberg, *All Deliberate Speed: Segregation and Exclusion in California Schools, 1855–1975* (Berkeley, Calif., 1976), pp. 28–47.

17. *Occident,* October 27, 1877.

18. Woman's Foreign Missionary Society, *Annual Report,* 1887, p. 34; WFMS-OBo, *Annual Report,* 1889, p. 34.

19. On the changes in racial thought in these years, see Frederick Hoxie, *A Final Promise: The Campaign to Assimilate the Indians, 1880–1920* (Lincoln, Nebr., 1984), pp. 115–45; John Higham, *Strangers in the Land: Patterns of American Nativism, 1860–1925* (1955; reprint, New York, 1978), chaps. 6–11; Stocking, *Race, Culture, and Evolution,* chaps. 3, 10; and Gossett, *Race,* chaps. 7, 14, 15.

20. Philip Jordan, "Immigrants, Methodists and a 'Conservative' Social Gospel, 1865–1908," *Methodist History* 17 (October 1978): 16–43; Seager, "Denominational Reactions"; Wilbert Ahern, "Assimilationist Racism:

The Case of the 'Friends of the Indian,' " *Journal of Ethnic Studies* 4 (1976–1977): 23–32; Hoxie, *A Final Promise,* pp. 115–45; Coleman, *Attitudes toward American Indians,* pp. 161, 164–65.

21. King, "Presbyterian Chinese Mission Home," p. 3: emphasis mine.

22. Resident to friend, September 23, 1927, file #158, CH.

23. Ethel Higgins to resident's mother, October 24, 1928, file #174, CH; *Women and Missions* 5 (1928–29): 184–85.

24. *Woman's Work,* July 1887, p. 169.

25. *Occidental Board Bulletin,* February 1, 1902, p. 4.

26. King, "Chinese Mission Home," p. 3.

27. The first scholars to study missionary women described them as largely unchanged by their encounters with women of different cultures, but recent research is revealing a more complicated pattern of interaction. See especially Deutsch, *No Separate Refuge,* pp. 63–86; Helen Bannan, "Newcomers to Navajoland: Transculturation in the Memoirs of Anglo Women, 1900–1945," *New Mexico Historical Review* 59 (April 1984): 165–185; and Hunter, *Gospel of Gentility,* pp. 128–173.

28. Sara Kinney to Alice Fletcher, Sept. 16, 1897, box 1, Fletcher-LaFlesche Papers, NAA.

29. Donaldina Cameron to Grace Abbott, March 30, 1923, 1923 correspondence file, CH.

30. WOBFM, *Annual Report,* 1904, p. 53.

31. Maddie* to Donaldina Cameron, June 10, 1915, file #269, CH.

32. Ah Ho* to Donaldina Cameron, June 10, 1915, file #269, CH.

33. See Fletcher's landmark anthropological work on the Omaha: Alice Fletcher and Francis LaFlesche, "The Omaha Tribe," *Twenty-seventh Annual Report of the Bureau of American Ethnology, 1905–06* (Washington, D.C., 1911).

34. Accounts of LaFlesche's life include Valerie Sherer Mathes, "Dr. Susan LaFlesche Picotte: The Reformed and the Reformer," in L. G. Moses and Raymond Wilson, eds., *Indian Lives: Essays on Nineteenth- and Twentieth-Century Native American Leaders* (Albuquerque, N.M., 1985), pp. 61–90; Valerie Sherer Mathes, "Susan LaFlesche Picotte: Nebraska's Indian Physician, 1865–1915," *Nebraska History* 63 (Winter 1982): 502–31; Laurence Hauptman, "Medicine Woman: Susan La-Flesche, 1865–1915," *New York State Journal of Medicine,* September 1978, pp. 1783–88; and Norma Kidd, *Iron Eye's Family: The Children of Joseph LaFlesche* (Lincoln, Nebr., 1969), pp. 122–221. See also Norma

---

*Pseudonym.

Kidd, "The Presbyterian Mission to the Omaha Indian Tribe," *Nebraska History* 48 (Autumn 1967): 267–88.

35. For the best recent assessment of the situation of the Omaha in the 1870s, see Clyde Milner, "Off the White Road: Seven Nebraska Indian Societies in the 1870s—A Statistical Analysis of Assimilation, Population, and Prosperity," *Western Historical Quarterly* 12 (January 1981): 37–53; and idem, *With Good Intentions: Quaker Work among the Pawnees, Otos, and Omaha in the 1870s* (Lincoln, Nebr., 1982).

36. "Eighth Annual Report of the CIA," November 5, 1889, Minute Book 2, CIA, Thomson-Kinney Papers, CSA.

37. *Southern Workman,* July 1886, pp. 78, 83.

38. *Hartford Courant,* June 15, 1886, Scrapbook 1, CIA, Thomson-Kinney Papers, CSA.

39. Susan LaFlesche to Sara Kinney, printed in *Hartford Courant,* June 25, 1886, Scrapbook 1, CIA, Thomson-Kinney Papers, CSA.

40. Sara Kinney to Commissioner of Indian Affairs, September 6, 1886, Bureau of Indian Affairs, Letters Received, #23847, 1886, NA.

41. Francis LaFlesche to Ed Farley, September 17, 1886, LaFlesche Papers, NSHS.

42. Sara Kinney to Rosalie LaFlesche Farley, October[?] 1886, LaFlesche Papers, NSHS; "Connecticut Indian Association," *Hartford Courant,* October 8, 1886, Scrapbook 1, CIA, Thomson-Kinney Papers, CSA.

43. Susan LaFlesche to Rosalie LaFlesche Farley, October 14, 1886, LaFlesche Papers, NSHS.

44. Susan LaFlesche to Sara Kinney, April 2, 1888, "Indian Letters, 1883–1891," Box 4, Thomson-Kinney Papers, CSA.

45. Sara Kinney to Commissioner of Indian Affairs, June 29, 1887, Bureau of Indian Affairs, Letters Received, #16996, 1887, NA. In that year, medical college faculty rated students on a scale of points ranging from 660 to 858; LaFlesche scored 777. Minutes of the Faculty Meeting, March 9, 1889, p. 42, MCP. I am grateful to Margaret Jerrido for providing me with this information.

46. Susan LaFlesche to Rosalie LaFlesche Farley: October 27, 1886, December 1, 1886, January 19, 1887, and undated, LaFlesche Papers, NSHS.

47. Susan LaFlesche to Rosalie LaFlesche Farley, undated fragment, LaFlesche Papers, NSHS.

48. "A Delightful Lawn Festival and Fair," *Hartford Courant,* October 5, 1887, Scrapbook 1, CIA, Thomson-Kinney Papers, CSA; *Indian's Friend,* April 1889, p. 2.

49. U.S. Commissioner of Indian Affairs, *Annual Report,* 1890, pp. 321–49, 1891, pp. 609 and 850, and 1893, p. 197; "Talks and Thoughts,"

clipping, circa August 1889, Scrapbook 1, CIA, Thomson-Kinney Papers, CSA.

50. *Hartford Post* clipping, November 26, 1889, Scrapbook 1, CIA, Thomson-Kinney Papers, CSA; *Bulletin,* April 1890; WNIA, *Annual Report,* 1891, p. 20; Sara Kinney, "Indian Home-Building," *Indian's Friend,* April 1889, p. 3; WNIA, *Report of Missionary Department* (Philadelphia, Pa., 1890), p. 9.

51. "A Delightful Lawn Festival and Fair," *Hartford Courant,* October 5, 1887, Scrapbook 1, CIA, Thomson-Kinney Papers, CSA.

52. WFMS-OBr, *Annual Report,* 1878, pp. 9–10.

53. Mrs. E. V. Robbins, *Ten Years Among the Chinese in California* (San Francisco, Calif., 1883), pp. 17–18.

54. WFMS-OBr, *Annual Report,* 1878, pp. 9–10.

55. *Occident,* November 13, 1878, p. 6.

56. *Occident,* January 30, 1884, p. 7.

57. WFMS-OBo, *Annual Report,* 1886, pp. 43–44.

58. Ibid.

59. *Occident,* February 20, 1889, p. 11, and October 28, 1897, p. 13; WOBFM, *Annual Report,* 1889, p. 49, 1891, p. 48, and 1920, pp. 22–23; Mrs. E. V. Robbins, *How Do the Chinese Girls Come to the Mission Home?* (n.p., n.d); Muriel Wing biographical file, POH. It is impossible to trace the date of Wing's husband's death through these sources, but she was a widow by the time she began working for the Mission Home.

60. WOBFM, *Annual Report,* 1894, pp. 38–39; Victor Nee and Brett de Bary Nee, *Longtime Californ': A Documentary Study of an American Chinatown* (New York, 1972), pp. 84–87.

61. "Tien Wu," clipping, Donaldina Cameron file, SFTS.

62. Untitled MS, January 1934, Tien Fu Wu biographical file #2, POH.

63. WOBFM, *Annual Report,* 1905, p. 64.

64. *Pacific Presbyterian,* August 10, 1905, p. 14; WOBFM, *Annual Report,* 1912, pp. 57–58; Nee and Nee, *Longtime Californ',* p. 89.

65. Nee and Nee, *Longtime Californ',* p. 86; WOBFM, *Annual Report,* 1917, p. 35.

66. On the creation of pan-Indian identity, see Hazel Hertzberg, *The Search for an American Indian Identity: Modern Pan-Indian Movements* (Syracuse, N.Y., 1971); Wilbert Ahern, " 'The Returned Indians': Hampton Institute and Its Indian Alumni, 1879–1893," *Journal of Ethnic Studies* 10 (Winter 1983): 101–24; and Sally McBeth, "Indian Boarding Schools and Ethnic Identity: An Example from the Southern Plains Tribes of Oklahoma," *Plains Anthropologist* 28 (May 1983): 119–28.

67. "Extract from Report on Condition of Omaha School," HIA.

68. Susan LaFlesche Picotte to R. G. Valentine, July 13, 1909, HIA.

69. "Translation of letter received by Miss Wu," December 14, 1914, file #44, CH.

70. Letter from resident's father-in-law, file #167, CH.

71. *Occident,* June 30, 1886, p. 11.

72. "From Dr. Susan LaFlesche," *Indian's Friend,* June 1893; "Testimony of Susan LaFlesche Picotte at the Investigation into the Death of Henry Warner, May 22, 1914," folder 1, box 3, LaFlesche Papers, NSHS.

73. *Indian's Friend,* March 1900, pp. 8–9; Rosalie LaFlesche Farley to Francis LaFlesche: January 28, 1894, May 4, 1893, and January 2, 1894; and Susan LaFlesche Picotte diary, September 26, 1910 and January 19, 1911, folder 2, box 3, all in LaFlesche Papers, NSHS.

74. *Indian's Friend,* February 1891, p. 3; "Letter from Dr. Susan LaFlesche," *Bulletin,* May 1894; Susan LaFlesche Picotte to Rev. Wilbur Crofts, October 16, 1905, Bureau of Indian Affairs, Letters Received, #84470, 1905, NA. Though Susan LaFlesche is widely believed to have been responsible for the temperance provision in Walthill, Nebraska, town-site leases, a note added to the Bureau of Indian Affairs correspondence cited above indicates that she may only have added her support to an action already intended by BIA officials.

75. Susan LaFlesche Picotte to R. G. Valentine, July 2, 1909.

76. *Far West,* March 1910, p. 2; Robbins, *How Do the Chinese Girls,* 4th ed.; WOBFM, *Annual Report,* 1910, pp. 28 and 62, and 1911, p. 32.

77. Him Mark Lai et al., *Island: Poetry and History of Chinese Immigrants on Angel Island, 1910–1940* (San Francisco, Calif., 1980), p. 16. See also Shih-Shan Henry Tsai, *The Chinese Experience in America* (Bloomington, Ind., 1986), p. 98; and Yung, *Chinese Women of America,* p. 54. I am grateful to Judy Yung, who generously shared with me a handwritten autobiography of Tye Leung Schulze.

78. "Tien Wu," clipping, Donaldina Cameron file, SFTS.

79. Edna Voss to Donaldina Cameron, August 21, 1934; and Edna Voss to Tien Fu Wu, August 7, 1934, in Tien Fu Wu biographical file #2, POH.

80. Nee and Nee, *Longtime Californ',* pp. 89–90.

81. Lorna Logan to Katharine Gladfelter, February 26, 1948, Tien Fu Wu biographical file #1, POH.

82. WOBFM, *Annual Report,* 1903, p. 44.

83. "Annual Reports on Missionary" and confidential comments of Board of National Missions personnel, 1935–1950, Tien Fu Wu biographical file #2, POH; "Reports on Workers" forms, 1924–1930, Muriel Wing biographical file, POH. To some extent, of course, these comments reflect, not only racial stereotypes, but also the missionary workers' shift in style.

For those working in the 1920s and 1930s, "domineering" missionary zeal that would have been applauded in previous decades often seemed outdated and counterproductive.

84. Susan LaFlesche Picotte to Francis Leupp, Bureau of Indian Affairs, Letters Received, #61405, 1907. See also #49760, 1907; #51403, 1907; and #66499, 1907.

85. *Indian's Friend,* March 1890, p. 1, and November 1890, p. 3.

86. DAR of Connecticut, *Sara Thomson Kinney,* p. 22.

87. Mrs. E. P. Gould to Alice Fletcher, April 1, 1891, Fletcher-LaFlesche Papers, NAA; J. M. Gould to Rosalie LaFlesche Farley, October 13, 1898, LaFlesche Papers, NSHS; Wanken, " 'Woman's Sphere' and Indian Reform," pp. 174–78.

88. Susan LaFlesche Picotte to Clara Folsom, February 15, 1910, HIA.

89. Susan LaFlesche Picotte to Alice Fletcher, n.d., and December 2, 1909, Fletcher-LaFlesche Papers, NAA.

90. *Indian's Friend,* July 1889, p. 1; "Dr. Picotte Discusses the New Policy," *Walthill Times,* December 31, 1909; "Omahas Will Seek Liberty in the Courts," *Omaha Sunday World Herald,* January 23, 1910, p. 6-M.

91. "Omaha Indians in Earnest," *Nebraska State Journal,* January 27, 1910.

92. Susan LaFlesche Picotte diary, December 21, 1910, folder 2, box 3, LaFlesche Papers, NSHS.

93. "Dr. Picotte at Omaha," *Walthill Times,* February 21, 1908; and Susan LaFlesche Picotte, "The Varied World of an Indian Missionary," *Home Mission Monthly,* August 1908.

94. House of Representatives Committee on Indian Affairs, *Peyote: Hearings Before a Subcommittee of the Committee on Indian Affairs on H.R. 2614* (Washington, D.C., 1918), p. 113. On the spread of peyote among the Omaha, see Omer Stewart, *Peyote Religion: A History* (Norman, Okla., 1987), pp. 162–65.

95. "Field Matrons," *Indian's Friend,* July 1890, p. 2.

96. "Tien Wu," clipping, Donaldina Cameron file, SFTS; Nee and Nee, *Longtime Californ',* p. 83; Martin, *Chinatown's Angry Angel,* pp. 282–93. After Cameron's death, Wu lived in a home for retired missionaries.

Chapter 5: Homes Outside the Rescue Homes

1. M.H.F., "A Christian Chinese Wedding," *Occident,* May 1, 1878, p. 6.

2. *Occident,* April 30, 1879, p. 6.

3. *Occident,* October 29, 1879, p. 6.

4. Ibid.

5. WFMS-OBr, *Annual Report,* 1878, p. 9.

6. *Occident,* April 27, 1881, p. 7.

7. "A Knight of the New Chivalry," *WCTU Messenger,* March 1915. For a discussion of the chivalry image in nineteenth-century middle-class courtship, see Rothman, *Hands and Hearts,* p. 198.

8. "A True Story," *WCTU Messenger,* February 1906.

9. Rosenberg, "Sexuality, Class, and Role"; Lewis Perry, " 'Progress, Not Pleasure, Is Our Aim': The Sexual Advice of an Antebellum Radical," *Journal of Social History* 12 (Spring 1979): 354–67; McCarthy, *Noblesse Oblige,* pp. 53–75.

10. Rosenberg, "Sexuality, Class, and Role"; E. Anthony Rotundo, "Body and Soul: Changing Ideals of American Middle-Class Manhood, 1770–1920," *Journal of Social History* 16 (Summer 1983): 23–38; idem, "Learning about Manhood: Gender Ideals and the Middle-Class Family in Nineteenth-Century America," in J. A. Mangan and James Walvin, eds., *Manliness and Morality: Middle-class Masculinity in Britain and America, 1800–1940* (Manchester, U.K. 1987), pp. 35–51.

11. "The Colorado Cottage Home," folder 7, box 7, CWCTU Collection, UC.

12. "Mrs. F. I. Smith, President," *WCTU Messenger,* April 1917.

13. "From the President of Cottage Home Board," *WCTU Messenger,* March 1915.

14. Susan LaFlesche to Rosalie LaFlesche Farley, October 24, 1886, LaFlesche Papers, NSHS.

15. Susan LaFlesche to Rosalie LaFlesche Farley, January 12, 1887, LaFlesche Papers, NSHS.

16. Susan LaFlesche to Rosalie LaFlesche Farley, January 12, 1887, January 19, 1887, February 2, 1887, all in LaFlesche Papers, NSHS.

17. Susan LaFlesche to Rosalie LaFlesche Farley, January 26, 1887, LaFlesche Papers, NSHS.

18. Susan LaFlesche Picotte to "my dear friend," October 12, 1905, HIA.

19. Mathes, "Susan LaFlesche Picotte," pp. 516–17, 520.

20. *Occident,* September 6, 1876, p. 285.

21. "Corrections on Tentative Report of the Presbyterian Chinese Mission Home," May 7, 1935, correspondence file, CH.

22. Donaldina Cameron to Mrs. Rodriguez, n.d., file #238, CH; see also Cameron to Mrs. Joseph Cochran, October 7, 1931, correspondence file, CH.

23. Evelyn Nakano Glenn, "Split Household, Small Producer, and Dual Wage Earner: An Analysis of Chinese American Family Strategies," *Journal of Marriage and the Family* 45 (February 1983): 37–38; Chan, "Chinese

Women in California" and "Exclusion of Chinese Women"; Megumi Dick Osumi, "Asians and California's Anti-Miscegenation Laws," in Nobuya Tsuchida, ed., *Asian and Pacific American Experiences: Women's Perspectives* (Minneapolis, Minn., 1982), pp. 2–8. For the testimony of one man who chose a bride from the Mission Home, see "Life History of Andrew Kan," Major Document #178, Box 27, Survey of Race Relations, HI.

24. Clara Swan to Donaldina Cameron, January 6, 1920, file #238, CH.

25. Tien Fu Wu to Donaldina Cameron, June 13, 1915, file #269, CH.

26. *Occident,* October 3, 1877, p. 5, and January 26, 1881, p. 7; Donaldina Cameron to Home resident, November 9, 1931, file #82, CH.

27. WOBFM, *Annual Report,* 1909, p. 77.

28. See, for example, WOBFM, *Annual Report,* 1905, p. 62.

29. WFMS-OBo, *Annual Report,* 1883, p. 41.

30. *Occident,* August 23, 1882, p. 7.

31. *Occident,* February 7, 1900, pp. 18–19; resident to Donaldina Cameron, May 10, 1916, file #85, CH.

32. Investigator to Donaldina Cameron about Mr. Jung*, September 19, 1929, file #75, CH.

33. Letters to Donaldina Cameron, August 8, 1929, and August 28, 1929, file #75, CH.

34. Lucie Cheng's figures indicate that in 1870, there were 3,536 adult Chinese women in California, 2,157 of whom were listed in the census as prostitutes and 753 of whom were listed as "keeping house." By 1880, when exclusionist sentiment was already beginning to take effect, there were 3,171 adult Chinese women in California, 759 of whom were listed in the census as prostitutes and 1,445 as "keeping house." Hirata, "Chinese Immigrant Women," pp. 227–28, 236. The total number of Chinese women in the United States did not increase until the 1920s. For later figures see Chan, "Chinese Women in California."

35. WFMS-OBo, *Annual Report,* 1888, pp. 52–61; WOBFM, *Annual Report,* 1901.

36. Mission Home officials reported a yearly total of marriages in 33 of the 54 annual reports issued between 1874 and 1928. A total of 163 marriages were reported, for an average of 4.9 marriages per year. If we assume that the same average number of marriages was performed in each of the 21 years for which marriage statistics are not available, 102.9 additional marriages would have occurred during these years; thus my estimated total of 266 marriages. This total would be smaller than the summary totals occasionally claimed by Mission Home officials.

---

*Pseudonym.

37. Ex-resident to Donaldina Cameron, June 1, 1928, file #111, CH.

38. June Mei, "Socioeconomic Developments among the Chinese in San Francisco, 1848–1906," in Lucie Cheng and Edna Bonacich, eds., *Labor Immigration Under Capitalism: Asian Workers in the United States Before World War II* (Berkeley, Calif., 1984), pp. 370–401.

39. Victor Nee and Brett de Bary Nee use the term *bachelor society* to describe the years from the beginning of Chinese immigration through the 1920s; George Peffer refers to a "century of bachelorhood" among Chinese immigrants in the United States. See Nee and Nee, *Longtime Californ'*, p. 11; Peffer, "Forbidden Families," p. 42. For a notable exception, see Chan, "Chinese Women in California."

40. On the Ng family, see *Occident,* May 18, 1892, p. 11; WOBFM, *Annual Report,* 1892, p. 52, and 1909, p. 76; *Occidental Board Bulletin,* July 1, 1902; *Far West,* November 1918, pp. 3–4; Mrs. E. V. Robbins, *How Do the Chinese Girls,* 4th ed.; Dumas Malone, ed., *Dictionary of American Biography* (New York, 1934), 15: 479–80; Corinne Hoexter, *From Canton to California: The Epic of Chinese Immigration* (New York, 1976); and Judy Yung, "The Social Awakening of Chinese American Women as Reported in *Chung Sai Yat Po,* 1900–1911," *Chinese America: History and Perspectives* (1988): 80–102.

41. *Occident,* February 7, 1900, pp. 18–19; *Occidental Board Bulletin,* November 1, 1901, p. 10, December 1, 1901, January 1, 1902, p. 12, and February 1, 1902, pp. 3–4; files #53 and #98, CH. According to the figures cited in Homer Ch'i-Ch'en Loh, "Americans of Chinese Ancestry in Philadelphia" (Ph.D. diss., Univ. of Pennsylvania, 1944), p. 198, Qui Ngun and Choi Qui would have been two of only 18 Chinese women who lived in the state of Pennsylvania at the time. On the development of a mission-influenced community in Minneapolis, see Sarah Mason, "Family Structure and Acculturation in the Chinese Community in Minnesota," in Lim, *Chinese American Experience,* pp. 177–79.

42. Rose Chan* correspondence, file #250, CH.

43. Foong Lon* correspondence, file #52, CH.

44. WOBFM, *Annual Report,* 1901.

45. Letter to Donaldina Cameron, January 3, 1923, file #62, CH.

46. *Occident,* January 27, 1886, p. 11, and April 4, 1887; WFMS-OBr, *Annual Report,* 1878, p. 9; WOBFM, *Annual Report,* 1915, pp. 87–88; files #12, #119, #189, #237, CH.

47. V. L. Hatfield to Donaldina Cameron, October 6, 1923, file #189, CH.

---

*Pseudonym.

48. "Admissions, 1923–1928," and "Dismissals, 1923–1928," folder 6, box 3, record group 101, POH.

49. WOBFM, *Annual Report,* 1900, p. 73.

50. Biographical sketch and newspaper clippings (*San Francisco Call,* March 4, 1924; *San Francisco Examiner,* March 4, 1924; and *San Francisco Chronicle,* March 5, 1924), file #56, CH.

51. Yung* correspondence, file #167, CH.

52. WOBFM, *Annual Report,* 1907, pp. 68–69.

53. "Statement by Miss Tien Fuh Wu," file #63, CH.

54. "Statement," file #63, CH.

55. *Occident,* September 6, 1876, p. 285, January 24, 1877, p. 5, December 23, 1885, p. 11, March 7, 1900, p. 18; WOBFM, *Annual Report,* 1910, p. 64. On the vulnerability of widows in the Chinese gender system, see Susan Mann, "Widows in the Kinship, Class, and Community Structures of Qing Dynasty China," *Journal of Asian Studies* 46 (February 1987): 37–56.

56. "Agreement," August 8, 1925, file #30, CH.

57. Information about Wong Ah So has been compiled from files #258 and #260, CH; *Women and Missions* 2 (1925–26): 169–72; and Major Document #146, box 26, Survey of Race Relations, HI, reprinted in Fisk University Social Science Institute, *Orientals and Their Cultural Adjustment* (Nashville, Tenn., 1946), pp. 31–35.

58. Wong Ah So to her mother, n.d., file #260, CH.

59. Wong Ah So to Donaldina Cameron, October 24, 1928, file #258, CH.

60. Ibid. On the Hop Sing Tong, see Jackie Day, "Boise, Idaho, 1900–1911: Factionalism and Community Reorganization Within an Idaho Chinatown," in Lim, *Chinese American Experience,* pp. 170–73.

61. David Katzman, *Seven Days a Week: Women and Domestic Service in Industrializing America* (New York, 1978); Evelyn Nakano Glenn, *Issei, Nisei, War Bride: Three Generations of Japanese American Women in Domestic Service* (Philadelphia, Pa., 1986); Hirata, "Chinese Immigrant Women."

62. This preference for domestic work can be seen in a wide variety of reform efforts of the period. See Faye Dudden, *Serving Women: Household Service in Nineteenth-Century America* (Middletown, Conn., 1983), p. 168; Freedman, *Their Sister's Keepers,* pp. 90–95; Brenzel, *Daughters of the State,* chap. 7; Hobson, *Uneasy Virtue,* pp. 64–65; and Robert Trennert, "From Carlisle to Phoenix: The Rise and Fall of the Indian

---

*Pseudonym.

Outing System, 1878–1930," *Pacific Historical Review* 52 (August 1983): 267–91.

63. Donaldina Cameron, "Salvaged for Service," *Women and Missions* 4 (1927–28): 168–70.

64. "Cottage Home Questions and Answers," *WCTU Messenger,* November 1903; "Mrs. F. I. Smith, President," *WCTU Messenger,* June 1915.

65. Historians have made the same point about middle-class reformers who tried to promote domestic work as alternative employment for prostitutes and for dance hall girls. See Rosen, *Lost Sisterhood,* pp. 62–63, and Gullett, "City Mothers, City Daughters," pp. 158–59.

66. "From the President of the Cottage Home Board," *WCTU Messenger,* October–November 1909.

67. WOBFM, *Annual Report,* 1901, p. 44.

68. Cameron, "Salvaged for Service."

69. "The First Year's Work," *Salt Lake Tribune,* October 6, 1887.

70. On mistress–servant relationships, see Dudden, *Serving Women,* pp. 163–71; Carol Lasser, "The Domestic Balance of Power: Relations Between Mistress and Maid in Nineteenth Century New England," *Labor History* 28 (Winter 1987): 5–22; Glenn, *Issei, Nisei, War Bride,* pp. 153–64; and Judith Rollins, *Between Women: Domestics and Their Employers* (Philadelphia, Pa., 1985), pp. 155–206.

71. Jane Ying* to Donaldina Cameron about Mrs. Webster*, January 31, 1923, file #141, CH.

72. Jane Ying* to Donaldina Cameron, March 3, 1923, file #141, CH.

73. Ng Shee* to Donaldina Cameron about Mrs. Anderson*, September 1918, file #209, CH.

74. Ng Shee* to Donaldina Cameron, September 22, 1918, file #209, CH.

75. Ng Shee* to Donaldina Cameron, December 3, 1918, file #209, CH.

76. "President," October–November 1909.

77. Ibid.

78. Dudden, *Serving Women,* pp. 206–7, 213–19, 227; Hobson, *Uneasy Virtue,* chap. 5.

79. "Cottage Home Incidents and Letters," *WCTU Messenger,* May 1906.

80. M.H.F., "A Christian Chinese Wedding."

---

*Pseudonym.

Chapter 6: The Crisis of Victorian Female Moral Authority, 1890–1939

1. WNIA, *Annual Meeting and Report,* 1901, pp. 35–36.

2. "Indian Association," *Litchfield Inquirer,* October 15, 1908, Scrapbook 3, CIA, Thomson-Kinney Papers, CSA.

3. Wanken, " 'Woman's Sphere' and Indian Reform," pp. 340–43. The few men who did take advantage of the welcome thus extended were, however, placed in high positions. In 1905, the Association elected its first male president; in later years, much of its work was handled by General Secretary John Clark.

4. WNIA, *Annual Meeting and Report,* 1901, pp. 35–36.

5. Ibid.

6. Baker, "Domestication of Politics." pp. 620–47.

7. Michael Quinn, "LDS Authority and New Plural Marriages, 1890–1904," *Dialogue* 18 (Spring 1985): 9–105; Thomas Alexander, *A History of the Latter-day Saints, 1890–1930* (Urbana, Ill., 1986), pp. 62–73.

8. Rosen, *Lost Sisterhood,* p. 128; Gullett, "City Mothers, City Daughters"; Neil Shumsky, "Vice Responds to Reform: San Francisco, 1910–1914," *Journal of Urban History* 7 (November 1980): 31–47.

9. In the Salt Lake City case, charity development depended on a rapprochement between Mormon and Gentile women. See Carol Cornwall Madsen, "Decade of Detente: Mormon-Gentile Female Relationships in Nineteenth Century Utah," paper presented to the Western History Association, Los Angeles, October 1987; and Maureen Ursenbach Beecher and Kathryn MacKay, "Women in Twentieth-century Utah," in Poll, *Utah's History,* pp. 563–86.

10. CWCTU, *Annual Report,* 1888, pp. 36–40.

11. "The State Treasury," *WCTU Messenger,* August 1903.

12. CWCTU, *Annual Report,* 1904, p. 82, 1905, p. 82, 1910, p. 115, 1911, p. 47; "Mid Year Meeting of Colorado WCTU Executive Committee," *WCTU Messenger,* April 1906.

13. "Cottage Home Notes," *WCTU Messenger,* December 1903; "Cottage Home," *WCTU Messenger,* March 1904; "My Travels," *WCTU Messenger,* June 1914.

14. WFMS-OBr, *Annual Report,* 1881, p. 45.

15. WOBFM, *Annual Report,* 1898, pp. 17–22.

16. "Minutes of Conference between Executive Council and Executive Committee of Central Committee," January 20, 1920, Minutes and Reports, Central Committee, Woman's Boards of Foreign Missions, POH.

17. On the "reintegration" of Presbyterian women's boards, see Boyd and Brackenridge, *Presbyterian Women,* pp. 123–27.

18. "Report of Mrs. F. S. Bennett on work among Chinese girls on Pacific Coast," Dec. 1921, folder 14, box 2, record group 101, POH.

19. "Transfer of Work Among the Orientals on the Pacific Coast to the Home Boards," and "List of Papers on the Transfer of the Work Among the Orientals in the U.S. Given to Dr. Brown, May 15, 1922," both in folder 8, box 1, record group 81, POH.

20. WOBFM, *Annual Report,* 1909, p. 23; Katharine Bennett to Mrs. George Kennedy, June 9, 1922; Mrs. Rawlins Cadwallader to Bennett, July 8, 1922; Evelyn Kech to Cadwallader, July 14, 1922; Bennett to Cadwallader, July 25, 1922, all in Cadwallader Papers, SFTS.

21. WNIA, *Annual Meeting and Report,* 1889, p. 11; WNIA, *Our Work—What? How? Why?* (Philadelphia, Pa., 1893), pp. 36–37.

22. See, for example, WNIA, *Annual Meeting and Report,* 1892, pp. 32–34, and 1893, pp. 32–33.

23. WNIA, *Annual Meeting and Report,* 1901, pp. 35–36.

24. "Mrs. Antoinette A. Hawley, for Years a Worker in Temperance Field, Retires," *WCTU Messenger,* June 1918.

25. CWCTU, *Annual Report,* 1896, pp. 13–14, 1915, pp. 46–47, 1921, p. 48, and 1928, p. 58; *WCTU Messenger,* October 1920.

26. See, for example, WFMS-OBr, *Annual Report,* 1881, p. 19; and WFMS-OBo, *Annual Report,* 1882, pp. 13–14.

27. "Admissions, 1923–1928," folder 6, and "Home Stats, 1936–1938," folder 13, both in box 3, record group 101, POH.

28. John Manion, " 'Lo Mo', Mother of Chinatown," *Women and Missions* 8 (1931–32): 387–389; Major Document #129, Box 26, Survey of Race Relations, HI, p. 4.

29. WOBFM, *Annual Report,* 1910, pp. 58–68.

30. "Report of Mrs. F. S. Bennett."

31. By 1917, requests for assistance (from Chinese immigrants as well as immigration officials) were so numerous that Cameron limited herself to those that concerned "friends of the Home." In at least three of the half-dozen cases she reported looking into in that year, the immigrants in question were allowed to stay on her recommendation. WOBFM, *Annual Report,* 1917, pp. 34–39.

32. Among the historians who have examined the rise of social work bureaucracies are Roy Lubove, *The Professional Altruist: The Emergence of Social Work as a Career, 1880–1930* (Cambridge, Mass., 1965); Thomas Haskell, *The Emergence of Professional Science: The American Social Science Association and the Nineteenth-Century Crisis of Authority* (Urbana, Ill., 1977); and Mary Furner, *Advocacy and Objectivity: A Crisis in the Professionalization of American Social Science, 1865–1905* (Lexington, Ky., 1975).

33. On Denver charity consolidation, see Bernard Rosen, "Social Welfare in the History of Denver," (Ph.D. diss., Univ. of Colorado, 1976); and Stefanco, "Pathways to Power," pp. 171–81.

34. On California charity consolidation, see Leiby, "State Welfare Administration"; Cahn and Bary, *Welfare Activities;* and Shinn, "Poverty and Charity, I and II."

35. Shinn, "Poverty and Charity II."

36. Rosen, "Social Welfare in Denver," p. 166; Efay Nelson Griff, "Social Legislation and the Welfare Program," in LeRoy Hafen, ed., *Colorado and Its People* 2 (New York, 1948): 333–68.

37. Cahn and Bary, *Welfare Activities,* chap. 2.

38. *Far West,* October 1908, p. 9.

39. King, "Presbyterian Chinese Mission Home."

40. Donaldina Cameron to Edna Voss, October 28, 1926, folder 14, box 3, record group 101, POH.

41. Katherine Gladfelter to Edna Voss, February 24, 1932; Ethel Higgins to Edna Voss, March 8, 1932, both in folder 12, box 3, record group 101, POH.

42. CWCTU, *Annual Report,* 1924, pp. 31–32.

43. CWCTU, *Annual Report,* 1929, p. 46.

44. On the distinctive ideals of Progressivism, see especially Kathryn Kish Sklar, "Florence Kelley and the Integration of 'Women's Sphere' into American Politics, 1890–1921," paper presented to the Organization of American Historians, New York City, April 1986; and Daniel Rodgers, "In Search of Progressivism," *Reviews in American History* 10 (December 1982): 113–32. Home mission workers never adopted the language of social interdependency some historians see as characteristic of Progressivism, and they retained a concern about race relations notably lacking in most reformers of their time.

45. For a sense of the variety of women's institutions that faced this dilemma, see Virginia Drachman, *Hospital with a Heart: Women Doctors and the Paradox of Separatism at the New England Hospital, 1862–1969* (Ithaca, N.Y., 1984); Meyerowitz, *Women Adrift,* pp. 48–55, 120–26; Pleck, *Domestic Tyranny,* p. 98; and Kunzel, "Seduced Victims to Sex Delinquents."

46. Baker, "Domestication of Politics," p. 644; Estelle Freedman, "Separatism as Strategy: Female Institution Building and American Feminism, 1870–1930," *Feminist Studies* 5 (Fall 1979): 512–29.

47. Daniel Walker Howe, "Victorian Culture in America," in Howe, *Victorian America* (Philadelphia, Pa., 1976), pp. 3–28; Daniel Joseph Singal, "Towards a Definition of American Modernism," *American Quarterly* 39 (Spring 1987): 7–26. See also John Higham,

"The Reorientation of American Culture in the 1890's," in Higham, *Writing American History: Essays on Modern Scholarship* (Bloomington, Ind., 1970); May, *End of American Innocence;* and Stanley Coben, "The Assault on Victorianism in the Twentieth Century," in *Victorian America,* pp. 160–81.

48. D'Emilio and Freedman, *Intimate Matters,* pp. 171–201, 222–38; Rosenberg, *Beyond Separate Spheres;* Carroll Smith-Rosenberg, "The New Woman as Androgyne: Social Disorder and Gender Crisis, 1870–1936," in Smith-Rosenberg, *Disorderly Conduct,* pp. 245–96.

49. Hal Sears, *The Sex Radicals: Free Love in High Victorian America* (Lawrence, Kan., 1977).

50. Meyerowitz, *Women Adrift;* Peiss, *Cheap Amusements.*

51. Christina Simmons, " 'Marriage in the Modern Manner' "; Ellen Kay Trimberger, "Feminism, Men, and Modern Love: Greenwich Village, 1900–1925," in Snitow et al., *Powers of Desire,* pp. 131–52.

52. Paula Fass, *The Damned and the Beautiful: American Youth in the 1920's* (New York, 1977); Lewis Erenberg, *Steppin' Out: New York Nightlife and the Transformation of American Culture, 1890–1930* (Westport, Conn., 1981).

53. John Modell, "Dating Becomes the Way of American Youth," in Leslie Moch, ed., *Essays on the Family and Historical Change* (College Station, Tex., 1983), pp. 91–126; Rothman, *Hands and Hearts,* chap. 7; Fass, *Damned and the Beautiful,* chap. 6.

54. May, *Great Expectations,* chap. 3; see also Simmons, "Companionate Marriage"; Epstein, "Family, Sexual Morality."

55. "From the President of the Cottage Home Board," *WCTU Messenger,* October–November 1909.

56. "From the President of Cottage Home Board," *WCTU Messenger,* August 1908.

57. Soo Ah Young* to Donaldina Cameron about Mr. Ping*, November 4, 1931, file #82, CH.

58. Ibid.

59. Stansell, *City of Women,* chap. 5.

60. "The Cottage Home," *Rocky Mountain News,* June 14, 1891, p. 13; CWCTU, *Annual Report,* 1914, p. 65; "YWCTU," *WCTU Messenger,* February 1901. See also Katherine Harris, "Feminine and Class Identity," p. 56.

61. Case of Amy Wong*, "Agreement, September 13, 1927," file #211, CH.

62. "Rescue Work," *WCTU Messenger,* December 1907.

---

*Pseudonym.

63. Rose Seen* to Bill Wong*, n.d., file #176, CH.

64. "Two Slave Girls Flee With $1000," *San Francisco Daily News,* December 22, 1925; "Slave Girls Turn Thieves," *San Francisco Chronicle,* December 23, 1925; clippings in file #115, CH.

65. Robert Handy, "The American Religious Depression, 1925–1935," in John Mulder and John Wilson, eds., *Religion in American History* (Englewood Cliffs, N.J., 1978), pp. 431–44; Martin Marty, *Righteous Empire: The Protestant Experience in America* (New York, 1970), chap. 6; Robert Crunden, *Ministers of Reform: The Progressives' Achievement in American Civilization, 1889–1920* (New York, 1982); Robert Mathisen, "Evangelicals and the Age of Reform, 1870–1930: An Assessment," *Fides et Historia* 16 (Spring–Summer 1984): 74–85.

66. Ferenc Szasz, *The Divided Mind of Protestant America, 1880–1930* (University, Ala., 1982); George Marsden, *Fundamentalism and American Culture: The Shaping of Twentieth-Century Evangelicalism: 1870–1925* (New York, 1980), pp. 85–93; William Hutchison, *The Modernist Impulse in American Protestantism* (Cambridge, Mass., 1976); Paul Carter, *The Decline and Revival of the Social Gospel: Social and Political Liberalism in American Protestant Churches, 1920–1940* (Ithaca, N.Y., 1954); Sue Lynn, "Women, Reform, and Feminism: The Young Women's Christian Association and the American Friends Service Committee, 1945–1960" (Ph.D. diss., Stanford Univ., 1986).

67. Welter, " 'She Hath Done What She Could' "; Beaver, *All Loves Excelling,* chaps. 2–3, 6; Hill, *World Their Household,* chap. 1; Boyd and Brackenridge, *Presbyterian Women,* chap. 4.

68. Ex-resident to Ethel Higgins, May 25, 1928, file #262, CH. For examples of similar stereotyping in other women's institutions, see Meyerowitz, *Women Adrift,* pp. 86, 125, and Gordon, *Heroes of Their Own Lives,* pp. 59–60.

69. Stocking, *Race, Culture and Evolution,* chaps. 8–9; Curtis Hinsley, *Savages and Scientists: The Smithsonian Institution and the Development of American Anthropology, 1846–1910* (Washington, D.C., 1981); Marshall Hyatt, "Franz Boas and the Struggle for Black Equality: The Dynamics of Ethnicity," *Perspectives in American History,* n.s. 2 (1985): 269–296.

70. Singal, "American Modernism," pp. 18–20; Erenberg, *Steppin' Out,* p. 256; Deutsch, *No Separate Refuge,* p. 190.

71. Ethel Higgins, "Proposed Changes at Ming Quong Home," June 13, 1936, folder 13, box 3, record group 101, POH.

72. Ethel Higgins to Edna Voss, December 29, 1934, folder 13, box 3, record group 101, POH.

73. Ethel Higgins to Edna Voss, June 13, 1936, folder 13, box 3, record group 101, POH.

74. Fletcher and LaFlesche, "Omaha Tribe," appendix.

75. Margaret Mead, *The Changing Culture of an Indian Tribe* (1932; reprint, New York, 1966), p. 114.

76. "Report of the Educational Committee," *Bulletin,* December 1891, p. 3; Charlotte Edgerton Swarthout, "Connecticut Indian Association," *Lend-a-Hand,* February 1894, Scrapbook 2, CIA, Thomson-Kinney Papers, CSA; *Indian's Friend,* May 1910, p. 4.

77. "Miss Scoville's Plan for New Work," typed MS, May 21, 1906, Minute Book 5, CIA, Thomson-Kinney Papers, CSA; "Indian Mission Schools," May 21, 1906, Minute Book 5, CIA, Thomson-Kinney Papers, CSA.

78. Executive and Mission Committee Minutes, February 2, 1906, Minute Book 5, CIA, Thomson-Kinney Papers, CSA.

79. "Indian Association," *Litchfield Inquirer,* October 5, 1908; "Hartford Branch of Indian Association," *Hartford Courant,* November 6, 1908, both in Scrapbook 3, CIA, Thomson-Kinney Papers, CSA.

80. Annual Meeting Minutes, December 3, 1909, Minute Book 5, CIA, Thomson-Kinney Papers, CSA.

81. "Christmas Dinner for Old Indians," *Waterbury American,* November 16, 1910, Scrapbook 3, CIA, Thomson-Kinney Papers, CSA.

82. Executive Committee Minutes, June 4, 1910[?], Minute Book 5, CIA, Thomson-Kinney Papers, CSA.

83. Minutes, October 19, 1923; "Famous Old Indian Association Will Soon Terminate Four Decades of Service," *Hartford Courant,* April 6, 1924; both in Minute Book 5, CIA, Thomson-Kinney Papers, CSA.

84. See Francis Prucha, "The Decline of the Christian Reformers," in Prucha, *Indian Policy in the United States* (Lincoln, Nebr., 1981), pp. 252–62; and Henry Fritz, "The Last Hurrah of Christian Humanitarian Indian Reform: The Board of Indian Commissioners, 1909–1918," *Western Historical Quarterly* 76 (April 1985): 147–62.

85. "WCTU Groups Row Over Retreat for Unwed Mothers," *Rocky Mountain News,* January 21, 1930; "Home for Unwed Mothers May Be Abandoned Here," *Rocky Mountain News,* January 22, 1931; "Bitter Dissension Breaks Up WCTU Peace Hearing," *Denver Post,* January 22, 1930; " 'Peace' Parley of WCTU Ends in Open Fight," *Rocky Mountain News,* January 23, 1930.

86. "Internal Feud Fails to Balk WCTU Fete," *Denver Post,* January 23, 1930; " 'Peace' Parley," *Rocky Mountain News,* January 23, 1930.

87. CWCTU, *Annual Report,* 1930, pp. 34–35, 43; "Insurgents Ousted

from State WCTU," *Denver Post,* January 24, 1930; "Six WCTU 'Rebels' Fired," *Rocky Mountain News,* January 25, 1930; "Audit of Treasurer's Books Vindicates State WCTU Officers," press release, folder 7, box 7, CWCTU Collection, UC.

88. "Two Factions in Battle to Rule Colorado WCTU," *Denver Post,* September 27, 1930; "National Officers Drawn into Colorado WCTU Dispute," *Denver Post,* September 28, 1930; "Mrs. Hungerford Again Is Elected Head of WCTU," *Denver Post,* October 2, 1930.

89. CWCTU, *Annual Report,* 1931, p. 37; "WCTU Will Close Cottage Home Hospital," *Denver Post* clipping, folder 7, box 7, CWCTU Collection, UC.

90. CWCTU, *Annual Report,* 1928, p. 55.

91. Donaldina Cameron to Edna Voss, October 6, 1927, folder 13, box 2, record group 101, POH.

92. H. N. Morse to Advisory Committee, December 22, 1927, folder 13, box 2, record group 101, POH.

93. "A New Avenue of Service," *Women and Missions* 7 (1930–1931): 163–68.

94. Anna Scott to Mrs. Henry Heylman, August 5, 1931, Donaldina Cameron file #1, POH; Edna Voss to Donaldina Cameron, May 29, 1934; Cameron to Voss, June 18, 1934; Voss to Cameron, June 21, 1934; all in Donaldina Cameron biographical file #2, POH.

95. Ethel Higgins to Edna Voss, June 2, 1934, folder 13, box 3, record group 101, POH.

96. "Minutes of Special Meeting of Advisory Committee on Oriental Work," June 3, 1936, folder 14, box 2, record group 101, POH.

97. Edna Voss to H. N. Morse, September 1, 1936, folder 13, box 3; Donaldina Cameron to Voss, October 12, 1936, folder 14, box 2; H. N. Morse memo *"Re* 920 Sacramento Street," December 4, 1936, folder 14, box 2; all in record group 101, POH.

98. Edna Voss to H. N. Morse, January 15, 1937, folder 13, box 2, record group 101, POH.

99. Philip Payne to H. N. Morse, January 13, 1937, folder 13, box 2, record group 101, POH.

100. Edna Voss to Lorna Logan, June 21, 1939, folder 9, box 4, record group 111, POH.

101. Presbyterian Church, *Board Reports,* 1939, pp. 96–98, 1940, p. 41. The quarters at Wetmore Street were abandoned in 1949, and all the Presbyterian social services for Chinese Americans were once again consolidated in the building at 920 Sacramento Street, where they remain to this day. The building was later renamed Cameron House.

Epilogue: A Legacy to Ponder: Female Moral Authority and Contemporary Women's Culture

1. Pleck, *Domestic Tyranny,* p. 10.

2. For one attempt to deal with this difficulty, see Sara Ruddick, "Pacifying the Forces: Drafting Women in the Interests of Peace," *Signs* 8 (Spring 1983): 471–89.

3. On the centrality of the women's culture model among feminist historians, see Linda Kerber, "Separate Spheres, Female Worlds, Woman's Place: The Rhetoric of Women's History," *Journal of American History* 75 (June 1988): 9–39. For an extended criticism of the concept, see Hewitt, "Beyond the Search for Sisterhood."

4. Gerda Lerner, *The Creation of Patriarchy* (New York, 1986), appendix.

Bibliography

Primary Sources

Manuscripts and Archival Collections

American Indian Correspondence: The Presbyterian Historical Society
   Collection of Missionaries' Letters, 1833–1893.
Cadwallader, Mrs. Rawlins. Papers, 1919–1922. SFTS.
Cameron, Donaldina. Biographical file. POH.
Cameron House files, circa 1900–1939. CH.
Church of Jesus Christ of Latter-day Saints. Journal History, 1880–1899.
   LDS.
Colorado Woman's Christian Temperance Union Collection. UC.
Culbertson, Margaret. Biographical file. POH.
Dyer, Frank. Scrapbooks, 1890s. USHS.
Fletcher-LaFlesche Papers. NAA.
Froiseth, Jennie. "Some Utah Women." Typed manuscript. SLCPL.
Galt, William. Manuscript. NSHS.
Hamilton, Mrs. W. H. "Historical Sketch of the Occidental Board for
   First Seven Years." Typed manuscript. SFTS.
LaFlesche Papers. NSHS.
LaFlesche, Susan. Alumnae file. MCP.
———. Student record. HIA.
Likens, Sadie. Papers. DPL.
Logan, Lorna. Biographical file. POH.
Nebraska Woman's Christian Temperance Union Collection. NSHS.
Nebraska Woman's Home Missionary Society. Records. NWU.
Nyman, Emil. "Westminster College: 100 Years." Typed manuscript.
   USHS.
"Polygamous Assembly." Circular of the Ladies Anti-Polygamy Society.
   LDS.

Presbyterian Board of Foreign Missions. Records, 1892–1965. Record Group 81. POH.

Presbyterian Board of National Missions. Files of the Department of Educational and Medical Work, 1878–1966. Record Group 101. POH.

———. Reports and Histories. Record Group 111. POH.

Presbyterian Woman's Board of Home Missions. Records, 1878–1948. Record Group 105. POH.

"The Public Buildings for Salt Lake City, Utah. A Plan for Limiting Its Cost to a Sum Not Exceeding $75,000.00." Carbon of original proposal. LDS.

Robbins, Mrs. E. V. "The Occidental Board, 1873–1911." Handwritten reminiscence, 1912. POH.

Survey of Race Relations. HI.

Thomson-Kinney Papers. CSA.

U.S. Bureau of Indian Affairs. Letters Received, 1881–1907. NA.

U.S. Department of the Interior. Territorial Papers. Utah, 1850–1902. Letters Received Relating to Polygamy, January 27, 1879–December 17, 1897. NA.

Wing, Muriel. Biographical file. POH.

Wu, Tien Fu. Biographical file. POH.

Women's Mission Organizations: Minutes, Annual Reports, and Periodicals

Anti-Polygamy Standard. Ladies' Anti-Polygamy Society of Utah. 1880–1883. LDS.

Bulletin. CIA. 1889–1899. CSA.

Colorado Woman's Christian Temperance Union. *Annual Report*, 1886–1931. UC.

Connecticut Indian Association. Handwritten minute books, scrapbooks, 1881–1923. CSA.

Far West. Woman's Home and Foreign Mission Boards of the Presbyterian Church of California. 1907–1920. SFTS.

Hensel, L. M. *Report of Our Omaha Mission*. Philadelphia, Pa.: WNIA, 1888.

Home Mission Monthly. Woman's Executive Committee of Home Missions, Presbyterian Church. 1886–1902. POH.

Indian's Friend. WNIA. 1888–1915.

"920" Newsletter. WOBFM. Scattered issues, 1933–1939. CH.

Occidental Board Bulletin. WOBFM. 1900–1903. SFTS.

Parsons, Ellen, ed. *One Year's Stewardship, 1912–1913: A United Report of the Woman's Boards of Foreign Missions.* Philadelphia, Pa.: Central Committee of Presbyterian Women for Foreign Missions, n.d. POH.

Presbyterian Church in the United States of America. *Board Reports,* 1920–1940. POH.

Robbins, Mrs. E. V. *Ten Years Among the Chinese in California: Decennial Report of the Occidental Board of the Woman's Foreign Missionary Society.* San Francisco, Calif.: A. J. Leary, 1883. POH.

Tileston, Laura. *Report of the Hospital Department.* Philadelphia, Pa.: WNIA, 1891.

Union Signal. Woman's Christian Temperance Union. 1883–1889.

WCTU Bulletin. CWCTU. 1891–1893. UC.

WCTU Messenger. CWCTU. 1897–1924. UC.

Woman's Christian Temperance Union. *Annual Report,* 1880–1892.

Woman's Foreign Missionary Society, Presbyterian Church. *Annual Report,* 1874–1890. POH.

———, California Branch. *Annual Report,* 1874–1876. SFTS.

———, Occidental Board. *Annual Report,* 1882–1888. SFTS.

———, Occidental Branch. *Annual Report,* 1877–1881. SFTS.

Woman's Home Missionary Society, Methodist Episcopal Church. *Annual Report,* 1881–1894. MCAH.

Woman's Home Missions. Woman's Home Missionary Society, Methodist Episcopal Church. 1884–1889. MCAH.

Woman's Occidental Board of Foreign Missions. *Annual Report,* 1889–1920. SFTS.

Woman's Work. Woman's Foreign Missionary Societies of the Presbyterian Church. 1885–1895. POH.

Woman's Work for Woman. Woman's Foreign Missionary Society and Woman's Presbyterian Board of Missions of the Northwest. 1875–1878. POH.

Women's National Indian Association. *Annual Meeting and Report,* 1883–1915.

———. Executive Board Minutes, 1890–1894. HFL.

———. *Report of Missionary Work,* 1886, 1888, 1889. Philadelphia, Pa.: WNIA, 1886–1889.

———. *Report of the Missionary Department.* Philadelphia, Pa.: WNIA, 1890, 1891.

———. *Work of the Missionary Department.* Philadelphia, Pa.: WNIA, 1892.

Women and Missions. Board of Missions, Presbyterian Church in the U.S.A. 1924–1939. POH.

Printed Government Documents

California State Senate, Special Committee on Chinese Immigration. *Chinese Immigration; Its Social, Moral, and Political Effect.* Sacramento, Calif.: State Printing Office, 1878.

U.S. Commissioner of Indian Affairs. *Annual Report,* 1889–1893.

U.S. Congress. House of Representatives. H. Mis. Doc. 104. 52nd Cong., 1st sess., February 24, 1892.

———. H. Mis. Doc. 6. 52nd Cong., 2nd sess., December 5, 1892.

———. H. Doc. 327. 54th Cong., 1st sess., March 30, 1896.

———. H. Rept. 1247. 55th Cong., 2nd sess., May 2, 1898.

———. Committee on Indian Affairs. *Peyote: Hearings Before a Subcommittee of the Committee on Indian Affairs on H.R. 2614.* Washington, D.C.: Government Printing Office, 1918.

U.S. Congress. Senate. S. Rept. 1279. 49th Cong., 1st sess., June 5, 1886.

———. *Woman Suffrage in Utah,* by Angie Newman. S. Mis. Doc. 122. 49th Cong., 1st sess., June 8, 1886.

———. S. Ex. Doc. 57. 50th Cong., 1st sess., January 24, 1888.

———. S. Mis. Doc. 201. 50th Cong., 1st sess., September 21, 1888.

———. S. Mis. Doc. 34. 51st Cong., 1st sess., December 19, 1889.

———. S. Mis. Doc. 15. 51st Cong., 2nd sess., December 9, 1890.

———. *Record of Indian Students Returned from Hampton Institute.* S. Ex. Doc. 31. 52nd Cong., 1st sess., February 9, 1892.

———. S. Mis. Doc. 7. 53rd Cong., 2nd sess., December 5, 1893.

U.S. Industrial Commission. *Report.* Vol. 15. Washington, D.C.: Government Printing Office, 1901.

Newspapers and Journals

Bancroft Blade. 1895–1901.

Christian Advocate. 1882–1910.

Denver Post. 1930–1931.

Denver Times. 1930–1931.

Occident. 1876–1899.

Pacific Presbyterian. 1903–1904.

Rocky Mountain News. 1930–1931.

Salt Lake Tribune. 1886–1890.

Southern Workman. 1882–1915.

Walthill Times. 1906–1915.

Woman's Exponent. 1886–1893.

Books, Pamphlets, and Articles

Bartlett, Jennie. *Elder Northfield's Home; or, Sacrificed on the Mormon Altar.* New York: J. Howard Brown, 1882.

Bass, Elizabeth. "These Were the First." *Journal of the American Medical Women's Association* 7 (November 1952): 432. MCP.

Bird's-Eye Views: Chinese Mission Home. New York: Presbyterian Board of National Missions, n.d. POH.

Brummitt, Stella Wyatt. *Looking Backward, Thinking Forward: The Jubilee History of the Woman's Home Missionary Society of the Methodist Episcopal Church.* Cincinnati, Ohio: Woman's Home Missionary Society, 1930.

Buckley, James. *Constitutional and Parliamentary History of the Methodist Episcopal Church.* New York: Methodist Book Concern, 1912.

Burton, Richard. *City of the Saints.* Edited by Fawn M. Brodie. London, 1861; reprint, New York: Alfred A. Knopf, 1963.

Cameron, Donaldina. "Challenge of the Open Door to the Door Thrice-Barred." *New Era Magazine,* July 1919. Reprinted by Woman's Board of Foreign Missions, New York, n.d.

————. *Chinese Girls as Witnesses from a Far Country.* N.p., n.d. POH.

————. *The Passing of the Occidental Mission Home.* San Francisco, Calif.: WOBFM, circa 1907. SFTS.

Condit, Mrs. I. M. *A Quarter of a Century* [pamphlet printed to accompany the Board's 25th Annual Report, 1898]. San Francisco, Calif.: WOBFM, 1898. SFTS.

Coyner, J. M., comp. *Handbook on Mormonism.* Salt Lake City, Utah: Hand-Book Publishing Company, 1882.

Craighead, R. C. "Refuge in Chinatown." *Presbyterian Life,* November 12, 1949.

Daughters of the American Revolution of Connecticut. *In Memoriam: Sara Thomson Kinney.* Windsor, Connecticut: DAR, 1923.

Edholm, M. G. C. "A Stain on the Flag." *The Californian* 1 (1914): 159–70.

Ferry, Jeannette. *The Industrial Christian Home Association of Utah.* Salt Lake City, Utah: n.p., 1893.

Finks, Theodora. "The First Indian Woman Physician." *Home Mission Monthly,* February 1924. POH.

"The First Indian Woman Physician." *Bulletin of Council of Women for Home Missions,* 1932, p. 447. MCP.

"The First Woman Physician Among Her People." *Medical Missionary Record* 4 (October 1889): 126. MCP.

Fisk University, Social Science Institute. *Orientals and Their Cultural Adjustment.* Nashville, Tenn.: Fisk University, 1946.

Fletcher, Alice. "Home Life Among the Indians." *Century Magazine* 54 (1897): 252–63.

———. "Lands in Severalty to Indians." *American Association for the Advancement of Science Proceedings* 33 (1884): 654–65.

Fletcher, Alice, and Francis LaFlesche. "The Omaha Tribe." *Twenty-seventh Annual Report of the Bureau of American Ethnology, 1905–1906.* Washington, D.C.: Government Printing Office, 1911.

Froiseth, Jennie. "The Home and Mormonism." *Home Science* 1 (October 1884): 226–32. LDS.

———, ed. *The Women of Mormonism; or, The Story of Polygamy as Told by the Victims Themselves.* With introduction by Frances Willard. Detroit: C. G. G. Paine, 1882.

Gibson, Reverend O. *The Chinese in America.* Cincinnati, Ohio: Hitchcock and Walden, 1877.

Higgins, Ethel. *From Bondage to Freedom.* New York: Presbyterian Board of National Missions, n.d. POH.

———. *Suey Ching: Lost and Found.* New York: Presbyterian Woman's Board of Home Missions, n.d. POH.

"Holiday Notes." *Woman's Tribune,* October 20, 1888.

How the Quest for Ah Yoke Discovered Yute Wah and Ah Oie. WOBFM, n.d. POH.

Johnson, Ellen. *Historical Sketch of the Connecticut Indian Association from 1881 to 1888.* Hartford, Conn.: Fowler and Miller, 1888. CSA.

Kelley, Mrs. L. A. *The Day's Work.* San Francisco, Calif.: WOBFM, n.d. POH.

Logan, Lorna. *Into Our Second Century.* N.p., 1974. SFTS.

———. *Ventures in Mission: The Cameron House Story.* Wilson Creek, Wash.: Crawford Hobby Print Shop, 1976.

Ludlow, Helen. *Ten Years' Work for Indians at Hampton Normal and Agricultural Institute.* Hampton, Va.: n.p., 1888.

Mead, Margaret. *The Changing Culture of an Indian Tribe.* New York, 1932; reprint, New York: Capricorn Books, 1966.

Meeker, Ruth Esther. *Six Decades of Service, 1880–1940: A History of the Woman's Home Mission Society of the Methodist Episcopal Church.* N.p.: Woman's Home Mission Society, 1969.

Mormon Women's Protest; An Appeal for Freedom, Justice and Equal Rights. Salt Lake City, Utah: [Deseret News Company], 1886.

Paddock, Cornelia. *The Fate of Madame LaTour: A Tale of Great Salt Lake.* New York: Fords, Howard, and Hulbert, 1881.

———. "An Industrial Home for Mormon Women." *Christian Register,* January 7, 1886. LDS.

"Pioneer Medical Woman: Dr. Susan LaFlesche Picotte." *Medical Woman's Journal* 37 (January 1930): 19–20. MCP.

Richards, Josephine. "The Training of the Indian Girl as the Uplifter of the Home." *National Educational Association Journal of Proceedings and Addresses.* Washington, D.C., 1900, pp. 701–5.

Robbins, Mrs. E. V. *Chinese Slave Girls: A Bit of History.* San Francisco, Calif.: WOBFM, n.d. POH.

———. *History of the Woman's Occidental Board of Foreign Missions.* N.p., 1905. SFTS.

———. *How Do the Chinese Girls Come to the Mission Home?* 4th and 5th eds. N.d. SFTS.

———. "The Occidental Board—A Retrospect and Prospect." *Far West.* February 1916, pp. 14–15.

Schwarz, Reverend Julius. *History of the Presbyterian Church in Nebraska.* Omaha, Nebr.: n.p., 1924.

Semple, James Alexander. *Representative Women of Colorado.* Denver, Colo.: Alexander Art Publishing, 1911.

Shinn, M. W. "Charities for Children in San Francisco." *Overland Monthly,* January 1890, pp. 78–100.

———. "Poverty and Charity in San Francisco, I & II." *Overland Monthly,* November 1889, pp. 535–47; December 1889, pp. 486–592.

Smith, Adelaide. *Womanhood and Polygamy.* New York: Woman's Home Missionary Society, n.d. LDS.

Smith, Bertha. "They Call Her Fahn Quai 'The White Spirit.' " Reprinted from *American Magazine* by Presbyterian Board of National Missions, n.d. SFTS.

Stenhouse, Fanny. *"Tell It All:" The Story of a Life's Experience in Mormonism.* With introductory preface by Harriet Beecher Stowe. Hartford, Conn.: A. D. Worthington, 1874.

The Story of Little Ah Fong. San Francisco, Calif.: WOBFM, n.d. POH.

Strange True Stories of Chinese Slave Girls. San Francisco, Calif.: WOBFM, n.d. SFTS.

Tanner, Annie Clark. *A Mormon Mother: An Autobiography.* Salt Lake City, Utah: University of Utah Press, 1969.

Tomkinson, Laura. *Twenty Years' History of the Woman's Home Missionary Society of the Methodist Episcopal Church, 1880–1900.* Cincinnati, Ohio: Woman's Home Missionary Society, 1903.

Tullidge, Edward. *The Women of Mormondom.* New York: n.p, 1877.

A Visit to the Occidental Board Mission Home for Chinese Girls. N.p., n.d. POH.

Waid, Eva Clark. *At Work Among the Chinese in America.* New York: Board of National Missions, n.d. POH.

Walworth, Jeannette. *The Bar-Sinister: A Mormon Study.* Rathway, N.J.: Mershon, 1885.

Whitney, Helen Mar. *Plural Marriage, as Taught by the Prophet Joseph. A Reply to Joseph Smith, Editor of the Lamoni "Herald."* Salt Lake City, Utah: Juvenile Instructor Office, 1882. LDS.

————. *Why We Practice Plural Marriage, by a "Mormon" Wife and Mother.* Salt Lake City, Utah: Juvenile Instructor Office, 1884. LDS.

Woman's Occidental Board of Foreign Missions. *Good News from "920."* N.p., 1915. CSL.

Women's National Indian Association. *Missionary Work of the Women's National Indian Association.* Philadelphia, Pa.: WNIA, 1884.

————. *Our Work: What? How? Why?* Philadelphia, Pa.: WNIA, 1893.

————. *Sunshine Work.* Philadelphia, Pa.: WNIA, 1894.

Young, Ann Eliza. *Wife No. 19, or The Story of a Life in Bondage, Being a Complete Exposé of Mormonism, and Revealing the Sorrows, Sacrifices and Sufferings of Women in Polygamy.* With introductory notes by John Gough and Mary Livermore. Hartford, Conn., 1875; reprint, New York: Arno Press, 1972.

Selected Secondary Sources

Abbott, Elizabeth Lee, and Kenneth Abbott. "Chinese Pilgrims and Presbyterians in the United States, 1850–1977." *Journal of Presbyterian History* 55 (Summer 1977): 125–44.

Ahern, Wilbert. "Assimilationist Racism: The Case of the 'Friends of the Indian.' " *Journal of Ethnic Studies* 4 (1976–77): 23–32.

————. " 'The Returned Indians': Hampton Institute and Its Indian Alumni, 1879–1893." *Journal of Ethnic Studies* 10 (Winter 1983): 101–24.

Alcoff, Linda. "Cultural Feminism vs. Post-Structuralism: The Identity Crisis in Feminist Theory." *Signs* 13 (Spring 1988): 405–36.

Alexander, Thomas G. *A History of the Latter-day Saints, 1890–1930.* Urbana: University of Illinois Press, 1986.

Armitage, Susan, and Elizabeth Jameson. *The Women's West.* Norman: University of Oklahoma Press, 1987.

Baker, Paula. "The Domestication of Politics: Women and American

Political Society, 1780–1920." *American Historical Review* 89 (June 1984): 620–47.

Bannan, Helen. "Newcomers to Navajoland: Transculturation in the Memoirs of Anglo Women, 1900–1945." *New Mexico Historical Review* 59 (April 1984): 165–85.

Barnhart, Jacqueline Baker. *The Fair But Frail: Prostitution in San Francisco, 1840–1900.* Reno: University of Nevada Press, 1986.

Barth, Gunther. *Instant Cities: Urbanization and the Rise of San Francisco and Denver.* New York: Oxford University Press, 1975.

Beaver, R. Pierce. *All Loves Excelling: American Protestant Women in World Mission.* Grand Rapids, Mich.: Wm. B. Eerdmans, 1968.

Beecher, Maureen Ursenbach. "The 'Leading Sisters': A Female Hierarchy in Nineteenth Century Mormon Society." *Journal of Mormon History* 9 (1982): 25–39.

Beecher, Maureen Ursenbach, and Lavina Fielding Anderson, eds. *Sisters in Spirit: Mormon Women in Historical and Cultural Perspective.* Urbana: University of Illinois Press, 1987.

Bennion, Lowell "Ben." "The Incidence of Mormon Polygamy in 1880: 'Dixie' versus Davis Stake." *Journal of Mormon History* 11 (1984): 27–42.

Berkhofer, Robert. *The White Man's Indian: Images of the American Indian from Columbus to the Present.* New York: Alfred A. Knopf, 1978.

Bitton, Davis. "Mormon Polygamy: A Review Article." *Journal of Mormon History* 4 (1977): 101–18.

Blocker, Jack, Jr. "Separate Paths: Suffragists and the Women's Temperance Crusade." *Signs* 10 (Spring 1985): 460–76.

———. *"Give to the Winds Thy Fears": The Women's Temperance Crusade, 1873–1874.* Westport, Conn.: Greenwood Press, 1985.

Blu, Karen. *The Lumbee Problem: The Making of an American Indian People.* London: Cambridge University Press, 1980.

Bordin, Ruth. *Woman and Temperance: The Search for Power and Liberty, 1873–1900.* Philadelphia, Pa.: Temple University Press, 1981.

Boyd, Lois, and R. Douglas Brackenridge. *Presbyterian Women in America: Two Centuries of a Quest for Status.* Westport, Conn.: Greenwood Press, 1983.

Boyer, Paul. *Urban Masses and Moral Order in America, 1820–1920.* Cambridge, Mass.: Harvard University Press, 1978.

Boylan, Anne M. "Women in Groups: An Analysis of Women's Benevolent Organizations in New York and Boston, 1797–1840." *Journal of American History* 71 (December 1984): 497–523.

———. "Timid Girls, Venerable Widows and Dignified Matrons:

Life Cycle Patterns among Organized Women in New York and Boston, 1797–1840." *American Quarterly* 38 (Winter 1986): 779–97.

Brandenstein, Sherilyn. "The Colorado Cottage Home." *Colorado Magazine* 53 (Summer 1976): 229–42.

Brenzel, Barbara. *Daughters of the State: A Social Portrait of the First Reform School for Girls in North America, 1836–1905.* Cambridge, Mass.: MIT Press, 1983.

Brumberg, Joan Jacobs. " 'Ruined' Girls: Changing Community Responses to Illegitimacy in Upstate New York, 1890–1920." *Journal of Social History* 18 (Winter 1984): 247–72.

———. "Zenanas and Girlless Villages: The Ethnology of American Evangelical Women, 1870–1910." *Journal of American History* 69 (September 1982): 347–71.

Brundage, David. "The Producing Classes and the Saloon: Denver in the 1880s." *Labor History* 26 (Winter 1985): 29–52.

Cahn, Frances, and Valeska Bary. *Welfare Activities of Federal, State, and Local Governments in California, 1850–1934.* Berkeley: University of California Press, 1936.

Cannon, Charles. "The Awesome Power of Sex: The Polemical Campaign Against Mormon Polygamy." *Pacific Historical Review* 43 (February 1974): 61–82.

Carter, Paul A. *The Decline and Revival of the Social Gospel: Social and Political Liberalism in American Protestant Churches, 1920–1940.* Ithaca, N.Y.: Cornell University Press, 1954.

Cheng, Lucie, and Edna Bonacich, eds. *Labor Immigration Under Capitalism: Asian Workers in the United States Before World War II.* Berkeley: University of California Press, 1984.

Coleman, Michael. *Presbyterian Missionary Attitudes toward American Indians, 1837–1893.* Jackson: University Press of Mississippi, 1985.

———. "Presbyterian Missionary Attitudes Toward China and the Chinese, 1837–1900." *Journal of Presbyterian History* 56 (Fall 1978): 185–201.

———. "Not Race, But Grace: Presbyterian Missionaries and American Indians, 1837–1893." *Journal of American History* 64 (June 1980): 41–60.

Cott, Nancy. *The Bonds of Womanhood: "Woman's Sphere" in New England, 1780–1835.* New Haven, Conn.: Yale University Press, 1977.

———. *The Grounding of Modern Feminism.* New Haven, Conn.: Yale University Press, 1987.

———. "Passionlessness: An Interpretation of Victorian Sexual Ideology, 1790–1850." *Signs* 4 (Winter 1978): 219–36.

Cumbler, John. "The Politics of Charity: Gender and Class in Late Nineteenth-Century Charity Policy." *Journal of Social History* 14 (Fall 1980): 99–112.

Decker, Peter. *Fortunes and Failures: White Collar Mobility in Nineteenth-Century San Francisco.* Cambridge, Mass.: Harvard University Press, 1978.

Degler, Carl. *At Odds: Women and the Family in America from the Revolution to the Present.* New York: Oxford University Press, 1980.

D'Emilio, John, and Estelle Freedman. *Intimate Matters: A History of Sexuality in America.* New York: Harper and Row, 1988.

Deutsch, Sarah. "Women and Intercultural Relations: The Case of Hispanic New Mexico and Colorado." *Signs* 12 (Summer 1987): 719–39.

———. *No Separate Refuge: Culture, Class, and Gender on an Anglo-Hispanic Frontier in the American Southwest, 1880–1940.* New York: Oxford University Press, 1987.

Donovan, Josephine. *Feminist Theory: The Intellectual Traditions of American Feminism.* New York: Frederick Ungar, 1985.

Donzelot, Jacques. *The Policing of Families.* New York: Pantheon, 1979.

Doyle, Don Harrison. *The Social Order of a Frontier Community: Jacksonville, Illinois, 1825–1870.* Urbana: University of Illinois Press, 1978.

DuBois, Ellen, Mari Jo Buhle, Temma Kaplan, Gerda Lerner, and Carroll Smith-Rosenberg. "Politics and Culture in Women's History: A Symposium." *Feminist Studies* 6 (Spring 1980): 65–75.

Dudden, Faye. *Serving Women: Household Service in Nineteenth-Century America.* Middletown, Conn.: Wesleyan University Press, 1983.

Dunfey, Julie. " 'Living the Principle' of Plural Marriage: Mormon Women, Utopia, and Female Sexuality in the Nineteenth Century." *Feminist Studies* 10 (Fall 1984): 523–36.

Eisenstein, Hester. *Contemporary Feminist Thought.* Boston, Mass.: G. K. Hall, 1983.

Embry, Jessie. *Mormon Polygamous Families: Life in the Principle.* Salt Lake City: University of Utah Press, 1987.

Epstein, Barbara. *The Politics of Domesticity: Women, Evangelism, and Temperance in Nineteenth-Century America.* Middletown, Conn.: Wesleyan University Press, 1981.

Erenberg, Lewis. *Steppin' Out: New York Nightlife and the Transformation of American Culture, 1890–1930.* Westport, Conn.: Greenwood Press, 1981.

Ewen, Elizabeth. *Immigrant Women in the Land of Dollars: Life and Culture on the Lower East Side, 1890–1925.* New York: Monthly Review Press, 1985.

Fass, Paula. *The Damned and the Beautiful: American Youth in the 1920s.* New York: Oxford University Press, 1977.

Fields, Barbara J. "Ideology and Race in American History." *Region, Race, and Reconstruction: Essays in Honor of C. Vann Woodward.* Edited by J. Morgan Kousser and James M. McPherson. New York: Oxford University Press, 1982, pp. 143–78.

Foster, Lawrence. *Religion and Sexuality: Three American Communal Experiments of the Nineteenth Century.* New York: Oxford University Press, 1981.

Foucault, Michel. *The History of Sexuality.* Volume 1: *An Introduction.* Translated by Robert Hurley. New York: Pantheon, 1978.

Freedman, Estelle. "Separatism as Strategy: Female Institution Building and American Feminism, 1870–1930." *Feminist Studies* 5 (Fall 1979): 512–29.

———. "Sexuality in Nineteenth-Century America: Behavior, Ideology, and Politics." *Reviews in American History* 10 (January 1982): 196–215.

———. *Their Sisters' Keepers: Women's Prison Reform in America, 1830–1930.* Ann Arbor: University of Michigan Press, 1981.

Freedman, Maurice. "The Family in China, Past and Present." *Pacific Affairs* 34 (Winter 1961–62): 323–36.

Furner, Mary. *Advocacy and Objectivity: A Crisis in the Professionalization of American Social Science, 1865–1905.* Lexington: University Press of Kentucky, 1975.

Gay, Peter. *The Bourgeois Experience: Victoria to Freud.* Volume 1: *Education of the Senses.* New York: Oxford University Press, 1984.

Gilligan, Carol. *In a Different Voice: Psychological Theory and Women's Development.* Cambridge, Mass.: Harvard University Press, 1982.

Glenn, Evelyn Nakano. "Split Household, Small Producer, and Dual Wage Earner: An Analysis of Chinese American Family Strategies." *Journal of Marriage and the Family* 45 (February 1983): 35–46.

Gordon, Linda. "Child Abuse, Gender, and the Myth of Family Independence: A Historical Critique." *Child Welfare* 64 (May–June 1985): 213–24.

———. "Family Violence, Feminism, and Social Control." *Feminist Studies* 12 (Fall 1986): 453–78.

———. *Heroes of Their Own Lives: The Politics and History of Family Violence, Boston, 1880–1960.* New York: Viking, 1988.

———. *Woman's Body, Woman's Right: A Social History of Birth Control in America.* New York: Penguin Books, 1976.

Gordon, Linda, and Ellen DuBois. "Seeking Ecstasy on the Battlefield:

Danger and Pleasure in Nineteenth-Century Feminist Sexual Thought." *Feminist Studies* 9 (Spring 1983): 7–26.

Gossett, Thomas. *Race: The History of an Idea in America.* Dallas, Tex.: Southern Methodist University Press, 1963.

Green, Rayna. "The Pocahontas Perplex: The Image of Indian Women in American Culture." *Massachusetts Review* 16 (1975): 198–214.

Griego, Andrew. "Mayor of Chinatown: The Life of Ah Quin, Chinese Merchant and Railroad Builder of San Diego." M.A. thesis, San Diego State University, 1979.

Griffen, Clifford S. "Religious Benevolence as Social Control, 1815–1860." *Mississippi Valley Historical Review* 44 (December 1957): 423–44.

———. *Their Brothers' Keepers: Moral Stewardship in the United States, 1800–1865.* New Brunswick, N.J.: Rutgers University Press, 1960.

Griswold, Robert. *Family and Divorce in California, 1850–1890: Victorian Illusions and Everyday Realities.* Albany: State University of New York Press, 1982.

Gronewald, Sue. "Beautiful Merchandise: Prostitution in China, 1860–1936." *Women and History* 1 (Spring 1982).

Grossberg, Michael. *Governing the Hearth: Law and the Family in Nineteenth-Century America.* Chapel Hill: University of North Carolina Press, 1985.

Gullett, Gayle. "City Mothers, City Daughters, and the Dance Hall Girls: The Limits of Female Political Power in San Francisco, 1913." *Women and the Structure of Society.* Edited by Barbara J. Harris and JoAnn R. McNamara. Durham, N.C.: Duke University Press, 1984, pp. 149–59.

Haller, John, Jr. *Outcasts from Evolution: Scientific Attitudes of Racial Inferiority, 1859–1900.* Urbana: University of Illinois Press, 1971.

Haltunnen, Karen. *Confidence Men and Painted Women: A Study of Middle-Class Culture in America, 1830–1870.* New Haven, Conn.: Yale University Press, 1982.

Handy, Robert. *A Christian America: Protestant Hopes and Historical Realities.* New York: Oxford University Press, 1971.

Harris, Katherine. "Feminism and Temperance Reform in the Boulder WCTU." *Frontiers* 4 (Summer 1979): 19–24.

———. "A Study of Feminine and Class Identity in the Woman's Christian Temperance Union, 1920–1970: A Case Study." *Historicus* 2 (Fall/Winter 1980): 55–87.

Haskell, Thomas. "Capitalism and the Origins of the Humanitarian Sensibility, Parts I & II." *American Historical Review* 90 (April 1985): 339–61; (June 1985): 547–66.

————. *The Emergence of Professional Science: The American Social Science Association and the Nineteenth-Century Crisis of Authority.* Urbana: University of Illinois Press, 1977.

Hauptman, Laurence. "Medicine Woman: Susan LaFlesche, 1865–1915." *New York State Journal of Medicine* (September 1978): 1783–88.

Hayner, Norman S., and Charles N. Reynolds. "Chinese Family Life in America." *American Sociological Review* 2 (October 1937): 630–37.

Hertzberg, Hazel. *The Search for an American Indian Identity: Modern Pan-Indian Movements.* Syracuse, N.Y.: Syracuse University Press, 1971.

Hewitt, Nancy. "Beyond the Search for Sisterhood: American Women's History in the 1980s." *Social History* 10 (October 1985): 299–321.

————. *Women's Activism and Social Change: Rochester, New York, 1822–1871.* Ithaca, N.Y.: Cornell University Press, 1984.

Higham, John. "The Reorientation of American Culture in the 1890's." *Writing American History: Essays on Modern Scholarship.* Bloomington: Indiana University Press, 1970, pp. 73–102.

Hill, Patricia R. *The World Their Household: The American Woman's Foreign Mission Movement and Cultural Transformation, 1870–1920.* Ann Arbor: University of Michigan Press, 1984.

Hinsley, Curtis, Jr. *Savages and Scientists: The Smithsonian Institution and the Development of American Anthropology, 1846–1910.* Washington, D.C.: Smithsonian Institution Press, 1981.

Hirata, Lucie Cheng. "Chinese Immigrant Women in Nineteenth-Century California." *Women of America: A History.* Edited by Carol Ruth Berkin and Mary Beth Norton. Boston, Mass.: Houghton Mifflin, 1979, pp. 223–41.

————. "Free, Endentured, Enslaved: Chinese Prostitutes in Nineteenth-Century America." *Signs* 5 (Autumn 1979): 3–29.

Hobson, Barbara Meil. *Uneasy Virtue: The Politics of Prostitution and the American Reform Tradition.* New York: Basic Books, 1987.

Hoexter, Corinne. *From Canton to California: The Epic of Chinese Immigration.* New York: Four Winds Press, 1976.

Horsman, Reginald. *Race and Manifest Destiny: The Origins of American Racial Anglo-Saxonism.* Cambridge, Mass.: Harvard University Press, 1981.

————. "Scientific Racism and the American Indian in the Mid-Nineteenth Century." *American Quarterly* 27 (May 1975): 152–68.

Howe, Daniel Walker, ed. *Victorian America.* Philadelphia: University of Pennsylvania Press, 1976.

Hoxie, Frederick. *A Final Promise: The Campaign to Assimilate the Indians, 1880–1920.* Lincoln: University of Nebraska Press, 1984.

Hunter, Jane. *The Gospel of Gentility: American Women Missionaries in Turn-of-the-Century China.* New Haven, Conn.: Yale University Press, 1984.

Hutchison, William. *The Modernist Impulse in American Protestantism.* Cambridge, Mass.: Harvard University Press, 1976.

Hyatt, Marshall. "Franz Boas and the Struggle for Black Equality: The Dynamics of Ethnicity." *Perspectives in American History,* n.s. 2 (1985): 269–96.

Ikels, Charlotte. "The Family Past: Contemporary Studies and the Traditional Chinese Family." *Journal of Family History* 6 (Fall 1981): 334–40.

Jaggar, Alison. *Feminist Politics and Human Nature.* Totowa, N.J.: Rowman and Allanheld, 1983.

Jardine, Alice. *Gynesis: Configurations of Woman and Modernity.* Ithaca, N.Y.: Cornell University Press, 1985.

Jeffrey, Julie Roy. *Frontier Women: The Trans-Mississippi West.* New York: Hill and Wang, 1979.

Johnson, Paul E. *A Shopkeeper's Millennium: Society and Revivals in Rochester, New York, 1815–1837.* New York: Hill and Wang, 1978.

Jordan, Philip. "Immigrants, Methodists, and a 'Conservative' Social Gospel, 1865–1908." *Methodist History* 17 (October 1978): 16–43.

Katzman, David. *Seven Days a Week: Women and Domestic Service in Industrializing America.* New York, 1978; reprint, Urbana: University of Illinois Press, 1981.

Kerber, Linda. "Separate Spheres, Female Worlds, Woman's Place: The Rhetoric of Women's History." *Journal of American History* 75 (June 1988): 9–39.

Kern, Louis. *An Ordered Love: Sex Roles and Sexuality in Victorian Utopias—The Shakers, The Mormons, and the Oneida Community.* Chapel Hill: University of North Carolina Press, 1981.

Kidd, Norma Green. *Iron Eye's Family: The Children of Joseph LaFlesche.* Lincoln, Nebr.: Johnson Publishing Company, 1969.

Lai, Him Mark, Genny Lim, and Judy Yung. *Island: Poetry and History of Chinese Immigrants on Angel Island, 1910–1940.* San Francisco, Calif.: HOC-DOI Project, 1980.

Lamar, Howard. *The Far Southwest: A Territorial History.* New Haven, Conn.: Yale University Press, 1966.

Lang, Olga. *Chinese Family and Society.* New Haven, Conn.: Yale University Press, 1946.

Larson, Gustive. *The "Americanization" of Utah for Statehood.* San Marino, Calif.: Huntington Library, 1971.

———. "An Industrial Home for Polygamous Wives." *Utah Historical Quarterly* 38 (Summer 1970): 263–75.

Lasch, Christopher. *Haven in a Heartless World: The Family Besieged.* New York: Basic Books, 1977.

Laslett, Peter, Karla Oosterveen, and Richard Smith, eds. *Bastardy and Its Comparative History.* Cambridge, Mass.: Harvard University Press, 1980.

Lasser, Carol. "The Domestic Balance of Power: Relations Between Mistress and Maid in Nineteenth-Century New England." *Labor History* 28 (Winter 1987): 5–22.

Lebsock, Suzanne. *The Free Women of Petersburg: Status and Culture in a Southern Town, 1784–1860.* New York: W. W. Norton, 1984.

Leiby, James. "State Welfare Administration in California, 1879–1929." *Pacific Historical Review* 41 (May 1972): 169–88.

Lerner, Gerda. *The Creation of Patriarchy.* New York: Oxford University Press, 1986.

———. *The Majority Finds Its Past: Placing Women in History.* New York: Oxford University Press, 1979.

Light, Ivan. "From Vice District to Tourist Attraction: The Moral Career of American Chinatowns, 1880–1940." *Pacific Historical Review* 43 (August 1974): 367–94.

Lim, Genny, ed. *The Chinese American Experience: Papers from the Second National Conference on Chinese American Studies.* San Francisco, Calif.: Chinese Historical Society of America and the Chinese Culture Foundation of San Francisco, 1984.

Limerick, Patricia Nelson. *The Legacy of Conquest: The Unbroken Past of the American West.* New York: W. W. Norton, 1987.

Logue, Larry. "A Time of Marriage: Monogamy and Polygamy in a Utah Town." *Journal of Mormon History* 11 (1984): 3–26.

Low, Victor. *The Unimpressible Race: A Century of Educational Struggle by the Chinese in San Francisco.* San Francisco, Calif.: East/West, 1982.

Lubove, Roy. *The Professional Altruist: The Emergence of Social Work as a Career, 1880–1930.* Cambridge, Mass.: Harvard University Press, 1965.

Luker, Ralph. "The Social Gospel and the Failure of Racial Reform, 1877–1898." *Church History* 46 (March 1977): 80–99.

Lyman, Stanford. "Conflict and the Web of Group Affiliation in San Francisco's Chinatown, 1850–1910." *Pacific Historical Review* 43 (November 1974): 473–99.

———. "Marriage and the Family Among Chinese Immigrants to America, 1850–1960." *Phylon* 29 (Winter 1968): 321–30.

McBeth, Sally. "Indian Boarding Schools and Ethnic Identity: An Example from the Southern Plains Tribes of Oklahoma." *Plains Anthropologist* (May 1983): 119–28.

McClain, Laurene Wu. "Donaldina Cameron: A Reappraisal." *Pacific Historian* 27 (Fall 1983): 25–35.

McDannell, Colleen. *The Christian Home in Victorian America, 1840–1900.* Bloomington: Indiana University Press, 1986.

McLoughlin, William G. *Revivals, Awakenings, and Reform: An Essay on Religion and Social Change in America, 1607–1977.* Chicago, Ill.: University of Chicago Press, 1978.

Mangen, J. A., and James Walvin, eds. *Manliness and Morality: Middle-Class Masculinity in Britain and America, 1800–1940.* Manchester, U.K.: Manchester University Press, 1987.

Mann, Ralph. "Frontier Opportunity and the New Social History." *Pacific Historical Review* 53 (November 1984): 463–91.

Mann, Susan. "Widows in the Kinship, Class, and Community Structures of Qing Dynasty China." *Journal of Asian Studies* 46 (February 1987): 37–56.

Mark, Joan. *A Stranger in Her Native Land: Alice Fletcher and the American Indians.* Lincoln: University of Nebraska Press, 1988.

Marsden, George. *Fundamentalism and American Culture: The Shaping of Twentieth-Century Evangelicalism, 1870–1925.* New York: Oxford University Press, 1980.

Marquis, Kathleen. " 'Diamond Cut Diamond:' Mormon Women and the Cult of Domesticity in the Nineteenth Century." *University of Michigan Papers in Women's Studies* 2, no. 2 (1976): 105–23.

Marsh, Margaret. "Suburban Men and Masculine Domesticity, 1870–1915." *American Quarterly* 40 (June 1988): 165–86.

Martin, Mildred Crowl. *Chinatown's Angry Angel: The Story of Donaldina Cameron.* Palo Alto, Calif.: Pacific Books, 1977.

Marty, Martin. *Righteous Empire: The Protestant Experience in America.* New York: Dial Press, 1970.

Mathes, Valerie Sherer. "A New Look at the Role of Women in Indian Society." *American Indian Quarterly* 2 (1975): 131–39.

———. "Susan LaFlesche Picotte: Nebraska's Indian Physician, 1865–1915." *Nebraska History* 63 (Winter 1982): 502–31.

———. "Dr. Susan LaFlesche Picotte: The Reformed and the Reformer." *Indian Lives: Essays on Nineteenth- and Twentieth-Century Native American Leaders.* Edited by L. G. Moses and Raymond Wilson. Albuquerque: University of New Mexico Press, 1985, pp. 61–90.

Mathisen, Robert. "Evangelicals and the Age of Reform, 1870–1930: An Assessment." *Fides et Historia* 16 (Spring–Summer 1984): 74–85.

Matthews, Glenna. *"Just a Housewife": The Rise and Fall of Domesticity in America.* New York: Oxford University Press, 1987.

May, Elaine Tyler. *Great Expectations: Marriage and Divorce in Post-Victorian America.* Chicago: University of Chicago Press, 1980.

May, Henry. *The End of American Innocence: A Study of the First Years of Our Own Time, 1912–1917.* New York: Alfred A. Knopf, 1959.

Medicine, Bea. "American Indian Family: Cultural Change and Adaptive Strategies." *Journal of Ethnic Studies* 8 (Winter 1981): 13–24.

Meyerowitz, Joanne. *Women Adrift: Independent Wage Earners in Chicago, 1880–1930.* Chicago, Ill.: University of Chicago Press, 1988.

Miller, Stuart. *The Unwelcome Immigrant: The American Image of the Chinese, 1785–1882.* Berkeley: University of California Press, 1969.

Milner, Clyde. "Off the White Road: Seven Nebraska Indian Societies in the 1870s—A Statistical Analysis of Assimilation, Population, and Prosperity." *Western Historical Quarterly* 12 (January 1981): 37–53.

———. *With Good Intentions: Quaker Work among the Pawnees, Otos, and Omahas in the 1870s.* Lincoln: University of Nebraska Press, 1981.

Mintz, Steven, and Susan Kellogg. *Domestic Revolutions: A Social History of American Family Life.* New York: Free Press, 1988.

Modell, John. "Dating Becomes the Way of American Youth." *Essays on the Family and Historical Change.* Edited by Leslie P. Moch. College Station: Texas A & M Press, 1983, pp. 91–126.

Morantz-Sanchez, Regina Markell. *Sympathy and Science: Women Physicians in American Medicine.* New York: Oxford University Press, 1985.

Morton, Marian. "Seduced and Abandoned in an American City: Cleveland and Its Fallen Women, 1869–1936." *Journal of Urban History* 11 (August 1985): 443–69.

Nee, Victor, and Brett de Bary Nee. *Longtime Californ': A Documentary Study of an American Chinatown.* New York: Pantheon Books, 1972.

Nicholson, Linda. "Women, Morality, and History." *Social Research* 50 (Autumn 1983): 504–36.

Noel, Thomas. *The City and the Saloon: Denver, 1858–1916.* Lincoln: University of Nebraska Press, 1982.

Peffer, George Anthony. "Forbidden Families: Emigration Experiences of Chinese Women Under the Page Law, 1875–1882." *Journal of American Ethnic History* 6 (Fall 1986): 28–46.

Peiss, Kathy. *Cheap Amusements: Working Women and Leisure in Turn-of-the-Century New York.* Philadelphia, Pa.: Temple University Press, 1986.

Perry, Lewis. " 'Progress, Not Pleasure, Is Our Aim': The Sexual Advice of an Antebellum Radical." *Journal of Social History* 12 (Spring 1979): 354–67.

Pivar, David. *Purity Crusade: Sexual Morality and Social Control, 1868–1900.* Westport, Conn.: Greenwood Press, 1973.

Platt, Anthony. *The Child-Savers: The Invention of Juvenile Delinquency.* 2nd ed. Chicago, Ill.: University of Chicago Press, 1977.

Pleck, Elizabeth. "Challenges to Traditional Authority in Immigrant Families." *The American Family in Social-Historical Perspective,* 3rd ed. Edited by Michael Gordon. New York: St. Martin's Press, 1983, pp. 504–17.

———. *Domestic Tyranny: The Making of Social Policy Against Family Violence from Colonial Times to the Present.* New York: Oxford University Press, 1987.

Poll, Richard, ed. *Utah's History.* Provo, Utah: Brigham Young University Press, 1978.

Prucha, Francis. *American Indian Policy in Crisis: Christian Reformers and the Indian, 1865–1900.* Norman: University of Oklahoma Press, 1976.

———. "The Decline of the Christian Reformers." *Indian Policy in the United States.* Lincoln: University of Nebraska Press, 1981, pp. 252–62.

———. "Scientific Racism and Indian Policy." *Indian Policy in the United States.* Lincoln: University of Nebraska Press, 1981, pp. 180–97.

Puzzo, Dante. "Racism and the Western Tradition." *Journal of the History of Ideas* 25 (October–December 1964): 579–86.

Quinn, D. Michael. "LDS Authority and New Plural Marriages, 1890–1904." *Dialogue* 18 (Spring 1985): 9–105.

Riley, Glenda. "Some European (Mis)Perceptions of American Indian Women." *New Mexico Historical Review* 59 (July 1984): 237–66.

Rodgers, Daniel. "In Search of Progressivism." *Reviews in American History* 10 (December 1982): 113–32.

Rosen, Ruth. *The Lost Sisterhood: Prostitution in America, 1900–1918.* Baltimore, Md.: Johns Hopkins University Press, 1982.

Rosenberg, Charles. "Sexuality, Class, and Role in Nineteenth-Century America." *American Quarterly* 25 (May 1973): 131–53.

Rosenberg, Rosalind. *Beyond Separate Spheres: Intellectual Roots of Modern Feminism.* New Haven, Conn.: Yale University Press, 1982.

Rothman, David. *The Discovery of the Asylum: Social Order and Disorder in the New Republic.* Boston, Mass.: Little, Brown, 1971.

———. *Conscience and Convenience: The Asylum and Its Alternatives in Progressive America.* Boston, Mass.: Little, Brown, 1980.

Rothman, Ellen. *Hands and Hearts: A History of Courtship in America.* New York: Basic Books, 1984.

Rotundo, E. Anthony. "Body and Soul: Changing Ideals of American Middle-Class Manhood, 1770–1920." *Journal of Social History* 16 (Summer 1983): 23–38.

Ruggles, Steven. "Fallen Women: The Inmates of the Magdalen Society Asylum of Philadelphia, 1836–1908." *Journal of Social History* 16 (Summer 1983): 65–82.

Ryan, Mary P. *Cradle of the Middle Class: The Family in Oneida County, New York, 1790–1865.* Cambridge, U.K.: Cambridge University Press, 1981.

———. "The Power of Women's Networks: A Case Study of Female Moral Reform in Antebellum America." *Feminist Studies* 5 (Spring 1979): 66–87.

Saxton, Alexander. *The Indispensable Enemy: Labor and the Anti-Chinese Movement in California.* Berkeley: University of California Press, 1971.

Schlossman, Steven, and Stephanie Wallach. "The Crime of Precocious Sexuality: Female Juvenile Delinquency in the Progressive Era." *Harvard Educational Review* 48 (February 1978): 65–94.

Scott, Anne Firor. *Making the Invisible Woman Visible.* Urbana: University of Illinois Press, 1984.

———. "Mormon Women, Other Women: Paradoxes and Challenges." *Journal of Mormon History* 13 (1986–87): 3–20.

Scott, Joan. "Gender: A Useful Category of Historical Analysis." *American Historical Review* 91 (December 1986): 1053–75.

Seager, Robert II. "Some Denominational Reactions to Chinese Immigration to California, 1856–1892." *Pacific Historical Review* 28 (February 1959): 49–66.

Sears, Hal. *The Sex Radicals: Free Love in High Victorian America.* Lawrence: Regents Press of Kansas, 1977.

Shipps, Jan. *Mormonism: The Story of a New Religious Tradition.* Urbana: University of Illinois Press, 1985.

Shumsky, Neil. "Vice Responds to Reform: San Francisco, 1910–1914." *Journal of Urban History* 7 (November 1980): 31–47.

Shumsky, Neil, and Larry Springer. "San Francisco's Zone of Prostitution, 1880–1934." *Journal of Historical Geography* 7, no. 1 (1981): 71–89.

Simmons, Christina. "Companionate Marriage and the Lesbian Threat." *Frontiers* 4 (Fall 1979): 54–59.

Singal, Daniel Joseph. "Towards a Definition of American Modernism." *American Quarterly* 39 (Spring 1987): 7–26.

———. *The War Within: From Victorian to Modernist Thought in the South, 1919–1945.* Chapel Hill: University of North Carolina Press, 1982.

Singleton, Gregory. *Religion in the City of the Angels: American Protestant Culture and Urbanization, Los Angeles, 1850–1930.* Ann Arbor, Mich.: UMI Research Press, 1979.

Sklar, Kathryn Kish. *Catharine Beecher: A Study in American Domesticity.* New Haven, Conn.: Yale University Press, 1973.

Smith, Daniel Scott. "The Dating of the American Sexual Revolution: Evidence and Interpretation." *The American Family in Social-Historical Perspective,* 2nd ed. Edited by Michael Gordon. New York: St. Martin's Press, 1978, pp. 426–38.

Smith, Daniel Scott, and Michael Hindus. "Premarital Pregnancy in America 1640–1971: An Overview and Interpretation." *Journal of Interdisciplinary History* 5 (Spring 1975): 537–70.

Smith-Rosenberg, Carroll. *Disorderly Conduct: Visions of Gender in Victorian America.* New York: Alfred A. Knopf, 1985.

———. *Religion and the Rise of the American City: The New York City Mission Movement, 1812–1870.* Ithaca, N.Y.: Cornell University Press, 1971.

Snitow, Ann, Christine Stansell, and Sharon Thompson, eds. *Powers of Desire: The Politics of Sexuality.* New York: Monthly Review Press, 1983.

Stansell, Christine. *City of Women: Sex and Class in New York, 1789–1860.* New York: Alfred A. Knopf, 1986.

Stefanco, Carolyn. "Pathways to Power: Women and Voluntary Associations in Denver, Colorado, 1876–1893." Ph.D. dissertation, Duke University, 1987.

Stocking, George, Jr. *Race, Culture, and Evolution: Essays in the History of Anthropology,* 2nd ed. Chicago, Ill.: University of Chicago Press, 1982.

Stoper, Emily, and Roberta Ann Johnson. "The Weaker Sex and the Better Half: The Idea of Women's Moral Superiority in the American Feminist Movement." *Polity* 10 (Winter 1977): 192–217.

Szasz, Ferenc Morton. *The Divided Mind of Protestant America, 1880–1930.* University: University of Alabama Press, 1982.

Tank, Robert. "Mobility and Occupational Structure on the Late

Nineteenth-Century Urban Frontier: The Case of Denver, Colorado." *Pacific Historical Review* 47 (May 1978): 189–216.

Takaki, Ronald. *Iron Cages: Race and Culture in Nineteenth-Century America.* New York: Alfred A. Knopf, 1979.

Thomas, Hilah, Louise Queen, and Rosemary Skinner Keller, eds. *Women in New Worlds: Historical Perspectives on the Wesleyan Tradition.* 2 vols. Nashville, Tenn.: Abingdon, 1982.

Tsuchida, Nobuya, ed. *Asian and Pacific American Experiences: Women's Perspectives.* Minneapolis: Asian/Pacific American Learning Resource Center and General College, University of Minnesota, 1982.

Vance, Carole, ed. *Pleasure and Danger: Exploring Female Sexuality.* Boston, Mass.: Routledge and Kegan Paul, 1984.

Van de Wetering, Maxine. "The Popular Concept of 'Home' in Nineteenth-Century America." *Journal of American Studies* 18 (April 1984): 5–28.

Wallace, Irving. *The Twenty-Seventh Wife.* New York: Simon and Schuster, 1961.

Watson, James. "Chinese Kinship Reconsidered: Anthropological Perspectives on Historical Research." *China Quarterly* 92 (December 1982): 589–622.

Weist, Katherine. "Beasts of Burden and Menial Slaves: Nineteenth Century Observations of Northern Plains Indian Women." *The Hidden Half: Studies of Plains Indian Women.* Edited by Patricia Albers and Beatrice Medicine. Washington, D.C.: University Press of America, 1983, pp. 29–52.

———. "Plains Indian Women: An Assessment." *Anthropology on the Great Plains.* Edited by W. Raymond Wood and Margot Liberty. Lincoln: University of Nebraska Press, 1980, pp. 255–71.

Welter, Barbara. "The Cult of True Womanhood: 1820–1860." *American Quarterly* 16 (Summer 1966): 151–74.

West, Elliott. *The Saloon on the Rocky Mountain Frontier.* Lincoln: University of Nebraska Press, 1979.

White, Richard. "Race Relations in the American West." *American Quarterly* 38 (Bibliography 1986): 396–416.

Wilson, Carol Green. *Chinatown Quest: The Life Adventures of Donaldina Cameron.* Stanford, Calif.: Stanford University Press, 1931.

Wolf, Margery, and Roxane Witke, eds. *Women in Chinese Society.* Stanford, Calif.: Stanford University Press, 1975.

Woo, Wesley. "Protestant Work Among the Chinese in the San Francisco Bay Area, 1850–1920." Ph.D. dissertation, Graduate Theological Union, 1983.

Young, Mary E. "Women, Civilization, and the Indian Question." *Clio*

Was a Woman: Studies in the History of American Women. Edited by Mabel E. Deutrich and Virginia C. Purdy. Washington, D.C.: Howard University Press, 1980, pp. 98–112.

Yung, Judy. *Chinese Women of America: A Pictorial History.* Seattle: University of Washington Press, 1986.

———. "The Social Awakening of Chinese American Women as Reported in *Chung Sai Yat Po,* 1900–1911." *Chinese America: History and Perspectives 1988.* San Francisco: Chinese Historical Society of America, 1988, pp. 80–102.

Index